Law and Society
Recent Scholarship

Edited by Melvin I. Urofsky

A Series from LFB Scholarly

Judicial Power and Institutional Constraints

A Comparison of Canadian and American Courts

Ryan Hurl

LFB Scholarly Publishing LLC
El Paso 2010

Library of Congress Cataloging-in-Publication Data

Hurl, Ryan, 1973-
Judicial power and institutional constraints : a comparison of Canadian and American courts / Ryan Hurl.
p. cm. -- (Law & society)
Includes bibliographical references and index.
ISBN 978-1-59332-384-4 (hardcover : alk. paper)
1. Judicial power--United States. 2. Political questions and judicial power--United States. 3. Indians of North America--Legal status, laws, etc.--United States. 4. Environmental law--United States. 5. Judicial power--Canada. 6. Political questions and judicial power--Canada. 7. Indians of North America--Legal status, laws, etc.--Canada. 8. Environmental law--Canada. I. Title.
KDZ3156.H87 2010
347.71'012--dc22

2010019615

ISBN 978-1-59332-384-4

Printed on acid-free 250-year-life paper.

Manufactured in the United States of America.

Table of Contents

List of Tables

CHAPTER ONE: INTRODUCTION

In the spring of 2007, the United States Supreme Court rendered a decision in the case of *Massachusetts v. EPA*,[1] in which a variety of state governments and environmental groups asked the court to push the national government to regulate "greenhouse gases" such as carbon dioxide. One might have thought that the issue of "global warming" would not come under the Court's jurisdiction, for the same reason that one would not expect the court to develop its own foreign policy. The issue of global warming is, after all, a global problem. As in the case of other global problems, solutions can only be reached through inter-government negotiation and compromise, and it is not clear whether courts can contribute much if anything to this process. Global warming raises complex issues that are not readily comprehended even by those who have enjoyed three years of law school. Yet the American Supreme Court—or at least a majority of its justices—argued that, due to the dictates of the Clean Air Act and its amendments, the court could not avoid taking a part in the debate over global warming. Many would regard this judicial intervention into climatology as illegitimate and even dangerous; climatology is difficult, even for climatologists. The decision might have been from a policy perspective. Yet the position of the majority was not implausible as an interpretation of the law. In a way, the law itself forced judicial power out of its normal institutional constraints; the law authorized this judicial foray into public policy.

The plaintiffs in *Massachusetts v. EPA* sought a declaration that, given the current state of scientific knowledge about the effects of carbon dioxide emissions on global warming, the Environmental Protection Agency must begin plans to regulate green house gas emissions from automobiles. The courts were asked to force a major development in public policy, despite Congress' inability to reach conclusions on green house gas emissions, despite the vast impact that such regulations would have on America's automobile dependent

---

[1] *Massachusetts v. EPA*, 127 S. Ct. 1438 (2007).

economy, and despite the international aspects of climate change. The key "legal hook" for the plaintiffs in *Massachusetts v. EPA* was found in the following language of the Clean Air Act:

> The EPA Administrator shall by regulation prescribe (and from time to time revise) in accordance with the provisions of this section, standards applicable to the emission of any air pollutant from any class or classes of new motor vehicles or new motor vehicle engines, which in his judgment cause, or contribute to, air pollution which may reasonably be anticipated to endanger public health or welfare. . . .[2]

Given this statutory language, Justice Stevens (writing for the majority in the case) argued that the EPA had not provided a sufficient explanation for its decision *not* to regulate the four green house gases identified by the plaintiffs. EPA had argued that its own decisions could not possibly affect the advance of global warming, as the increase in global temperatures was a consequence of developments occurring in all industrial and developing nations. In addition, the EPA argued that carbon dioxide is not a kind of pollutant covered by the Clean Air Act. Both arguments were dismissed by the Court. Relying extensively on its interpretation of scientific consensus, but even more extensively on the language of the Clean Air Act, the Supreme Court ruled that the EPA's inaction on greenhouse gas regulation was unlawful.

Environmentalists undoubtedly regard this ruling as an important victory, and are understandably unconcerned with the legal niceties of the case. For those more concerned with the proper scope of judicial power, *Massachusetts v. EPA* is an example of judicial overreach. But it would be difficult, in this instance, to argue that the court was simply ignoring or creating the law. The majority of five made the plausible argument that the Environmental Protection Agency was given the power, under federal law, to regulate greenhouse gas emissions from automobiles; and if it had the power, circumstances dictated that it had to act. This had been the position of two of the EPA's general counsels

[2] Clean Air Act, 42 U.S.C. §7521 (a)(1) (2000)

in 1998 and 1999 under the Clinton administration.[3] Under the Bush administration, EPA officials came to the opposite conclusion, arguing that there was nothing in the Environmental Protection Act that gave the EPA the power to regulate "greenhouse gases."[4] Even if the EPA did possess the authority to regulate gases such as carbon dioxide, it would not have been prudent for it to do so, as Congress was attempting to address global warming through new (though certainly not always successful) legislative initiatives. The majority's position in *Massachusetts v. EPA* was that, as a matter of law, the Clinton administration had been correct. Though green house gases may not have been of specific concern to the legislators who created the EPA, the regulation of such gases fell within the EPA's power. This did not mean that the EPA would be forced by the court to issue specific regulations of automobile emissions. But the EPA could no longer avoid addressing the issue of carbon dioxide emissions from automobiles and their contribution to global warming. Congress had already given it the responsibility to investigate and, if necessary, regulate pollutants that affected the environment, and the contemporary scientific consensus was that green house gases were pollutants of that kind. Thus, the majority opinion cannot simply be dismissed as judicial law-making, or as an example of the "capture" of the Court by environmentalist interest groups and their allies. The intervention of the judiciary was enabled by the language of American environmental law, language which constrained the discretion of executive officials and experts. Whether it makes sense for courts to intervene into such a complicated policy arena is an entirely separate question. For better or worse, the American political system has structured environmental policy in such a way that it invites the exercise of judicial power.

---

[3] See Jonathan Z. Cannon, "The Significance of Massachusetts v. EPA." *Virginia Law Review*, Volume 93, Issue 3, pp 53-62 and Veronique Bugnion and David M. Reiner, "A Game of Climate Chicken: Can the EPA regulate Greenhouse Gases before the U.S. Senate passes the Kyoto Protocol?" *Environmental Law*, Volume 30, Issue 3, p. 498.

[4] Jennifer S. Lee, "EPA Says It Lacks Power to Regulate Some Gases." *New York Times*, 29 August, 2003.

Reports of the "demise of environmentalism" in American law have, after *Massachusetts v. EPA*, been revealed as premature.[5] While it is certainly the case that there is a coterie of judges opposed to the "judicialization"[6] of environmental policy, the advocates of judicial deference in environmental policy are apparently outnumbered on the Supreme Court (at least in regards to some momentous issues, such as the scope of EPA duties). They are unlikely to gain reinforcements in the immediate political future, even if one of the sitting liberal justices should choose to leave the bench. Personnel, in *Massachusetts v. EPA* as in so many other cases, seemed more important than precedent.

The demise of environmentalism in American law was exaggerated, at least in part, because some scholars overestimated the impact of judicial precedent or "stare decisis," the principle that courts should generally adhere to the rules laid down in earlier decisions. The scope of environmentalism in American law was not settled by precedents from the Rehnquist and Burger eras, precedents which suggested that courts should exercise extreme deference when evaluating the discretionary and scientific decisions of bureaucratic policy-makers.[7] In addition, the majority in *Massachusetts v. EPA* did not conform to those precedents which established a more restrictive conception of legal standing, precedents which appeared to raise further hurdles against those who might wish to direct public policy through litigation.[8] Those who thought that the heyday of environmentalism in American law was over by the late 1990s were, perhaps, guilty of

---

[5] Michael Greve, *The Demise of Environmentalism in American Law.* Washington: AEI Press, 1996.

[6] Judicialization has been described by Ran Hirschl as "the ever-accelerating reliance on courts worldwide for addressing core moral predicaments, public policy questions, and political controversies" Ran Hirschl, "The New Constitutionalism and the Judicialization of Pure Politics Worldwide." *Fordham Law Review*, Vol. 75, No. 2, pp. 721-754, 2006.

[7] E.g. *Chevron v. Natural Resources Defense Council, Inc.* 467 U.S. 837 (1984) see also Cass Sunstein "Law and Administration After Chevron." *Columbia Law Review*. Vol. 90, No. 8. (Dec. 1990) pp 2071-2120.

[8] E.g. *Lujan v. Defenders of Wildlife*, 504 U.S. 555 (1992) see also Cass Sunstein "What's Standing After Lujan? Of Citizen Suits, 'Injuries,'and Article III." *Michigan Law Review*, Vol. 91, No. 2 (Nov. 1992) pp 163-236.

excessive legal idealism. Environmental litigation continues in American courts, and it continues to succeed on occasion, despite the decisions of the Burger and Rehnquist courts that seemed to limit the legal bases for environmental litigation.

Massachusetts v. EPA might give pleasure to environmentalists, but it might also make us more cynical about the role of courts. The U.S. Supreme Court, in this case as in many others, appears to mirror the public controversies over environmentalism. Or, to use a slightly different metaphor, the case reveals the court to be an arena for ideological combat. The dissenting justices would argue, to the contrary, that their position had little or nothing to do with the science of global warming or political differences over environmentalism. Yet, for many observers, the political persuasion of the four dissenting justices cannot escape notice. Surely it is not a coincidence that only Justices Scalia, Thomas, Roberts, and Alito, conservatives all, found legal reasons to rule in favor of the Bush Administration. *Massachusetts vs. EPA*, in other words, illustrates the political character of the Supreme Court. When momentous questions reach the courtroom—the proper response to global warming, say, or the selection of the President of the United States—partisan lines are drawn, and the meaning of law and the outcome of legal cases depends upon the political affiliations and preferences of judges. If we wish to know how the courts will resolve these major issues, then we need only to inquire into the ideologies or "political preferences" of judges.

The connection between politics and law is important, and obvious. Less obvious is the way in which institutions—the structure of government, and the nature of law itself—place limits on the politics of jurisprudence. Particularly in the contemporary era, when the political and the ideological aspects of jurisprudence are highlighted by both scholars and journalists, it is easy to overlook or downplay the ways in which institutional structures constrain judicial power. The best way to remind us how institutions limit political jurisprudence is to compare how different kinds of political institutions shape the law. Comparisons between Canadian and American jurisprudence are particularly useful in this regard. If we compare American courts with courts in Canada, courts that operate in a very similar culture but in a very different institutional environment, it is easier to discern the ways in which judicial decision-making is shaped by political institutions and ultimately by the law itself.

For instance, if we take a political perspective on courts and law, we might expect that environmental activism would be at least as prevalent in Canadian law as in American. But this is not the case. Environmentalism is a popular cause in Canada,[9] but courts have rarely become its champion. The Canadian environmental record is not so great that environmentalists could ask for nothing more from the courts; in fact, Canadian environmental protections are probably less effective, and less severe, than many equivalents in the United States. Yet one searches in vain for the equivalent to *Massachusetts v. EPA* in Canadian law—that is, an example of litigation initiating major changes in the direction of environmental policy..

If legal decisions really are determined by politics and ideology, it is somewhat curious that the left-leaning Canadian polity has produced a judiciary that is hesitant to help advance one of the most central left-leaning political causes. What accounts for this relative absence of environmentalism in Canadian jurisprudence? And what does this absence tell us about the relationship between politics and law?

The timidity of the Canadian judiciary in environmental policy cannot be ascribed to a general unwillingness to intervene into politics. The *Constitution Act of 1982* and the *Canadian Charter of Rights and Freedoms* introduced "American style" judicial activism into the Canadian political system, and in many instances Canadian courts have made rulings that emulate the liberal jurisprudence of the Warren and Burger courts.[10] In some areas of policy, the impact of Canadian courts is far more apparent than in the United States. Consider, for instance, the role played by Canadian courts in regards to the Indian law.[11] In

---

[9] Judith I. McKenzie, *Environmental Politics in Canada: Managing the Commons into The 21st Century*. Oxford University Press: London, 2002. pp 91-99.

[10] The most prominent area of "judicial activism" in Canada, at least in terms of number of decisions has been the investigation and prosecution of criminal suspects. (James Kelly, *Governing with the Charter*. UBC Press: Vancouver, 2005. Pp 107-136.) However, the courts have also engaged in major interventions into abortion policy, the rights of women, rights related to freedom of speech, the rights of gays and lesbians.

[11] My use of the term "Indian law" deserves some explanation, due to the fact that in Canada the term "Indian" has often been replaced by terms and phrases such as "aboriginal," "First Nations," or "Native Canadian." First, the term

contrast to the example of environmental policy, Canadian courts have transformed the relationship between "First Nations" and the Canadian state. The best example of the Court's transformative role in aboriginal policy is *Delgamuukw v British Columbia,*[12] a complicated land claim case decided in 1997. While the case did not resolve the specific land claims of the Gitksan and Wet'suwet'en Nations who initiated the litigation, the court's opinion did elaborate a broad conception of "aboriginal title" that would form the basis for subsequent litigation. The implications of the expansive definition of aboriginal title were immediately seized upon by aboriginal leaders and academic commentators. According to some legal academics, the Court's definition of aboriginal title confirms not only ownership rights over land, but also the existence of an inherent right of self-government for aboriginal people.[13] A summit of First Nations leaders informed the federal government that, as a consequence of the *Delgamuukw* decision, the court had confirmed aboriginal title to the whole of British Columbia, along with "complete authority, jurisdiction, and decision-making in our territories and over our resources."[14] *Delgamuukw*

Indian is still commonly used in the United States, in particular by scholars. Secondly, and most importantly, in Canadian law the term "Indian" (as opposed to more inclusive terms such as aboriginals) refers to individuals who have a distinct bundle of legal and financial rights. See Gordon Gibson, *A New Look at Canadian Indian Policy.* Vancouver: Fraser Institute, 2009. Pp 18-29

[12] *Delgamuukw v. British Columbia,* (1997) CanLII 3 S.C.R. 1010.

[13] E.g. Kent McNeil "Aboriginal Rights in Canada: From Title to Land to Territorial Sovereignty." *Tulsa Journal of Comparative and International Law.* Volume 5, 1998. pp 278-98 The idea of an inherent right of aboriginal self-government is by no means a marginal idea amongst aboriginal leaders and legal elites. Less than sufficient attention has been paid to the practical details of implementing this right: "(T)he amount of attention paid by the First Nation political elite and scholarly supporters of their position to the search for a viable political and constitutional arrangement with the non-Aboriginal majority is minimal compared to the effort and advocacy devoted to self-determination, self-government, and a third order of government." Alan Cairns, *First Nations and the Canadian State.* Kingston: Queen's University, The Institute of Inter-Governmental Relations, 2005 p. 31.

[14] The Globe and Mail, 17 February 1998, p. A-18, quoted in Gurston Dacks, "British Columbia after the *Delgamuukw* Decision: Land Claims and Other

certainly did not resolve the various problems of aboriginal-state relations in Canada, but through this decision and others like it the court has shaped the options and expectations of both Native Canadians and political elites. Unlike the case of environmental policy, Canadian courts have not been hesitant to play a leading role in shaping rights and policies related to indigenous peoples.

The situation in American jurisprudence is quite different. American courts have not followed the Canadian example in reforming the relationship between Native Americans and the state. Academic commentators do not think it likely that American courts will endorse a revolution in Indian rights.[15] The simplest explanation for this situation is that the litigation prospects of Native Americans have been hampered by the strength of conservative jurists on the court—individuals such as Justice Clarence Thomas and Justice Antonin Scalia, joined recently by allies such as Chief Justice Roberts and Justice Samuel Alito, as well as their occasional compatriots such as Justice Anthony Kennedy, the recently deceased Chief Justice Rehnquist, and the recently retired Justice Sandra Day O'Connor. The absence of progressive Indian rights jurisprudence can, in other words, be explained in political terms. This situation could be reversed with changes in Congress and the Presidency, changes that would ultimately lead to more liberal appointees and thus to a jurisprudence more supportive of aboriginal claims.

The problem with this political interpretation of American Indian rights jurisprudence is simple as well: the so-called "conservatives" on the American Supreme Court are often joined by their more "liberal" colleagues in their opinions that limit and circumscribe the scope of Indian claims. At least for the last decade and half, liberal justices on the American Supreme Court— Justices Stevens, Souter, Breyer, and Ginsburg—have refrained from developing an ambitious Indian rights jurisprudence. This explains why some of the most prominent proponents of Indian rights jurisprudence have aimed their venom at

---

Processes." *Canadian Public Policy*. Volume 28, No. 2, (June, 2002) pp 239-255.

15 Steven Paul McSloy, "The Miner's Canary: A Bird's Eye View of American Indian Law and Its Future." *New England Law Review*, Volume 37, (Spring, 2003).

American Supreme Court justices who provide reliable votes for liberal political positions.[16] The obstacles to Canadian-style judicial intervention into Indian policy lies within American law itself, and not merely in the political balance of power on the court. Perhaps this is why some legal scholars suggest that only appeals to authorities outside of the American constitutional and legal tradition can lead to an American revolution in Indian rights.[17] It would be premature to suggest that a revolution in Indian rights will never occur within American law. But it would be overly simplistic to say that this revolution has been foreclosed solely because of the presence of conservative or "new right" justices on the American Supreme Court.

The divergence between Canadian and American jurisprudence in environmental and Indian law is worthy of note, not merely because they touch upon two of the central issues in contemporary political life, but also because of what the differences tell us about the nature and limits of judicial power. If courts are primarily driven by politics, we would expect that judges who support Indian rights would also support environmentalism, and vice versa. This is because support for Indian interests (or the interests of minority groups in general) and environmentalism are in many ways central to what it means to be liberal or progressive in contemporary North America.[18] A general divergence between Canadian and American jurisprudence in the last three decades would not be surprising for those who interpret courts in purely political terms. Canada has, in general, elected more left-leaning

---

[16] Robert A.Williams, *Like A Loaded Weapon: The Rehnquist Court, Indian Rights, and the legal history of racism in America.* Minneapolis: University of Minnesota Press, 2005. Pp 143-148

[17] E.g. Note, "International Law as an Interpretive Force in Federal Indian Law." *Harvard Law Review*, Vol. 116, No. 8, (June, 2003) pp 1751-1773.

[18] E.g. Richard Ellis, "Romancing the Oppressed: The New Left and the Left Out." *Review of Politics*. Volume 58, Number 1, (Winter, 1996) pp 109-154. Ellis notes the strong connection between environmentalism and support for indigenous peoples as a defining of marker of the "new left" that emerged in the post-1960s era: "Among the strongest contemporary manifestations of the of this perennial egalitarian tendency is the radical environmental movement, whose adherents routinely argue that dispossessed indigenous peoples offer an authentic model of a truly ecological society." p. 118.

governments during the past two decades, and presumably this would lead to a more left- leaning judiciary. This is what makes the differing responses of the Canadian and American courts to environmental and Indian litigatin so intriguing: it shows that the politics of jurisprudence does not always develop in ways we might expect, at least if our expectations have been shaped by cynical or "realistic" theories which assert the dependence of law upon politics. Despite the undoubted significance of political ideology and preferences, constitutional structures and legal norms continue to place constraints on the powers of courts, and they explain some of the important differences that separate the jurisprudence of Canada and the United States.

Institutional Constraints on Judicial Power: Two Facets of Constitutional Architecture

The central insight of the advocates of political interpretations of jurisprudence—whether mid-20th century legal realists, the advocates of the "attitudinal" and "rational choice" models in political science, or the proponents of critical legal studies—is that the language of law cannot constrain judicial discretion. I am not proposing that a pure legal model of judicial decision making provides a better explanation for the decisions made by judges. My goal is to illustrate how judicial politics is shaped by institutional structures or "constitutional architecture." Differing kinds of constitutional architecture provide differing opportunities for judges to exercise their policy preferences. "Constitutional architecture" is not synonymous with "law" or constitutional rights; the concept is meant to encompass the ways in which laws are made, the ways they are enforced, and how these features either inhibit or enable judicial policy-making. But legal language is part of constitutional architecture as well, and the proponents of political jurisprudence often overstate the interpretive flexibility of Constitutional documents. By paying attention to the different rights that are protected by the Canadian and American constitutions, we can see that, in some instances, the inclusion of specific rights in a nation's constitutional architecture can shape how courts influence policy.

There are two general ways in which institutions or "constitutional architecture" might shape the politics of jurisprudence in Canada and the United States: first, the structure and relationship of the law-making and policy-implementation process, and secondly, the specific language of constitutional rights-provisions. The law-making and law-enforcement process—the way in which legislatures create law and policy, and the relationship between the legislative branch and the executive branch—are of course very different in Canada and the United States. Differing means of law-creation and law-enforcement have the potential to create very different opportunities for legal interpretation. There are at least two key ways in which the differences between the Canadian Parliamentary system and the American "separation of powers" system affect the scope of judicial power:

1) Statutory language and executive discretion: The American Congress has a greater incentive to place restraints upon executive discretion, the American executive branch is separate from and not directly accountable to the legislature. In many instances, different political parties will control the legislative and executive branches, and this gives Congress an additional motive to shackle executive discretion through law. Two of the most common ways in which this occurs are through increasing the detail and specificity of law, and by allowing private groups to play a role in enforcing public law.

2) The limited legitimacy of bureaucratic discretion in the American administrative state.

Despite the fact that Congress has incentives to cabin executive discretion as much as possible, it is impossible to eliminate the discretionary character of public policy in the modern state. Given what the public wants the state to accomplish, Congress cannot possibly create all of the various rules and restrictions that govern the activities of individuals and organizations. Most law-making (euphemistically referred to as "rule-making" or "policy-making") is thus undertaken by executive branch bureaucracies. However, the legitimacy of bureaucratic decision-making is hampered by the separation of the executive and legislative branches. American courts are less inclined to regard administrative interpretations of American law as authoritative, because, unlike in parliamentary systems, the American executive is not directly controlled by those with the primary responsibility for making law. American courts have an institutional justification for intervention into administrative politics that is not available to courts in parliamentary systems of government. When American courts challenge executive discretion, they can make the plausible claim that they are insuring that executive officials are faithful to the intention of legislators. In a parliamentary system, where the executive is directly responsible to the legislature, it is more difficult for courts to claim that they must act to restrain executive discretion in order to uphold the intentions of legislators.

The opportunities for judicial intervention into environmental policy are affected by these most general features of government in Canada and the United States. In regards to Indian rights, however, we find a different facet of constitutional architecture: here, the Canadian Constitution Act of 1982 confers explicit protections for Indian rights, while the American Constitution is largely silent on the status of Indian rights and Indian treaties. My argument is that the recognition of Indian rights in the Constitution Act has provided Canadian courts with a necessary justification for the judicialization of Indian policy, a justification that is not available for environmental policy. In contrast, Indian rights have not been made part of American constitutional architecture, at least not in the same way. This does not mean that judicial power and judicial politics are irrelevant in American Indian policy. The same tensions that promote judicial power in other areas—the tension between executive discretion and legislative intent, the tension between national and state policies—also provide opportunities for judicial power and displays of judicial politics in Indian law. But the judicial role in the development of Indian law in the United States has been limited, because courts must operate under a different set of institutional limits.

The general absence of "environmental activism" in Canadian jurisprudence, and the general absence of "Indian rights activism" in American law, is a product of institutional differences between the two nations, not the political balance of power on the courts or the idiosyncratic policy preferences of judges. My intent in this study is not to deny the role of politics in judging, however. There is no doubt that political preferences, beliefs, ideologies, and personal experience colors the ways in which judges interpret the law. As there is no way to eliminate the opportunities for judicial discretion that emerge from gaps in the law, confusion in legal language, or conflicts between various laws, it is always unrealistic to expect that politics is completely irrelevant to judging. But it is also unrealistic to ignore the real differences that separate judges from other political actors. It is important to recognize the inevitability of judicial politics, without being overwhelmed by the inevitable role that politics plays in law. By paying attention to the institutional structures that variously enable or inhibit judicial power, we can gain a better appreciation of the institutional constraints on judicial power.

Outline

In chapter two, I explain in greater detail why a comparison of Canadian and American Indian and environmental law decisions can help to illustrate some important elements of judicial politics. Theorists of judicial politics who focus solely on the American polity are tempted to emphasize the political influences on courts, as they study courts that operate in only one institutional setting. By looking at some of the ways courts operate in differing political regimes, we can better appreciate the ways in which institutions affect what issues become the subject of judicial power and judicial discretion. Those few comparativists who, in recent years, have paid attention to the role of courts, have tended to focus on the similarities between judges in various regimes, or to interpret the scope of judicial power as a consequence of social factors. The Canadian and American regimes are typically regarded as "converging" towards a single model of judicial power; differences in judicial outcomes can be explained as a consequence of political struggles, as opposed to institutional differences. In contrast, I argue that a comparison of judicial politics in Canada and the United States reveals that differences in constitutional architecture help explain some of the continuing differences between the jurisprudence of Canada and the United States.

Chapter three deals with various aspects of Indian law in Canada and the United States. In this section I compare cases dealing with Indian law (defined as cases which involve claims related to unwritten aboriginal rights, claims based on Indian treaties, and statutory cases involving Indian litigants) decided by the Canadian and American Supreme Courts between 1985 (when the Canadian Constitution Act of 1982 and the Charter of Rights and Freedoms went into effect) and 2008. My central claim is that Canadian constitutional reforms have created a greater space for judicial activism regarding Indian legal claims, particularly in the area of aboriginal and treaty rights. However, the court's support for Indian claimants remains limited in many respects—the expansion of Indian rights over the previous two decades is not a result of the court having been "captured" by aboriginal interest groups or their supporters in the legal academy. Similarly, decisions by the United States Supreme Court which affect the interests of Native Americans show the constraints imposed by constitutional architecture. Unlike the case in the Canadian Supreme Court, there are clearer "voting blocs" in American Indian law, composed of judges with distinctly different levels of support for Native American legal claims. But even amongst American judges who are most likely to support these claims, there are few signs of support for anything like the Canadian revolution in Indian rights.

In chapter four, I examine a variety of environmental law decisions in Canadian and American courts. My argument is that the Canadian parliamentary system creates fewer opportunities, and fewer justifications, for intervention into environmental policy-making by Canadian courts. While Canadian courts have adopted some legal innovations that have led, in American politics, to a massive increase in the exercise of judicial power through statutory interpretation, those innovations have not had a similar effect in Canada. Canadian courts tend to adopt a deferential approach to government power in environmental law that follows the "centralization" and "governing coalition" theories of judicial decision making.[19] American courts, in contrast, are more likely to support challenges to the environmental decisions made by executive bureaucracies such as the EPA. However, these decisions do not simply mirror the intense partisan differences over environmental policies that are so prominent in Congress, academia, and mass media. Rather, the decisions show a pattern in which judges are motivated by a desire to restrain executive discretion and insure fidelity to Congressional intent. The environmental law decisions of American appellate courts, for the most part, do not reveal the influence of either "green" or "free market" approaches to environmentalism. The problems of political activism emerge not because courts are imposing their own policy preferences, but because of the way American courts have constructed the scope of judicial power, the way they have conceptualized the Congressional-Presidential relations, and the way in which they understand the requirements of the rule of law.

---

[19] E.g. Martin Shapiro, *Courts: A Comparative and Political Analysis*. Chicago: University of Chicago Press, 1986; Robert Dahl, "Decision-Making in a Democracy: The Supreme Court as a National Policy-Maker." *Journal of Public Law*, Vol. 6, (1957).

This comparison of environmental and Indian law in Canadian and American courts reveals that differing institutional environments create different forms of judicial power, and differing opportunities for interest groups interested in using litigation to pursue their goals. Environmental law decisions in Canadian and American courts show that the political differences between the two nations continue to create differing opportunities for judicial activism. The continuing deference of Canadian courts towards environmental policy-makers, despite some shifts in the Court's approach to procedural questions, illustrates how the rise in judicial activism in Canada is constrained by the Constitution Act and the Charter, and is not merely a consequence of the judicial usurpation of power. This is not intended to refute critics of the Court's Charter jurisprudence. However, in response to those who criticize the judicial activists for "making law," I argue that the environmental law decisions of Canadian courts shows that judicial activism depends upon the opportunities that judges have been given , as opposed to opportunities that judges have created for themselves.

In Indian law, by way of contrast, Canadian courts have been empowered by the "interpretive flexibility"[20] of the *Constitution Act of 1982*, which gave courts the authority to transform Indian law (though not necessarily the conditions of aboriginal peoples) and encouraged Indian litigants to seek judicial enforcement and elaboration of their rights. The limited development of Native American rights in the United States is a consequence of both political divisions and constitutional constraints. Without the kind of constitutional transformations that have occurred in Canada, it is unlikely that the success of Native Canadian litigants could be repeated in American courts, even if "conservative" justices are one day replaced by "liberals." The most important barriers to a revolution in American Indian law are the Constitution and the doctrines and precedents built upon it, not the ideological predisposition of judges.

[20] Christopher Manfredi, *Feminist Activism in the Supreme Court: legal mobilization and the Women's Legal Education Action Fund.* Vancouver: UBC Press, 2004. pp 36-37

CHAPTER TWO: THE INSTITUTIONAL LIMITS OF JUDICIAL POLITICS

The insight that courts and judges are political is not new. Perhaps it is no longer even shocking. Martin Shapiro's discussion of the American judiciary as just another potential venue for interest group politics was, in the early 1960's, intended to be impish, if not scandalous.[1] Several decades of experience with judicial activism and academic debunking of "legal formalism" have made his observations less jarring. Scholars and the public have become accustomed to the idea that interest groups attempt to influence policy through the legal system. Similarly, the notion that the political beliefs and preferences of judges shape how they address legal issues is common wisdom for students of judicial politics in the academy and in journalism. Yet while it is important to see the functional similarities between the various branches of government—that is, the ways in which legislators, executive officials, and judges are similar insofar as they are makers of policy—it is also crucial to consider how the forms of government shape what kinds of policies can be made and by whom. Political scientists have focused on how courts are similar to other political institutions, and this has been a fruitful corrective to the danger of excessive legal idealism. But it is also crucial to remember that courts engage not in politics simply, but in judicial politics. In comparison with other political actors, courts face unique constraints in regards to their ability to enforce their decisions, in regards to the kinds of decisions they have the opportunity to make, and in regards to the kinds of decisions that they are willing to make. To give two extreme examples: no interest group will ever appeal to courts in order to declare a war, and no court would ever endorse a litigant who wanted a judicial order to bring a conflict to an end. The issue of foreign policy is the starkest reminder of the limits placed upon judicial politics, whatever the desires and preferences of judges. But there are other limits as well. If we wish to understand what

[1] Martin Shapiro, *Law and Politics in the Supreme Court: New Approaches to Political Jurisprudence*. New York: Free Press of Glencoe, 1964.

courts do, it is necessary to pay attention to how institutional structures create opportunities for courts to exercise power, and how, in some areas of politics, institutional constraints prevent courts from exercising much power at all.

My comparison of American and Canadian judicial power will attempt to assess some of the ways institutional differences between these two nations shape the exercise of judicial power. I do not claim to refute the theories that stress the inherently political character of Supreme Court decision-making; indeed, I accept that the role of political ideology is central to judicial decision making. I am even inclined to think that it would be politically salutary for Americans and particularly Canadians to be more cognizant of the political dimensions of law-enforcement and judging. However, the view that courts are *only* determined by politics is misleading; as political ideology is not the source of judicial decisions in some crucial fields of law. Before turning to a discussion of how institutions constrain judicial power, and how this can be illustrated through a comparison of the jurisprudence of Indian rights and environmental law in Canada and the United States, it is worthwhile to consider the "political" approach to judicial decision-making in more detail, in order to appreciate its insights and to understand its limits.

Explaining without Evaluating? Political Science, the attitudinal model, and the study of Courts

Within political science, the "attitudinal model" refers to a half-century old research tradition which claims that the legal decisions of courts are primarily determined by the policy preferences of judges. In contrast to legal scholars who emphasized the role of precedent and constitutional language, the attitudinalists marshaled an impressive array of data which suggested that jurisprudence exists, for the most part, as an elaborate smoke-screen for judges who, consciously or not, make decisions based upon their own political preferences.

The attitudinal model has been described as the reigning research paradigm for those political scientists who study law and courts.[2] The

---

[2] E.g. Jeffrey A. Segal and Harold J. Spaeth, *The Supreme Court and the Attitudianl Model Revisited.* (Cambridge: Cambridge University Press, 2002).

idea that jurisprudence can be reduced to the psychology of individual judges (as manifested in their political preferences) is certainly not the only variety of "political" interpretations of law. Some political scientists suggest that Supreme Court decisions tend to track shifts in public opinion.[3] Others focus on the connections between Supreme Court justices and the "governing regimes" that they are part of.[4] All of these approaches are rooted in the idea that judicial-decision making, at least for appellate courts, is driven by considerations of public policy, whether idiosyncratic and personal or connected to shifts in the elite and public moods.

Other political scientists have responded to the work of the attitudinalists by emphasizing the ways in which institutions shape and constrain judicial politics. One variant of the "post-attitudinal New Institutionalism" is the strategic or rational choice model of judicial decision-making. The rational choice approach is, in pith and substance, quite similar to the attitudinal model: both are based upon the premise that judicial decisions are rooted in political preferences. However, the proponents of the strategic model emphasize that judges are constrained in pursuing their preferences on account of institutional factors, such as the possibility of appellate review, the process of collegial decision making in appellate courts, and the potential for responses to judicial decisions by other political actors. Thus, while courts are still primarily political, the politics of courts is determined not only by what judges think is politically preferable, but also by what they think is politically possible given their overall political environment.[5]

---

[3] E.g. Herbert M. Kritzer, "Federal Judges and their Political Environment: The Influence of Public Opinion," 23 American Journal of Political Science, (1979), Willima Mishler and Reginald S. Sheehan, "Public Opinion, the Attitudinal Model, and Supreme Court Decision Making: A Micro-Analytic Perspective," 58 *Journal of Politics* 169 (1996), Roy B. Flemming and B. Dan Wood, "The Public and the Supreme Court: Individual Justice Responsiveness to American Policy Moods," 41 *American Journal of Political Science* 468 (1997).

[4] Lucas Powe, *The Warren Court and American Politics*. Cambridge: Harvard University Press, 2001.

[5] For a survey of the development of the "strategic model" of judicial decision-making, see Lee Epstein and Jack Knight, "Toward A Strategic Revolution in

In light of the apparent strength of political interpretations of judicial power, other scholars have attempted to re-assess the ways in which law, constitutional forms, and legal doctrine continue to shape the ways in which courts exercise political power.[6] The political implications of this debate are important, even though they are not often stressed by the scholars themselves.[7] The structure of the judiciary in both Canada and the United States is premised on the idea that judges, when interpreting constitutional and statutory law, aim to discover the meaning of the law instead of creating that meaning themselves. This is an ideal, and one that can never be fully achieved in practice. But the institutional structure of federal courts—in particular, the insulation of judges from direct democratic control after they have been appointed—is based on the premise that courts exercise power in a way that is distinct from other political actors. The fact that impeachment, "court packing," or any other direct attempt by political actors to affect the courts are usually regarded by the public as illegitimate cannot be reconciled with a judiciary that is solely or even primarily motivated by political preferences. To the extent that courts are motivated purely by political preferences, the legitimacy of the "anti-democratic" aspects of judicial tenure is brought into question.

Whether of the attitudinalist or rational choice school, the proponents of "political jurisprudence" have not, for the most part, emphasized the normative implications of their findings. Perhaps this

---

Judicial Politics: A Look Back, a Look Ahead." *Political Research Quarterly*. Vol. 53, No. 3, (September, 2000) pp 625-661.

[6] E.g. Howard Gillman, *The Constitution Besieged: The Rise and Decline of Lochner Era Police Powers Jurisprudence*. (Durham: Duke University Press, 1993).

[7] Consider the following observation by Segal and Spaeth: "Although we live in a representative democracy, the extent to which either representation or democratic elections have force and effect depends on the will of a majority of the nine unelected, life-time serving justices...Although the justices conventionally claim for public consumption that they do no not make public policy... the truth conforms to Chief Justice Charles Evan Hughes's declaration, 'We are under a Constitution, but the Constitution is what the judges say it is.'" *The Supreme Court and the Attitudinal Model Revisited*, pp 2-3.

illustrates their own rational, preference maximizing strategy—that is, scholars who study courts for a living, having come to the conclusion that the major justifications for judicial independence are ill-founded, have chosen not to emphasize or publicize this normative conclusion, thereby insuring that they do not destroy or alter their preferred object of study in the course of studying it.

While the language of the attitudinalists is mostly dry and their methodology mostly statistical, their ultimate findings are not so different from the more fashionable advocates of "Critical Legal Studies" who dress up their conclusions in Marxist and post-structuralist idioms and are not shy about denouncing the myth of impartial law.[8] In defense of Critical Legal Studies, one could say that its practitioners are alive to the de-legitimizing implications of their arguments. In contrast, political scientists who claim to have discovered the political character of judicial decision-making have usually not emphasized the clear institutional implications of those findings. But it is far from clear whether it makes sense for political scientists to be "value neutral," at least in this instance. If judicial institutions are founded on faulty premises, it only makes sense for political scientists to point out the need to re-arrange those institutions.

I once thought that the insights of political jurisprudence could be usefully extended and developed by examining the expansion of judicial power in Canada, where the legitimacy of judicial review is at least somewhat of an open question. In examining aboriginal and environmental litigation in Canadian and American courts, I expected that the development of law could be explained as a consequence of successful interest group "capture" of like-minded judges; the success or failure of interest group lobbying of the court would ultimately be traced back to the ideology and preferences of judges. Against the legalistic model of judicial decision making, I thought it would be possible to show that both Canadian and American courts are interest group battle grounds, where outcomes are determined not so much by

---

[8] For a discussion of the relationship between political interpretations of law (such as legal realism) and the eventual move towards radicalism made by the Critical Legal Studies movement, see G. Edward White, "The Inevitability of Critical Legal Studies." *Stanford Law Review*. Volume 36, Number 2, pp 649-672.

law as by the array of political forces. I expected to write another chapter in the history of political jurisprudence. Unlike the attitudinalists and their rational choice counterparts, I was eager to stress the unavoidable normative conclusions of political jurisprudence: the idea of an independent judiciary, the idea that judges should be insulated from political pressures, or that they somehow represent neutral arbiters of law and rights, is every bit as mythical as the divine right of kings. My anticipated conclusions turned out to be incorrect, because I underestimated the influence of institutional constraints—constitutional structures and constitutional language, or "constitutional architecture"—which limit and shape judicial power in ways that cannot be accounted for by a purely political understanding of jurisprudence.

A Global Rights Revolution or a Globalized Juristocracy? Judicial Power in a Comparative Context

My initial hunch was that a comparison of judicial power in Canada and the United States would illustrate Alexis de Toqueville's view that democratic societies are, over time, likely to become hostile to the forms of political life, that is, the particular ways of doing things in law, politics, and society that structure our actions, and prevent the direct expression of power or even desire. According to Toqueville, "men living in democratic ages do not readily comprehend the utility of forms; they feel an instinctive contempt for them."[9] He argued that, in consequence, the public in democratic societies would become increasingly hostile towards, or at least impatient with, the political, social and legal forms that placed obstacles in the path of popular will. The unfortunate paradox was that, as government became more powerful, society would both be in greater need of political and legal forms for the protection of liberty, and more likely to chafe at the restraints those forms imposed.

What de Toqueville did not anticipate was the way in which courts would aid and abet the assault on the forms of government and law. He

[9] Alexis de Toqueville, *Democracy In America*, Translated by Harvey Mansfield and Delba Winthrop. Chicago and London: University of Chicago Press, 2000. Book 4, p. 669.

anticipated that the assault on political and legal forms would come from majorities eager to violate individual rights, not from courts. According to contemporary critics of judicial power, the key form of liberal democratic government is self-government, and it is this which is potentially most threatened by judicial power. Thus, while I did not think that "political jurisprudence" could account for the role of the judiciary in American and Canadian political history as a whole, it appeared that Toqueville's ideas about the weakness of forms in democratic societies could help us to understand why jurisprudence became increasingly politicized in the 20th century.

The politicization of courts and the judicialization of politics have expanded in many countries since the mid-20th century, but nowhere has this development been more prominent than in Canada and the United States.[10] The question is whether the breakdown in legal and political forms—in particular, the collapse of the distinction between what courts can decide and what they cannot, the distinction between political issues and "cases and controversies in law"—was leading to a convergence between Canada and the United States regarding the political power of courts. A convergence in the role of the judiciary might not be the same as a convergence in the outcomes in the court rooms of North America, due to the greater strength of left-wing liberalism in Canada, and thus to the left-leaning character of the Canadian judiciary. However, I expected that the forms and developments of Canadian legal liberalism would parallel the high tide of American legal liberalism. In Canada, I expected to see the subterranean transformation of judicial power that America had experienced decades earlier, transformations that could not be directly connected to the language of the *Constitution Act* and the *Charter of Rights and Freedoms*, or the intentions of those who created it.

The transformation of judicial power in the United States in the late 20th century proceeded along four separate but related fronts. Most prominent was the transformation in the judiciary's approach to enumerated and implied rights related to the rights of criminal suspects, freedom of speech and expression, equality rights, and the right to

---

[10] C. Neal Tate and Torbjorn Vallinder,editors. *The Global Expansion of Judicial Power*. New York: NYU Press, 1995.

privacy.[11] It is these aspects of constitutional law which have drawn the attention of Canadian "Charterphobes," as the principles of the "rights revolution" have migrated North in the post-Charter era.[12] Secondly, American courts transformed what it means for something to be a legal case, and what it means for someone to have a legal claim. In other words, they transformed the rules of justiciability regarding standing, adverseness, mootness, political questions, etc.[13] Third, American courts became more active through interventions in administrative law and statutory interpretation, largely (though not entirely) as a consequence of choices made by Congress.[14] Finally, the courts became more willing to use their power not only to prevent government action that was un-Constitutional or illegal, but to prescribe specific policy solutions for legal violations, and to oversee the implementation of those solutions.[15]

---

[11] Aside from freedom of speech, these are the major areas addressed in Gerald Rosenberg's assessment of the American Supreme Court's judicial activism, *The Hollow Hope: Can Courts Bring About Social Change?* Chicago: University of Chicago Press, 1991 In response to the question that is the sub-title of his book, Rosenberg's answer is a no. The most plausible defense of the *legitimacy* of the Court's new approach to enumerated and implied rights that developed over the course of the Warren and Burger Courts, is Bruce Ackermann's *We The People, Volume Two: Transformations*. Cambridge: Harvard University Press, 1998.

[12] E.g. Morton, F.L. and Rainer Knopff. *The Charter Revolution and the Court Party*. Peterborough, Ontario: Broadview Press, 2000.

[13] For a good discussion of this topic and its relationship to the expanded power of the court, and thus the increased controversies over judicial appointments, see Mark Silverstein, *Judicious Choices: The New Politics of Supreme Court Appointments*. New York: Norton Press, 1994.

[14] Martin Shapiro *Who Guards the Guardians? Judicial Control of Administration*. Athens, Ga.: University of Georgia Press, 1988, Jeremy Rabkin, *Judicial Compulsions: How Public Law Distorts Public Policy*. (New York: Basic Books, 1989; R. Shep Melnick, *Between the Lines: Interpreting Welfare Rights*. Washington, D.C.: Brookings Institution, 1994.

[15] E.g. Donald Horowitz, *The Courts and Social Policy* Washington, D.C.: The Brookings Institution, 1977, Malcolm M. Feeley and Edward L. Rubin,

Other authors who have studied the growing role of courts in political life have tended to focus on the similarities between the development of judicial power in Canada and the United States.[16] In fact, the similarities between the "rights revolution" in Canada and the United States—successful revolutions both, in contrast with the partial or abortive revolutions in judicial power that have occurred in Britain and India—was one of the central themes in Charles Epp's aptly titled *The Rights Revolution.*[17] The similarities between the development of judicial power in Canada and the United States, according to Epp, are a result of the confluence of three factors:

1) the presence, in both nations, of court-empowering constitutional documents;

2) the rise of an activist, pro-rights judiciary; and

3) the development of a legal support structure composed of activists, lawyers, and governments that are willing to support them.

Thus while it is true that not all rights revolutions are the same, the rights revolutions that have occurred in Canada and the United States have been more similar than any other. They did not occur at the same time—the expansion of judicial power in Canada in areas such as

---

Judicial Policy-Making and the Modern State. Cambridge: Cambridge University Press, 2000, Ross Sandler and David Schoenbrod, *Democracy by Decree.* New Haven: Yale University Press, 2003.

[16] E.g. Ran Hirschl *Towards Juristocracy: The Origins and Consequences of the New Constitutionalism.* Cambridge: Harvard University Press, 2004 In his comparative analysis of the rise of judicial power, Hirschl argues that the common thread of "judicialization" is the desire of political and "influential economic stakeholders" (p. 213) to shelter decisions from popular decision-making. Hirschl's "hegemonic preservation thesis" does not address the way judicial power functions in different institutional contexts–a consequence of the fact that he only looks at parliamentary systems of government that have introduced judicial review in recent decades. Canadian critics of judicial power have also tended to focus on the ways in which judicial review in Canada has mirrored American constitutional developments (e.g. W.A. Bogart. *Good Government? Good Citizens? Courts, Politics, and Markets in a Changing Canada.* Vancouver: UBC Press, 2005, pp 30-31).

[17] Charles Epp, *The Rights Revolution.* Chicago: University of Chicago Press, 1998.

criminal rights, abortion rights, and freedom of expression had to wait, according to Epp, for the introduction of the court-empowering *Charter of Rights and Freedoms*—but they have followed along similar paths.

While political scientists have in recent years paid increased attention to the conditions that allow for increased judicial power, the ways in which "rights revolutions" *differ* in those places where they occur has not been as thoroughly explored. We know that rights revolutions are occurring around the globe, but we know less about how different institutional and cultural contexts affect the revolutionary process. Even if Epp's conditions for a "rights revolution" are fulfilled, we cannot be sure that the expansion of judicial power will take the same form in different institutional contexts.

There are some reasons to anticipate a convergence of rights revolutions, however. The influence of the American legal academy shapes the consciousness of judges around the world, though its influence is particularly prominent in Canada; according to H.W. Arthurs, the influence of the United States is a recurring theme in the history of Canadian legal education.[18] The pressure groups that play such a vital role in Epp's explanation are often part of international issue networks.[19] The circulation of information and individuals through these networks helps to solidify their ideological similarities and unify their programmatic goals. Given the fact that the legal elites who fuel the worldwide rights revolutions are so homogenous, it seems possible that when the conditions for a rights revolution exist, the "legal support structure" will push for similar kinds of changes within the governing regime.

Epp's comparative study of the development of judicial power can be read as a supplement to the attitudinal and rational choice models of political jurisprudence. While acknowledging the role of judicial ideology, *The Rights Revolution* stresses that the capacity of courts and the willingness of judges to make policy depends on both institutional

---

[18] H.W. Arthurs, "The Political Economy of Canadian Legal Education." *Journal of Law and Society*. Volume 25, Number 1, p. 15.

[19] E.g. Robert Rohrschneider and Russell Dalton, "A Global Network? Transnational Cooperation Amongst Environmental Groups." *The Journal of Politics*. Volume 64, Number 2. May 2002. pp 510-533.

and social pre-conditions, such as court-empowering constitutions that enshrine fundamental rights, and legal support structures that help to advance novel understandings of those rights. Epp also suggests that, in light of his analysis, concerns with the anti-democratic character of judicial power are exaggerated, as courts are only able to exercise power if other political actors take steps to empower courts. Thus, Epp explains not only why courts become politically active in some times and places but not others; he is also able to address, if not resolve, the question of the legitimacy of judicial power in democratic societies.

The development of judicial power analyzed (and celebrated)[20] by Epp has of course been subject to varying levels of criticism and scrutiny. In the United States, critics of judicial power have focused on both the legitimacy and the effectiveness of judicial activism, usually (though certainly not always) from the conservative end of the political spectrum.[21] In Canada, "Charterphobes" have been more evenly distributed across the political spectrum. Left wing critics tend to argue

---

[20] Epp's book can be read as an attempt to address the theoretical problems with modern judicial activism–in particular, the claim that non-interpretivist judicial review is suspect in a democracy because of its counter-majoritarian character: "Constitutional rights in general, and rights revolutions in particular... rest on a support structure that has a broad basis in civil society." (Epp, *The Rights Revolution*, p. 199) His argument is as follows: constitutional rights provisions cannot be effectively enforced unless a legal support structure (litigants, interest groups, public interest lawyers, academics) exists to mobilize those rights; such a legal support structure will be weak unless it is provided government support; government support for the legal support structures that make "rights revolutions" possible undercuts the claim that those rights revolutions are counter-majoritarian.

[21] E.g. John Agresto, *The Supreme Court and Constitutional Democracy*. Ithaca: Cornell University Press, 1984, Christopher Wolfe *The Rise of Modern Judicial Review: From Constitutional Interpretation to Judge-Made Law*. Lanham, Md.: Rowan and Littlefield, 1994., Matthew Franck *Against the Imperial Judiciary: The Supreme Court vs. The Sovereignty of the People* Lawrence: University Press of Kansas, 1996 For examples of theoretical criticisms of judicial power from a liberal perspective, see Mark Tushnet, *Taking the Constitution Away from the Courts*. Princeton: Princeton University Press, 1999 Jeremy Waldron, *The Dignity of Legislation* Cambridge: Cambridge University Press, 1999.

that the rise of judicial power has been part of a project to insulate elites from populist pressure on economic issues.[22] Those on the right are undoubtedly pleased that courts have not imposed a greater degree of socialism on Canadian citizens, but they have otherwise found little to applaud in the Court's *Charter* jurisprudence. Conservative critics have applied the doctrinal criticisms developed in the United States to the jurisprudence of the Supreme Court, and have found post-Charter Canadian jurisprudence similarly wanting in terms of its fidelity to the text of the Constitution, its underlying philosophical justifications, and its tendency to expand the scope of state power. The ultimate conclusion of right-wing Canadian critics is, in essence, that the Courts have become "captured" by organized interests and, perhaps most alarmingly, even captured by the legal academy itself.[23]

Conservative Charter critics have focused on the ways in which the Canadian Supreme Court has been influenced by liberal American jurisprudence in areas of law such as criminal rights, abortion, women's rights, and freedom of speech.[24] In regards to some issues, such as criminal disenfranchisement and gay rights, the Canadian

---

[22] E.g. Michael Mandel, *The Charter of Rights and the Legalization of Politics in Canada.* Toronto: Thompson Press, 1994. Consider also the views of Ran Hirschl: "As long as representative political-decision making institutions were kept safely in the hands of the established social circles... parliamentary sovereignty was praised by politicians and constitutional theorists alike as the most sacred of democratic values....As political representatives of the established interests started to lose control of these institutions (at different times in different polities), they started to worry about the 'tyranny of the majority.'" (Hirschl, *Towards Juristocracy*, p. 217).

[23] E.g. F.L. Morton and Troy Riddell, "Reasonable Limitations, Distinct Society, and the Canada Clause: Interpretive Clauses and the Competition for Constitutional Advantage." *Canadian Journal of Political Science.* Volume 31, Number 3, (April, 1998) pp 467-493.

[24] E.g. Christopher Manfredi, *Judicial Power and the Charter.* (Toronto: McLelland and Stewart, 1993); F.L. Morton *Pro-Choice vs. Pro-Life: Abortion and the Courts in Canada* Norman, Ok: University of Oklahoma Press, 1992; F.L. Morton and Avril Allen, "Feminists and the Courts: Measuring Success in Interest Group Litigation in Canada." *Canadian Journal of Political Science.* Volume 34, Number 1, 2001 pp 55-84.

Supreme Court has endorsed liberal or progressive positions that have not received the same recognition in American courts.[25] The proponents of the "rights revolution" have responded to these criticisms along two different fronts. First, there is the position of the "rights fundamentalists," who argue that the Supreme Court's Charter jurisprudence reflects a correct understanding of fundamental rights, in the sense that the framers of the Constitution Act of 1982 endorsed an evolutionary, court-centered approach to Constitutional law.[26] A second group of scholars have argued that Charter critics—and the rights fundamentalists—have exaggerated the extent to which the Courts have undermined Parliamentary sovereignty. These scholars suggest that Parliament has played a more active and voluntary role in the development of rights policies; post-Charter jurisprudence has thus emerged through a "dialogue" between Courts and the elected branches of government.[27]

The debate over judicial power in Canada has taken place over issues that are generally familiar to American students of constitutional law and judicial politics; the complaints of the critics ultimately turn on philosophical issues about the meaning and scope of rights, and thus any complaint that courts have engaged in illegitimate activism in regards to freedom of speech, women's rights, or the rights of suspects turns into an argument over "original intentions," living

---

[25] Christopher Manfredi, "Judicial Review and Criminal Disenfranchisement in Canada and the United States." *The Review of Politics*, Volume 60, Number 2, 1998 pp277-305 Jason Pierceson, *Courts, Liberalism, and Rights: Gay Law and Politics in Canada and the United States.* Philadelphia, Pa.: Temple University Press, 2005.

[26] E.g. David Beatty, *Talking Heads and the Supremes: The Canadian Production of Constitutional Review.* Toronto: Carswell, 1990. Lorraine Weinrib, "The Supreme Court of Canada and Section One of the Charter." The *Supreme Court Law Review.* Volume 10, 1998 pp 469-513 and "Canada's Constitutional Revolution: From Legislative to Constitutional State." *Israel Law Review.* Volume 33, Number 1, 1999 pp 13-50.

[27] Janet L. Hiebert, *Charter Conflicts: What Is Parliament's Role?* Montreal: McGill-Queen's University Press, 2002; James B. Kelly, *Governing with the Charter.* Vancouver: UBC Press, 2005.

constitutionalism, and the source and foundations of rights. The debate over American judicial activism has often proved most fruitful, however, when scholars have considered how courts have exercised power over public policy in ways that are not clearly connected to the individualistic, rights-oriented issues that are the traditional domain of the courts.[28] While the attempts to assess the "policy impact" of courts end up being as controversial as more theoretical and doctrinal debates over the legitimacy of judicial activism, they have helped to illustrate the full scope of judicial power in American politics. It also raises the question of whether Canada, which has experienced something like an American rights revolution, is likely to experience all aspects of the American revolution in judicial power. Similarly, it is useful to consider whether the textual differences between the Canadian and American constitutions limit judicial power in ways that cannot be explained by the differing ideologies or policy preferences of judges. In assessing these issues, we can shed light not only on the concerns of scholars who study the relative influence of constitutional architecture and political ideology in judicial decision making, but also on the legitimacy of judicial power. As I will explain next, environmental law and aboriginal rights provide two useful cases for assessing the role of "constitutional architecture" in Canadian and America courts.

The Separation of Powers, Parliamentary Government and Constitutional Language

The expansion of judicial power in the United States came about not merely as a consequence of new judicial approaches to questions of

---

[28] cf the work of Horowitz, Rabkin, Melnick, Sandler and Schoenbrod, and Feeley and Rubin. It is interesting to note that, in shifting to a defense of judicial activism that is entirely based on the politically beneficial outcomes of that activism, Feeley and Rubin argue that the theoretical criticisms leveled against judicial activism–that it violates principles of federalism, the separation of powers, and the rule of law–are correct: "the admitted divergence between the judiciary's actions and accepted legal principles reveals an underlying weakness in those principles...Judicial policy-making, by virtue of its brute existence, thus casts doubt not only on the individual principles, but on the general image of law and government from which they are derived." *Judicial Policy-Making and the Modern State*. p. 336.

fundamental rights, but also as a consequence of new judicial approaches to statutory interpretation and executive power. Thus, it is useful to consider whether the very different institutional architecture of the Canadian political system presents differing obstacles (or opportunities) for judges engaged in interpreting statutes and evaluating executive law-enforcement and policy implementation. While many rights recognized by the Canadian *Charter of Rights and Freedoms* parallel those found in the American Bill of Rights,[29] the repatriation of the Canadian constitution in 1982 did not change the parliamentary form of government.[30] Canadians were given American-style judicial review in 1982, but they were not given the American legislative process, or the American separation of powers. Thus, while authors like Epp, Manfredi, and Morton have focused on the overlap between American and Canadian judicial power in areas such as criminal and abortion rights, they represent only the tip of the legal iceberg in American political life. In addition, the Canadian *Charter of Rights and Freedoms* differs significantly from the American Bill of Rights. The latter was a product of the sectional and political differences amongst 18th century revolutionaries, the former a product of negotiations amongst late 20th century political and bureaucratic elites.31 It is worth considering whether textual differences in constitutional language affect the work of judges, or whether the language of constitutional

---

[29] Christopher Manfredi, "The Use of United States Decisions by the Supreme Court of Canada under the Charter of Rights and Freedoms." *Canadian Journal of Political Science*. Volume 23, Number 3. 1990 pp 499-518.

[30] For a discussion of "mega-constitutional" politics in Canada, see Peter H. Russell, *Constitutional Odyssey: Can Canadians Become a Sovereign People?* Toronto: University of Toronto Press, 1992. See also Ronald L. Watts, "Canada: Three Decades of Periodic Federal Crises." *International Political Science Review*. Vol. 17. No. 4, (Oct, 1996) pp 353-371.

31 For an interesting discussion of the Framers of the Canadian *Charter*, see James Kelly, *Governing with the Charter* , pp 88-95. Kelly argues the Framers (or, at least the intent of those who triumphed during constitutional negotiations) intended the Charter to produce judicial activism in at least two ways: first, the Charter would empower courts to challenge other governmental and bureaucratic actors, and the content of the Charter would be modified, altered, and adapted by the courts over time.

rights is so malleable that judges are not really restrained by the language and intentions of constitutional framers. To what extent have these continuing institutional differences prevented the "rights revolutions" of North America—or, more accurately, the revolutions in judicial power—from converging?

According to scholars such as R. Shep Melnick, there are several reasons to think that the American "separation of powers" system creates greater opportunities for the expression of judicial power. Focusing on the differences between American and British practices, Melnick argues that a variety of factors allow for American courts to engage in judicial activism through statutory interpretation. In contrast with Britain, American courts have authority equal to administrators in the interpretation of statutory law, whereas British courts are expected to focus on the ordinary meaning of words in statutes, American courts are much more likely to look to the history, purpose, and spirit of statutes when interpreting them.[32] As a consequence, American judges avail themselves of a wide range of diverging and contrary statements made by elected and unelected officials regarding the meaning of the law and the intentions of Congress, which in turn become the basis for judicial challenges to the statutory interpretations of the executive branch.[33] These contrary approaches to statutory interpretation are rooted in political differences between the two nations. Parliamentary government, by virtue of the strength of political parties, the respect afforded to the civil service, and the centralization of power within the cabinet, creates a situation which reduces judicial discretion: "Not only is legislation drafted by the ministries, but it is ordinarily passed in much the same form as presented. . . . The legislation that emerges from Parliament also tends to be more coherent and drafted with more care than is the legislation passed by Congress."[34] Finally, British

[32] Patrick Atiyah and Robert S. Summers, *Form and Substance in Anglo-American Law: A Comparative Study in Legal Reasoning, Legal Theory, and Legal Institutions.* London:Clarendon Press, 1987 pp 100-101.

[33] E.g. Robert Katzmann, *Institutional Disability: The Saga of Transportation Policy for the Disabled.* Washington, D.C.: The Brookings Institution, 1986.

[34] R. Shep Melnick, *Between the Lines: Interpreting Welfare Rights.* Washington, D.C.: The Brookings Institution, 1994 p. 10.

judges are aware that decisions a cabinet minister regards as adverse can be readily overturned through corrective legislation. The American legislative process is far more fragmented, and this often produces statutes that are more ambiguous. While presidents and administrators claim the authority to resolve ambiguities, courts are just as willing to claim that they possess a responsibility to uphold the intentions of Congress. The fragmented legislative process makes it difficult for the elected branches to respond to judicial statutory interpretations. Finally, the complexities of federalism, and the power of judicial review of legislation for violations of Constitutional rights, provide additional avenues for the exercise of judicial power in statutory interpretation.[35]

What are the implications of Melnick's study of judicial statutory activism in the United States for a comparative study of judicial power in Canada and the United States? The most important implication is that judges only have the capacity to exercise power depending upon the legal or Constitutional environment that they find themselves in. Despite the introduction of the court-empowering *Constitution Act* and *Charter*, the power of Canadian courts is likely to be restricted by the parliamentary form of government. Canadian courts have always played a role in adjudicating the respective spheres of federal and provincial power.[36] The introduction of the *Charter* has empowered courts to engage in review of legislation for rights violations, which has allowed Canadian courts to follow the American "rights revolutions" in a large numbers of areas. But the legislative process in Canada still remains parliamentary; in fact, the legislative process has become increasingly centralized in the Prime Minister's Office in recent decades.[37] In regards to statutory interpretation, this highly centralized

---

[35] Ibid pp 11-13.

[36] E.g. Peter Russell, *Constitutional Odyssey: Can Canadians Become a Sovereign People?* Toronto: University of Toronto Press, 1993 p. 42 See also Ronald L. Watts, "The American Constitution in Comparative Perspective: A Comparison of Federalism in Canada and the United States." *The Journal of American History*. Vol. 74, No. 3 (December, 1987) pp 769-792.

[37] Donald Savoie, *Governing from the Center: The Concentration of Power in Canadian Politics*. Toronto: University of Toronto Press, 1999.

legislative process creates less space for the assertion of judicial power, space that is created in American law by the tensions between the executive and the legislative branch, the chaotic nature of the legislative process, and the relative weakness of political parties and party leaders. Melnick's institutional analysis of the sources of American statutory judicial activism implies that, while American and Canadian courts might converge in areas of enumerated rights in the post-Charter era, the two political systems offer very different opportunities for the expression of judicial power in regards to statutory interpretation. Thus, based upon these institutional considerations, we have reasons to suspect that environmental policy-making by Canadian courts will be quite limited, regardless of what we might expect based upon the broader ideological predispositions of those judges.

The Canadian constitution does provide some avenues for judicial power that are not present in the American constitution. The written constitutions of Canada and the United States provide protections for rights that are broadly similar, but some of the most obvious differences between the two can be seen in the treatment of aboriginal treaties and aboriginal rights. Stated briefly, the Canadian *Constitution Act of 1982* made both aboriginal treaties and un-enumerated aboriginal rights part of the nation's "higher law." Unlike many of the rights protected by the Canadian *Charter*, judicial determinations of aboriginal rights cannot be overturned through recourse to the Section 33 "notwithstanding clause," which allows both federal and provincial governments to insulate legislation (in some circumstances, and in regards to certain rights) from legal challenges based on the *Charter*. Those who lobbied for and those who approved the protections for aboriginal rights in the *Constitution Act* were not certain what the content of those rights would be. But the explicit constitutional protections for indigenous rights provided a legal basis for judicial intervention into Indian policy that is not present in the American constitutional order.

The status and rights of American Indian tribes have always been uncertain. Native Americans are neither ordinary citizens nor separate peoples; in the famous and puzzling words of Chief Justice John Marshall, the Indians in the United States are "domestic dependent nations."[38] American policy towards the Indian tribes has been characterized by a variety of different approaches over time: military conflict and forced expulsion in the early 19th century, accommodation and the promotion of assimilation in the late 19th and early 20th century, and recognition and support for the continuing existence of the special political status of Native Americans in the late 20th century. What has not changed, however, is the dominant role played by Congress in determining the status of Indian tribes. In practice, this means that the treaties and "aboriginal rights" that are part of Canada's "higher law" are, in America, more akin to statutes. Treaties between the American government and Native American tribes can be altered and abridged by unilateral Congressional action. The plenary power of Congress in Indian policy leaves considerable potential for judicial influence, in the sense that courts must still adjudicate between conflicting claims of Congress, the executive branch, and state governments. The Canadian constitutional system, however, provides a much broader basis for judicial interventions into aboriginal policy.

From the perspective of the "attitudinal model," the presence or absence of specific constitutional provisions should matter very little, if at all. Judges who wish to advance or retard the legal claims of Native Americans or Canadians will have no trouble finding constitutional provisions upon which to hang their rhetorical hats. What matters is not the constitutional text, which can be interpreted in a manifold if not infinite number of ways, but whatever individual justices might happen to think about the political advantages and disadvantages of Indian claims.[39] The claim that I will defend is that, at least in the context of Indian rights, institutional constraints rooted in constitutional politics place limits on political jurisprudence. The patterns of Indian law decisions in Canadian and American courts, as in the case of environmental law, cannot be accounted for without paying attention to the role played by institutional architecture.

---

[38] *Cherokee Nation v. Georgia*, 30 U.S. 1 (1831)

[39] I note again the similarity, in the study of law, between the staid social scientists and their literary-theoretical equivalents in law schools and English departments (e.g. Stanley Fish), all of whom are in agreement over the radically indeterminate character of textual interpretation, and the priority of politics over law in judicial decision making.

Evaluating the Institutional Constraints on Judicial Power: How a Cross-National Study of Indian and Environmental Law Illustrates the Significance of Political Institutions

The institutional structures that this study will consider are the differences between the Canadian and American constitutions, both in the sense of the specific rights recognized or framed by these instruments, and the ways in which the two country's differing legislative processes, and differing executive-legislative relationships, create different spaces for judicial activism. The central argument is that the exercise of judicial power in Canada and United States diverges in Indian law and environmental law because of the continuing significance of constitutional differences between the two nations—differences that have been reduced, but not eliminated, by the "rights revolutions" of the late twentieth century.

The comparison also helps to illustrate some of the limits of purely political interpretations of judicial decision making, because the patterns of Canadian and American environmental and aboriginal law do not follow the patterns that one would expect to see, assuming that the courts are guided primarily by their policy preferences. What would we expect from a purely political court? That is, what patterns would we expect from judicial decisions, if judicial attitudes, preferences, and ideologies were more important than institutional and legal factors? A political court would reveal judges who make decisions that are, by and large, ideologically consistent across issues. If we know that the American Supreme Court is staffed by a conservative majority, we can expect that the court will tend to reach conservative conclusions in a broad range of controversial cases; if a liberal majority on the court comes to predominate, the reverse will be true.

One might object that "conservative" and "liberal" are too broad, and too ill-defined, to provide useful guidance in assessing the predispositions of judges. The first response to this objection is that the concepts of "liberal" and "conservative" predispositions are useful, even if they are imperfect. Political scientists should not be too quick to simply dismiss these popular terms of political discourse when considering judicial politics. Despite the imprecision of ideological classifications, they do capture something about the way individuals orient themselves towards political life. In commenting on the synergy amongst various progressive movements in the 1960s, Samuel

Huntington observed that "an individual or group that has a specific concern with one particular reform also usually has a generally reformist weltanschauung which induces the individual or group to be favorably disposed to all reforms."[40] While not all supporters of labor unionism support gay marriage (to give but one example), ideological classifications are useful in describing political attitudes.

It is not necessary to give a comprehensive definition of liberalism and conservatism in order to ascertain the political meaning of liberalism in relation to environmentalism and issues affecting native North Americans. The common sense answer is that "liberals" will tend to support both "green causes" and the claims of minority groups such as Indians; conservatives are far more likely to be suspicious of those causes and claims. Scholars have mostly confirmed this common sense conclusion.[41] Most importantly for this study, environmentalism and aboriginal rights (or perhaps minority rights in general) are both "post-materialist" issues associated with the rise of "new politics" in the post-1960s era.[42] Post-materialism is a concept that is used to explain the shift away from "class based" politics that has occurred in many industrial democracies. If materialist politics is based upon conflicts over how to expand the economic pie (and how to divide it up amongst

---

[40] Huntington, *American Politics: The Promise of Disharmony*, New York: Belnap Press, 1981 p. 110.

[41] "Environmental concern" ("the degree to which people are aware of environmental problems and support efforts to solve them..." R.E. Dunlap and R.E. Jones, "Environmental attitudes and values." in R. Fernandez-Ballesteros, editor, *Encyclopedia of Psychological Assessment* Volume One. Sage Publishers, London. p. 365) has been shown, unsurprisingly, to be positively associated with left-wing or liberal political attitudes (e.g. J.D. Skrentny, "Concern for the Environment: A Cross-National Perspective." *International Journal of Public Opinion Research* Volume 5, Number 4, 1993. pp 335-352). Few studies have found any strong relationship between occupational sector, social class, or income and environmental concern (e.g. Dietz T., et al. "Social structural and social psychological bases of environmental concern." *Environment and Behavior*, Volume 30, Issue 4, 1998.

[42] Ronald Inglehart, "Public Support for Environmental Protection: Objective Problems and Subjective Values in 43 Societies." *PS: Political Science and Politics*, Vol. 28, No. 1 (Mar., 1995), pp. 57-72

economic classes), post-materialist politics centers on the cultural claims or "identity politics" of groups that are not defined strictly by class (women, gays and lesbians, minorities) as well as the consequences of economic growth (such as consumer protection and environmentalism.) Just as we expect that broad public support for environmentalism would be joined with broad public support for aboriginal rights, so too would we expect that, if jurisprudence is determined by ideology, then courts that produce pro-environmental decisions will also tend to support aboriginal rights claimants. American and Canadian politics have become (too a great extent) constituted by conflicts between the post-materialist left and the still materialist right, and judicial politics will be characterized by the same schism.

The first supposition of this study, then, is that support for environmentalism tends to be linked with support for Indian rights. The second is that the ideological differences between Canada and the United States are minimal. Canada differs from the United States in the way that New York state differs from the United States as a whole—both are more liberal, but not fundamentally different.[43] So, while it is

---

[43] Mildred A. Schwartz, in her *Party Movements in the United States and Canada(* Lanham, Md.: Rowan and Littlefield, 2006) also suggests that a Canadian-American comparison allows for the consideration of the effects of institutional differences (e.g. the absence of primary elections in Canadian politics) because of the close similarities between northern American states and Canadian provinces in terms of "culture, economics, and voter dispositions." p. 15 See also Mildred Schwartz, "Canadian Policy Studies in Comparative Perspective," in *Policy Studies in Canada: The State of the Art* ed. Laurent Dobuzinskis, Michael Howlett, and David Laycock. Toronto: University of Toronto Press, 1996. Consider as well the conclusion of Mebs Kanji and Neil Nevitte in their study of attitudes towards authority in Canada and the United States: "The two cultures are virtually indistinguishable when it comes to their protest inclinations, their confidence in governmental institutions, their support for worker expressiveness and their views on parent-child relations." Mebs Kanji and Neil Nevitte, "Who are the most deferential: Canadians or Americans?" in *Canada and the United States: Differences that Count.* ed. David M. Thomas Peterborough, ON: Broadview Press, 2000 Other studies that emphasize the increasing similarities between the political values of Canadians and Americans include D. Baer, E. Grabb, and W. Johnston, "Reassessing Differences in Canadian and American Values." in *Images of Canada: The Sociological Tradition.* ed. J. Curtis and I Tepperman Scarborough, ON:

true that both libertarian anti-statism and religious conservatism have a greater presence in the American ideological spectrum, there is little reason to think that Canadian liberal elites have fundamentally different policy preferences than American liberals.

The case I want to make is thus based upon certain assumptions about the nature of political ideology in North America. Assumption #1 is that "liberalism" tends to imply support for aboriginal rights and a tendency to support environmentalism. Assumption #2 is that the meaning of liberalism, and the preferences of liberals, is to a considerable extent consistent across national boundaries in North America. Given the patterns of judicial decision-making identified in this study, a political explanation of the patterns of aboriginal and environmental law in Canada and the United States would have to be based upon the following claims:

a) The greater support for Indian litigants, as opposed to environmental interests, in the Canadian Supreme Court shows that judges have an ideological pre-disposition to support aboriginal claims, but not the goals of environmentalist groups.

b) Liberal or moderate justices on the American Supreme Court have policy preferences (regarding aboriginal and environmental

---

Prentice-Hall Canada, 1999., J.P Alston, T.M. Morris, and A Vedlitz, "Comparing Canadian and AmericanValues: New Evidence from National Surveys." *American Review of Canadian Studies* Volume 26, Number 3, 1996 pp 301-314.

There is an emerging literature on the supposedly increasing ideological and cultural differences between Canada and the United States. Michael Adams, in *Fire and Ice: The United States, Canada, and the Myth of Converging Values* (Toronto: Penguin, 2003) makes the argument that the cultural differences between Canada and the United States have been markedly distinct in the past, and are not converging despite the increased similarities between the Canadian and American political systems that have resulted from Canada's court-empowering Constitution Act of 1982. Phillip Resnick's more scholarly *The European Roots of Canadian Identity* (Peterborough, Ontario: Broadview Press, 2005) also endorses the view on the significance of cultural differences between the two countries, albeit in a more qualified form. My own view is closer to that of Christian Boucher ('Canada-U.S. Values: Distinct, Inevitably Carbon Copy, or Narcissism of Small Differences? *Horizons* Vol. 7, No. 1 (2004).

policy) that are the reverse of their liberal or moderate Canadian counterparts.

This political interpretation, I will argue, is difficult to sustain. In regards to environmental law and aboriginal rights, the differences between Canadian and American jurisprudence can be explained only if institutional differences are taken into account. The Canadian and American political systems afford different opportunities for political activism—and what this means, in substantive political terms, is that while Canada has experienced something like the American "rights revolution" in areas such as criminal law, abortion policy, and freedom of speech, it is unlikely to undergo the full American experience of an "imperial judiciary" that arbitrates a vast range of policy questions. All rights revolutions are not the same. Canadian courts have been empowered by constitutional changes, and they have converged with American courts in some ways, but the power exercised by Canadian courts is still restrained by constitutional language, and by the constitutional form of parliamentary government.

In regards to Indian law, the most salient aspects of "constitutional architecture" are those special protections for aboriginal rights that are so prominent in the Canadian Constitution Act of 1982, protections that are not present in the American Constitution. It is this constitutional difference which explains the prominence of the Canadian judiciary in the development of aboriginal rights. Unlike the case of Indian law, there is no reason to think that the transformative effects of the Constitution Act and the Charter should extend to environmental law—unless we assume, as some do, that the Charter has emboldened judges to invent rights as they see fit, in response to interest group pressures. Judicial activism in environmental law, in Canada, would be a troubling development, judged from the perspective of legal or constitutional legitimacy. The underlying political conditions that promote judicial deference in statutory interpretation were not altered by the re-patriation of the Canadian constitution. As the Canadian constitution contains no environmental equivalent to the aboriginal rights specifically protected in Section 35 of the Constitution Act, there is no legal reason to think that Canadian environmental law decisions would be encompassed by Canada's rights revolution. If Canadian courts have engaged in an environmental rights revolution, it would be further support for the Charter-phobes who see the courts as engaged in an essentially political role, guided solely by judicial policy preferences. The limits of judicialization in Canadian environmental law (as well as the limits of the "rights revolution" in American Indian law) show that, in some crucial instances, the role of courts cannot be understood in terms of political ideology and partisan differences.

The method and goals used in this project are similar in some ways to Howard Gilman's *The Constitution Besieged*, a study of the "laissez-faire" jurisprudence in late 19th and early 20th century America.[44] The common interpretation of this era—repeated by progressive jurists and scholars of various stripes—is that federal courts were dominated by anti-statist ideologues, influenced by Social Darwinism and Manchester-school economics, who waged a judicial war against the development of the modern state. Through a careful analysis of the legal arguments used by judges, and the patterns of judicial decision-making, Gilman demonstrates that courts during this era were not motivated by any particular animus against state power as a whole. Instead, their decisions reflected long established legal rationales, rooted in the political theories of the Founding generation and developed by early 19th century jurists, regarding the proper form of national and state regulatory power. Courts invalidated government actions that attempted to confer economic benefits on some at the expense others. The fact that the vast majority of state and federal regulations were upheld when subjected to judicial challenge illustrates the limits of purely political interpretations. What Gilman did in *The Constitution Besieged* was to ask a simple question: "If courts are political, and if the dominant narrative about judicial ideology during the laissez-faire era is correct, what would we expect to see in the jurisprudence of this era?" The answer to this question is that we would expect to see courts that are inveterately opposed to statism. What Gilman found instead was a jurisprudence that circumscribed state power in a consistent, principled, and infrequent manner.

This study of environmental and Indian law in Canada and the United States asks a similar question, and comes to a similar conclusion: the actual pattern of judicial decision-making in these areas

[44] Howard Gillman, *The Constitution Besieged: The Rise and Demise of Lochner-Era Jurisprudence*. Durham: Duke University Press, 1994.

of law confounds expectations based upon political interpretations of jurisprudence. This study challenges contemporary myths about judicial power, myths that have been promoted, perhaps unintentionally, by scholars who emphasize the political character of decision-making. Political preferences and ideology certainly play a role in jurisprudence, but a comparison of environmental and aboriginal law in Canada and the United States illustrates that institutional constraints continue to place limits on judicial power.

CHAPTER THREE: CONSTITUTIONAL CONSTRAINTS AND INDIAN LAW IN CANADA AND THE UNITED STATES

Constitutional Language and the Historical Development of Canadian and American Indian law

Canada and the United States share a similar political culture, and a common "Machiavellian" foundation: they exist as nations because European settlers displaced the various indigenous peoples who inhabited North America prior to the arrival of European settlers.[1] Nevertheless, there are some differences between the colonial experience in Canada and the United States. The displacement of Indian tribes was more violent in the United States than in Canada, though this does not give Canadians any grounds for self-righteousness. The expansion of the Canadian state preceded the expansion of the Canadian settlers, and this made "winning the west" a fairly orderly process.[2] This happened only because the north of the continent was not particularly attractive to any settlers prior to the very late 19th century, if then.[3] In addition, the aboriginal peoples who lived in what was to become Canada were much less numerous than their counterparts in the South.[4] Whether through a process orderly or disorderly, the native peoples of North America found their lands

---

[1] One commentator has described the difference between the colonization of Canada and the United States as follows: "An oversimplification, though not much of one, would be to say that the historical difference between American and Canadian handling of their native populations was that the United States decimated theirs by war, Canada theirs by starvation and disease." C.E.S Franks, "Indian Policy: Canada and the United States Compared." in Cook and Lindau, editors, *Aboriginal Rights and Self-Government*. McGill University Press: Montreal, 2000 p. 227.

[2] Jeanne Guillemin, "The Politics of National Integration: A Comparison of United States and Canadian Indian Administrations." *Social Problems*, Volume 25, Number 3, (February, 1978).

[3] "Land, Labour and Capital in Pre-Confederation Canada." pp 44-46 in Gary Teeple, *Capitalism and the National Question in Canada*. University of Toronto Press: Toronto, 1972.

[4] Franks, "Indian Policy: Canada and the United States Compared." p. 235.

diminished by the expansion of the settler societies. But native peoples were not simply conquered, and not simply assimilated. In both Canada and the United States, they remained both separate from the emerging settler societies, and subject to them; in the words of Chief Justice John Marshall, aboriginal peoples were "domestic dependent nations" in both Canada and the United States.[5]

This anomalous legal arrangement—nations within a nation—created a similar set of legal questions and problems in Canada and the United States. How should the "settler states" address the displacement of peoples that accompanied the founding of their societies? Is this a problem that should be solved by extending equal citizenship to Native Americans and Native Canadians, perhaps even without their consent?[6] Or do native communities deserve, as a matter of right, certain distinct privileges under the law?[7] Or should the native populations be kept separate and unequal, as subjects of management instead of partners in citizenship? The answers to these questions have consequences that extend beyond First Nations communities themselves, especially insofar as they touch upon question of rights to land and natural resources.

The status and rights of indigenous peoples raise questions about the meaning of citizenship, multi-culturalism, and even the legitimacy of the modern state. The dispossession of native peoples by settler societies, if not the outright conquest and slaughter of those peoples, remains one of the bleakest episodes in the history of North America, rivaled only by the history of slavery and Jim Crow. Traditional justifications for conquest, dispossession, and genocide are no longer regarded as legitimate; we no longer trust the old stories of how the West was won. Yet it is far from clear whether or how the settler

---

[5] This phrase was first used by Marshall to describe the status of American Indians in *Cherokee Nation v. Georgia* 30 U.S. 1 (1831)

[6] Tom Flanagan, *First Nations? Second Thoughts*.McGill University Press: Montreal, 2000; Alan Cairns, *Citizens Plus: Aboriginal Peoples and the Canadian State*. UBC Press: Vancouver, 2000.

[7] E.g. Michael Murphy, "Culture and Courts: A New Direction in Canadian Jurisprudence on Aboriginal Rights?" *Canadian Journal of Political Science*. Vol. 34, Number 1 (Mar. 2001) pp 109-129.

societies of North America should respond to historical injustices committed against Native Americans and Native Canadians.

There are, broadly speaking, two ways in which the state has attempted to respond to the injustices of the "settler contract," the doctrine that the property and lives of native North Americans were not fully deserving of protection under the law.[8] Until very recently, the "progressive" or "liberal" position emphasized the need for assimilation of native communities within liberal democratic society, a process which would allow for the native culture to sustain itself in the same manner as other ethnic groups.[9] The liberal assimilationist

---

[8] For a relatively sympathetic (though still critical) treatment of some of the ideological justifications for European colonization of the New World, see Flanagan, *First Nations? Second Thoughts* pp. 48. The idea that European colonization of North America was justified by the limited economic and political development of Indians has been rejected even by critics of aboriginal rights such as Flanagan. More theoretically interesting is the claim that many aboriginal tribes did not possess the attributes of sovereignty due to lack of a state or fixed territories–the doctrine of "terra nullius." In practice, this doctrine has of course been applied to settled agricultural communities as well as to stateless peoples; in the Berlin conference of 1885, for instance, European states declared all of sub-Saharan Africa to be "terra nullius." Most contemporary scholars regard the doctrine of terra nullius to be irrelevant to the question of aboriginal rights and self-government. E.g. James Tully, "A Just Relationship between Aboriginal and Non-Aboriginal Peoples of Canada." in *Aboriginal Rights and Self-Government: the Canadian and Mexican experience in North American Perspective.* Montreal and Ithaca: McGill-Queen's University Press, 2000 pp 39-72. Tully argues that once the "Eurocentric biases" of colonialism are abandoned, it is necessary to conclude that "Aboriginal peoples should be recognized as equal, coexisting, and self-governing nations" (p. 43).

[9] For discussion of the early assimilationist stage of American Indian policy, see Frederick E. Hoxie, *A Final Promise: The Campaign to Assimilate the Indians, 1890-1920.* Lincoln: University of Nebraska Press, 1984. American Indian policy retreated from the assimilationist paradigm during the New Deal era. For this period, see Lawrence C. Kelly *The Assault on Assimilation: John Collier and the Origins of Indian Policy Reform.* Albuquerque: University of New Mexico Press, 1983. American policy shifted towards assimilation once again by the 1950s, and this second period of tribal "termination" itself came to an end by the late 1960s. See Dan Russell, *A People's Dream.* Vancouver: UBC Press, 2000. pp 28-29. In Canada, the assimilationist paradigm for Indian policy was the mainstream or progressive position until well into the 1960s; the

position has been attacked on the grounds that Indians have not in fact accepted the sovereignty of the state, and that there are specific legal protections for the autonomy of native communities (embodied in both treaties and constitutional documents) that give them the right to a distinct status in North American society.[10] Even those who reject the doctrine of "terra nullius,"[11] however, encounter difficulties establishing the precise scope of native rights. The meaning of constitutional provisions, even recently adopted provisions such as the Canadian Constitution Act of 1982, are ambiguous, as are many of the relevant treaties (some centuries old) that provide the basis for aboriginal territorial claims.[12]

The Indian law cases that raise the most significant legal and political stakes are those dealing with the ownership of land. From the perspective of Indian litigants, the resolution of their claims has the potential to provide some form of redress for the sins of colonization, as well as the potential to restore economic well-being and perhaps even some form of political autonomy to native communities. Yet there

---

alternative tended to be neglect, benign or otherwise. See Alan C. Cairns, *Citizens Plus: Aboriginal Peoples and the Canadian State*. Vancouver: UBC Press, 2000 pp 47-77.

[10] Patrick Macklem, *Indigenous Difference and the Constitution of Canada*. Toronto: University of Toronto Press, 2001.

[11] The doctrine, developed in various ways, which asserted that aboriginal peoples of the "New World" lacked the attributes of sovereignty, and thus new world territory could be seized legitimately by European states. For a discussion, see Anthony Pagden, "Human Rights, Natural Rights, and Europe's Imperial Legacy." *Political Theory*. Vol. 31, No. 2, pp 171-199.

[12] Dan Rusell, an aboriginal lawyer, has observed that Section 35 of the *Constitution Act* provided both good news and bad news for the aboriginal peoples of Canada: "The good news was that they were recognized within the Constitution as Aboriginal peoples, but the bad news was that they had no understanding of what was intended by this new stature. Although they now had their respective Aboriginal and treaty rights recognized and entrenched, no one knew what this meant legally or practically." Dan Russell, *A People's Dream: Aboriginal Self-Government in Canada*. Vancouver: UBC Press, 2000 p. 5 The uncertainty extended to the federal and provincial governments as well.

are significant legal and political obstacles to these claims. It can be difficult, in many instances, to determine what ownership of land meant for peoples who did not live under a system of written law. Even if title can be established, there is the question of why claims of this kind are not barred by relevant statutes of limitation. Furthermore, and even more significantly, there is the problem of those who currently occupy the land. While it might seem painful and costly for governments to transfer public land and resources to aboriginal peoples (whether based on statutory, treaty, or claims to aboriginal title to land) there is at least some connection between the "legal personality" who committed the wrong and the legal personality being held to account. The sovereign that violated rights in the past is still in relevant measure the same sovereign who stands before the courts today. For individual land owners, however, the justice of being forced to pay for the decades-old crimes of others is far more in doubt.

My goal in this chapter, however, is not to resolve the question of what Indian law should be. Rather, it is to consider how two sets of judicial institutions, sharing a similar legal and political heritage, address a similar set of problems regarding the status and claims of aboriginal peoples. The central question I will consider is whether the differences in constitutional language create differing patterns of Indian law decisions in Canadian and American courts, or whether those patterns can best be explained by political divisions within the courts themselves. The central argument is that, particularly in regards to aboriginal rights (rights to certain practices, immunities from state regulation, and title to land not based upon specific written commitments such as treaties or statutes) and treaty rights, the Canadian courts have endorsed an "aboriginal rights" revolution.[13] In particular, the Courts have adopted novel standards of evidence that

---

[13] For the official statement that nicely encompasses "aboriginal rights orthodoxy" amongst Canadian academic, legal, and progressive political elites, see Canada, *Report of the Royal Commission on Aboriginal Peoples* 5 vols. Ottawa: Canada Communication Publishing Group, 1996. The thrust of the massive report is simple: aboriginal peoples have the right to cultural and political autonomy in Canada. For an in-depth analysis of the report, see Cairns, *Citizens Plus: Aboriginal Peoples and the Canadian State*. UBC Press: Vancouver, 2000. pp 116-152. Again, it should be noted that the rights and claims we are dealing with apply exclusively to status Indians in Canada, as opposed to those who identify as aboriginal, indigenous, First Nations etc.

make it easier for Native Canadians to sustain claims to aboriginal and treaty rights. In the United States, this aboriginal rights revolution has not taken place, and this cannot be explained as a consequence of the political composition of the court and the ideological preferences of American Supreme Court justices. This is because justices that are usually regarded as having left-leaning or liberal preferences in other contexts have not uniformly endorsed the expansion of aboriginal rights. American courts are unlikely to initiate an American aboriginal rights revolution, even with the appointment of more liberal judges on the Supreme Court. There are some judges who have endorsed "revolutionary" approaches to Indian law; however, the willingness of judges to endorse Indian claims varies in response to legal factors, even when the underlying policy dimensions are the same. This is because, in American Indian law, aboriginal and treaty rights are ultimately subordinate to Congressional sovereignty—and thus the willingness of judges to endorse aboriginal claims will vary, depending upon the legal environment created by Congressional statutes and actions of the national government. This is not to deny that there are no "attitudinal" dimensions to American and Canadian Indian law. As I will show, the limits that Canadian courts in particular have placed upon the aboriginal rights revolution stem from a desire to balance aboriginal claims against the political imperatives of both provinces and national governments; the Canadian Supreme Court has not been "captured," at least not completely, by the academic proponents of aboriginal sovereignty in Canadian law schools and philosophy departments. But the differences between Canadian and American Indian law must be traced to the differences between Canadian and American constitutionalism, not simply to differences in the policy preferences of judges.

Indian Law in the Supreme Court of Canada and the Supreme Court of the United States: Basic Doctrines and Recent Patterns

The development of Indian law in Canada and the United States offers an interesting contrast. In the United States, supporters of the rights and claims of Native Americans can often appeal to the past, that is, they can make some use of the doctrines and decisions of eminent nineteenth century jurists such as John Marshall and Joseph Story.[14] Commentators have noted that the late 20th century "rights revolution" has not, for the most part, provided new sources of support for the proponents of Native American sovereignty.[15] In Canada, however, the rights revolution supported by many new social movements has had a greater impact on indigenous peoples. The burden of this section will be to illustrate in greater detail the nature of the differences between Canadian and American Indian law. At the same time, I will attempt to show how (and to what extent) differences in Indian law decisions can be traced to constitutional differences and constitutional doctrine. The key issue is this: why, in regards to questions related to the power and status of Native communities, have the Canadian and American rights revolutions gone in different directions? My answer is that, contrary to the expectations of many students of judicial politics, constitutional language has determined, to a considerable extent, the differing patterns of Indian law in North America.

The special status of Native Americans and Native Canadians is recognized by both the American and Canadian constitutions, though in very different ways. The American Constitution's commerce clause, which grants Congress the power "to regulate commerce with foreign nations, and among the several states, and with the Indian tribes," implicitly recognizes the existence of Indian communities as distinct societies.[16] According to one commentator, the entire history of American Indian law is an attempt to develop—or perhaps deny—the implications of the "Indian commerce clause."[17] But the commerce clause, and the Constitution as a whole, is entirely unclear about the

---

[14] Petra T. Shattuck and Jill Norgren, *Partial Justice: Federal Indian Law in a Liberal Constitutional System*. New York and Oxford: St. Martin's Press, 1990 pp 23-56

[15] E.g. Vine Deloria and David E. Wilkins, *Tribes, Treaties and Constitutional Tribulations*. Austin: University of Texas Press, 1999 pp vii-viii

[16] See the discussion in Nell Jessup Newton, " Federal Power over Indians: Its Sources, Scope, and Limitations." *University of Pennsylvania Law Review*, Vol. 132, No. 2 (Jan., 1984), pp. 195-288

[17] N. Bruce Duthu, *American Indians and the Law*. New York: Penguin Press, 2008 p. xi

precise relationship between Indian tribes, the national government, and state governments. Indian tribes are neither "foreign nations"—entities which interact with, but are otherwise separate from the national government-- nor "states"—entities which are explicitly subordinated to the national government in regards to the latter's enumerated powers, but which also have various means of influencing and restraining the national government.

The status of Native Americans in U.S. constitutional law shifted dramatically in the nineteenth century. Broadly speaking, there was a shift from judicial recognition of tribal sovereignty in the first part of the 19th century, to an acceptance of Congressional "plenary power" over Native American communities by the beginning of the 20th century.[18] Early decisions of the U.S. Supreme Court established a legal basis for the relationship between the U.S. government and Indian tribes, a relationship that gave considerable scope for tribal sovereignty. Perhaps most importantly, the court ruled that the doctrine of "discovery" only gave the United States government the power to obtain title to Indian land with the consent of Indian tribes themselves.[19] This doctrine placed limits on the sovereignty of Indian tribes (insofar as the American government claimed the power to prevent the sale of tribal lands within the USA to other nations), and in this sense Indian tribes were not simply treated as sovereign nations. In the words of John Marshall the limits on the powers of Indian tribes in relation to foreign affairs made them "domestic dependent nations."[20] Yet the United States still approached its relations with Indians through the rubric of foreign affairs and the use of treaties. While not a matter beyond dispute, most jurists did not think that the doctrine of discovery or the "domestic dependent nation" status of Native American tribes gave the U.S. government the power to dictate the forms of tribal government. The constitution did not appear to grant the national

---

[18] David E. Wilkins, *American Indian Sovereignty and the U.S. Supreme Court.* Austin: University of Texas Press, 1997 pp 23-24

[19] Shattuck and Norgren, *Partial Justice*, pp 110-111

[20] For a discussion of the Marshall Court's treatment of the legal claims of Native Americans, see Jill Norgren, *The Cherokee Cases: two landmark decisions in the fight for sovereignty.* Norman, OK: Oklahoma University Press, 2004.

government any such power. While the U.S. government possessed the power to regulate commerce with Indian tribes, it was not yet the practice of American jurists to assume that "commerce" extended to any and all activities that might affect economic activity.[21] The commerce clause gave the American federal government power to create rules for the interaction of tribes and American society, but just as in the case of American states, the commerce clause did not give the national government the power to regulate the internal affairs of Indian tribes. The doctrine of discovery, the notion of domestic dependent nation, the use of treaties, and the constrained understanding of the commerce clause were all principles of law that established a basis for Native American sovereignty, a sovereignty limited in some respects, but a form of sovereignty compatible with the self-government and territorial integrity of Indian tribes.[22]

As is well known, the Supreme Court doctrines that provided some support for Indian sovereignty often proved little more than parchment barriers in practice.[23] The notion that Indian tribes should be treated justly, their land and peoples respected under the norms of constitutional and international law, was an idea that often crumpled before the powerful forces of western expansion. By the end of the 19th century even the doctrines themselves had been revised.24 Though the details of the transformation are complex, the outcome is relatively simple to relate: the doctrines of the early 19th century Marshall court were largely repudiated by the 20th century, and the Supreme Court

---

[21] The literature on this issue is immense. For a succinct presentation of the issues, see Howard Gillman, "More on the Origins of the Fuller Court's Jurisprudence: Reexamining the Scope of Federal Power over Commerce and Manufacturing in Nineteenth-Century Constitutional Law." *Political Research Quarterly*, Vol. 49, No. 2 (Jun., 1996), pp. 415-437

[22] It should be noted that not all scholars accept that the early principles of American Indian law were in any way supportive of tribal sovereignty. See Robert A. Williams, *Like a Loaded Weapon: The Rehnquist Court, Indian Rights, and the Legal History of Racism in America.* Minneapolis: University of Minnesota Press, 2005

[23] See Daniel Walker Howe, *What Hath God Wrought? The Transformation of America, 1815-1848.* New York: Oxford University Press, 2007 pp 411-415.

[24] Wilkins, *American Indian Sovereignty*, pp 64-118.

increasingly accepted Congressional plenary power—that is, "unlimited jurisdictional power"-- over Indian affairs. [25]This power, in a variety of guises, was used to undermine American Indian sovereignty, both in order to assist the expansion of the United States and to promote the assimilation of Indian peoples.

Unlike the case of many other "second class" citizens—most importantly, African Americans, but also women, gays and lesbians, the disabled, and other minorities— courts in the late 20th century United States have typically not been seen as strong supporters of the rights and interests of Native Americans. While there may be a Native American equivalent to *Dred Scott*[26], few scholars can identify with any confidence the Native American equivalent to *Brown v. Board of Education.* And therein lies the puzzle: why have American Indians been less successful than other groups at getting American courts—in particular, the American Supreme Court— to promote their interests? The answer to this puzzle, or at least the beginning of an answer, can be found by contrasting how native peoples are addressed in the constitutional structures of Canada and the United States.

The status of Native Canadians in early Canadian constitutional law mirrored late 19th century American doctrines, and insofar as Canadian law and policy differed from that of the USA, it tended to be more severe towards Native peoples, and more indifferent to violations of their basic rights. The tentative gestures towards Indian sovereignty made by the Marshall court made little impact upon the Canadian state, or the formation of the British North America Act (Canada's first Constitution). Prior to Canadian confederation in 1867, colonial governments had used the treaty process to segregate and isolate Native Canadian communities on reservations, for the purpose of opening up territory to settlement. After Confederation, the Canadian state pursued these policies in an even more authoritarian fashion, unleavened by any concerns for the sovereignty of Indian communities or the rights of individual Indians. The British North America Act of 1867 granted to the federal government power over "Indians and lands reserved to the Indians." In practice, Ottawa exercised despotic power over Indian peoples. Native Canadians were denied the vote; in many instances they were essentially imprisoned in reservations; children could be

---

[25] Williams, *Like a Loaded Weapon*, pp 71-75

[26] Wilkins, *American Indian Sovereignty* pp 42-49

removed from their parents by state dictat; the rights of assembly, petition, and legal representation were all limited if not eliminated. The Canadian state engaged in relatively few attempts to integrate or assimilate Native peoples into the broader Canadian community, relying instead, well into the 20th century, on a quasi-totalitarian "management" of Native Canadians. [27]

The transformation of the constitutional status of Native Canadians began in the post-war period, but this transformation did not lead in the direction of assimilation and integration. During the 1960s, in an attempt to move away from the authoritarian and segregationist legacies of the past, the Trudeau government investigated the possibility of ending the subordinate status of native peoples, and adopting instead a universal standard of citizenship for native and non-native alike.[28] These proposals, articulated in the unfortunately titled "White Paper" of 1969, were rejected by an overwhelming chorus of prominent Indian leaders. The Liberal government retreated almost immediately.

Instead of assimilation and equal citizenship, the Canadian constitutional revolution of the 1970s and 1980s created a special constitutional status for Indians in Canada. In law they would be the objects of government domination no longer, but not merely citizens. In the words of one eminent scholar, Native Canadians would be "citizens plus." The special status of Indians is codified in Sections 25 and Sections 35 of the Constitution Act:

> (Section 25)
> The guarantee in this Charter of certain rights and freedoms shall not be construed so as to abrogate or derogate from any aboriginal, treaty or other rights or freedoms that pertain to the aboriginal peoples of Canada including a) any rights or freedoms that have been recognized by the Royal Proclamation of October 7, 1763; and b) any rights or freedoms that now exist by way of land claims agreements or may be so acquired.

---

[27] Gordon Gibson, *A New Look at Canadian Indian Policy* pp 36-42

[28] Alan C. Cairns. *Citizens Plus : Aboriginal Peoples and the Canadian State* . Vancouver : UBC Press, 2000 pp 47-53.

Section 35.1)
The existing aboriginal and treaty rights of the aboriginal peoples of Canada are hereby recognized and affirmed.

While the precise meaning of these provisions was unclear (as was true of much of the Charter and Constitution Act), they seemed to reject the options of both authoritarianism and assimilation.

It is important to note that the Constitution Act places Indian rights in a particularly privileged category. Section 35 of the Constitution Act "constitutionalizes" both the treaty rights and unwritten aboriginal rights of Native Canadians. Prior to the Constitution Act, these rights were treated as common law rights that could be regulated and annulled through statute.29 Furthermore, the Constitution Act insulates these rights from the Section 33 "notwithstanding clause," which empowers both provincial and federal governments to exempt legislation from challenges based upon the Charter of Rights. Thus it is not merely the case that Indian rights in Canada are recognized more explicitly than in the United States. Indian rights are, in the Canadian constitutional system, protected from the lingering elements of parliamentary sovereignty that limit the scope of other rights.30

To what extent do these differences in "constitutional language" affect how Supreme Court justices resolve questions regarding the rights and powers of Indian tribes? Have Native Canadians gained an advantage from explicit recognition of their constitutional rights, not only at a symbolic level, but in terms of judicial decision-making? One

---

29 See e.g. John Borrows, "Let Obligations be Done." In Hamar Foster, Heather Raven, and Jeremy Webber, ed. *Let Right Be Done: Aboriginal Title, the Calder Case, and the Future of Indigenous Rights*. Vancouver: UBC Press, 2007. Pp 201-216

30 For a variety of reasons, the use of the Section 33 override clause has proven enormously controversial. Some commentators have suggested that a constitutional convention against the use of the clause has emerged (Andrew Heard, *Canadian Constitutional Conventions: The Marriage of Law and Politics*. Toronto: Oxford University Press, 1991. p. 147) For a defense of and a discussion of the political sources of opposition to Section 33, see Christopher Manfredi, *Judicial Power and the Charter*. Toronto: McLelland and Stewart, 1993 pp 188-212.

possible answer is that these constitutional differences, like all differences in constitutional language, affect judicial decision-making not at all. This is the answer that is most plausible for many political scientists who study judicial power. Stated with utmost brevity, scholars who adhere to the "attitudinal model" model of judicial power argue that, at least regarding the decisions made by courts at the pinnacle of the appellate pyramid, policy-preferences are the most important factor affecting their decisions.[31] This is not to say that constitutionalism is irrelevant to the exercise of judicial power. Charles Epp has argued that the presence of "court-enhancing" constitutional documents is a necessary pre-condition for the exercise of judicial power. In regards to how courts use the power that constitutions grant them, however, Epp does not think that differences in constitutional language merit much consideration.[32] Thus, while most political scientists would accept Epp's contention that Canada's "rights revolution" was precipitated by the "mega-politics of constitutional amendment," most would argue that it is naïve, or worse, "legalistic," to assume that subsequent differences in Canadian and American jurisprudence are a consequence of constitutional language. Law, from this viewpoint, should be seen through the lens of "political jurisprudence."[33] Mega-constitutional amendment politics—the struggle over the inclusion and wording of specific constitutional provisions— does not determine subsequent patterns of judicial decision-making.[34]

---

[31] Segal, Jeffrey and Harold Spaeth. *The Supreme Court and the Attitudinal Model.* Cambridge: Cambridge University Press, 1992.

[32] Charles Epp *The Rights Revolution.* Chicago: University of Chicago Press, 1998. Epp's central claim is that scholars of judicial politics place too much emphasis upon the power of judges to shape legal meaning, to the neglect of the "legal support structures" that allow various interests to shape the development of law. He suggests that constitutional provisions can become "rallying points" for interest group mobilization, or perhaps "hooks" for legal argumentation (p. 5), but he does not consider directly how differences in constitutional language might shape the outcomes of interest group litigation.

[33] See the discussion in Martin Shapiro and Alec Stone Sweet, *On Law, Politics, and Judicialization.* Oxford: Oxford University Press, 2002 pp 3-13.

[34] For an example of this argument, see F.L. Morton "The Supreme Court's Promotion of Sexual Equality: A Case Study of Institutional Capacity." *Polity,*

My argument is that, though politics and political ideology play a considerable role in judicial decision-making, the language used in the Canadian and American constitutions create differing opportunities for judicial intervention and activism in the realm of Indian law. While judicial ideology and policy preferences have played an important role in the development of Indian law in North America, the particular patterns of Canadian and American Indian law are also a consequence of the particular opportunities and constraints created by constitutional language.

In the remainder of this chapter, I will survey some recent developments in Canadian and American Indian law in order to consider how constitutional language can shape judicial decision making. The first section will survey the development of Indian law in Canadian and American jurisprudence since the 1980s, an overview which will demonstrate the greater degree of support for Indian litigants in the Supreme Court of Canada's decisions during this time. In the second section, I will suggest that these differences cannot be attributed to either the dominance of "conservative" appointees on the U.S. Supreme Court, or to the greater "conservatism" of American legal culture. While judicial ideology is not irrelevant, the differences between Indian law in Canada and the United States presents something of an anomaly for the proponents of "political jurisprudence." In the third section, I will present a theory about how doctrine and "constitutional language" place limits upon the development of American Indian law and jurisprudence; in particular, I will suggest that the limits of aboriginal rights litigation in American law is related to the broader features the post-New Deal constitutional order. Most importantly, I will argue that an expansive conception of national government power under the commerce clause—a central tenet of liberal jurisprudence-- is at odds with many aspects of Indian sovereignty. Given the current state of constitutional development, and given the specific political agenda of American Indian tribes, it may be difficult for liberal justices in the United States to advance the interests and rights of Indian communities in the absence of specific constitutional provisions protecting those interests and rights.

The claim that "constitutional language" matters in the case of Indian law is not to deny the impact of non-constitutional factors such

---

Vol. 16, No. 3 (Spring, 1984), pp. 467-483. Morton argues that judicial decisions were for the most part unaffected by the failure of the ERA.

as judicial ideology play in Indian law in Canada and the United States. The "litigation agenda" of American Indian tribes, rooted in their comparative economic prosperity and level of political organization, differs in important ways from that of First Nations peoples in Canada. The muted number of litigation victories for American tribes, I will suggest, may also be a consequence of their more complex and more radical legal claims

Indian Law Decisions in the Supreme Court of Canada and the Supreme Court of the United States

Between 1985 and 2008, the first two decades of the "Charter Era" in Canadian politics, the Supreme Court of Canada decided 45 cases dealing with the claims of Indian litigants (or cases in which Indian organizations were parties). During the same period, the United States Supreme Court decided 63 cases of a similar nature.[35] The cases involve disputes between Indian litigants and the national government, state or provincial governments, private parties or organizations, or other aboriginal individuals; the types of cases are summarized in Table 1:

Table 1: Indian Litigants in the Canadian and American Supreme Courts, 1985-2008

	National Gov't	Province/State	Private Parties
Canada	13	30	2
United States	15	36	10

In order to get a sense of the kinds of issues that have been raised in these cases, it is useful to divide them up into the underlying claims

[35] The cases were assembled by conducting keyword searches on Lexis Nexis (for the American Supreme Court) and the Canadian Legal Information Institute website for the Canadian Supreme Court using the terms "aboriginal," "aboriginals," "First Nations," "Indian," and "Indians." I then selected all of those cases in which an Indian tribe or individual was a party to a case, as well as those cases in which an issue related to the jurisdiction or rights of Indians was at stake even though the parties were not themselves Indian tribes.

made by the litigants (as well the legal issues at stake in those few cases which deal with aboriginal rights, even though the parties are not themselves aboriginal tribes or individuals). I have grouped both the Canadian and Amèrican cases into three broad categories, based upon the central legal claims raised by the parties. Table 2 illustrates the frequency of the different kinds of claims raised in 45 cases decided by the Canadian Supreme Court and the 63 cases decided by the American Supreme Court.

Table 2: Issues in Indian Law Cases in the Supreme Court of Canada and the Supreme Court of the United States, 1985-2008

	Treaty	**Statute**	**Aboriginal Rights**	**Proced ural**	**Constituti onal Rights**
Can.	10	14	14	5	4
USA	7	41	10	1	7

The Canadian court resolved 48 distinct legal issues in these cases, and it supported the position of First Nations litigants or interveners in regards to 21 of those issues.[36] Indians thus succeeded on 44% of their legal claims. In the United States, the court resolved 65 legal questions, supporting the position of aboriginal litigants or amici curiae on 19 of those issues, for a success rate of 29%. The success rate for Canadian Indian litigants in these cases is higher than the overall success rate for Charter claims in the Canadian Supreme Court (which is 33%[37]), but lower than the success rate for the major women's legal advocacy group in Canada (LEAF) which had a success rate of 70% in the 50

[36] I have interpreted 2 of those wins as "partial," as the Court did not entirely endorse the legal position of the aboriginal litigants.

[37] James B. Kelly, "The Charter of Rights and Freedoms and the Re-balancing of Liberal Constitutionalism in Canada, 1982-1997." *Osgood Hall Law Journal*, Number 37, 1999: p. 641.

legal issues which it contested before the Canadian Supreme Court between 1985 and 2000.[38]

The key issue is whether the patterns of wins and losses for Indian litigants was determined primarily by the policy preferences or political ideologies of the judges themselves; if this is the case, then it is plausible to discount the influence of constitutional differences. Tables 3 and 4 summarize judicial voting patterns in aboriginal law cases in the Canadian and American Supreme Courts between 1985 and 2008.

Table 3: Individual Judicial Support for Indian Litigants: Supreme Court of Canada, 1985-2008 (+= ruling in favor of Indian litigant; %= percentage of decisions in favour of Indian litigants)

Justice	Issues	+	-	%	Ideology
Dickson	6	5	1	83%	lib
Beetz	2	1	1	50%	con
Estey	2	1	1	50%	con
McIntyre	3	2	1	66%	con
Chouinard	2	1	1	50%	con
Wilson	5	5	0	100%	lib
LeDain	1	1	0	100%	con
Lamer	24	9	15	38%	lib
LaForest	20	7	13	35%	con
L'Heureux-Dube	24	14	10	58%	mod
Sopinka	18	9	9	50%	mod
Gonthier	30	11	19	37%	con
Cory	24	10	14	42%	con

[38] Christopher Manfredi, *Feminist Activism in the Supreme Court: Legal Mobilization and the Women's Legal Education Action Fund.* Vancouver: UBC Press, *2004*. p.20.

Table 3 (continued): Individual Judicial Support for Indian Litigants: Supreme Court of Canada, 1985-2008 (+= ruling in favor of Indian litigant; %= percentage of decisions in favour of Indian litigants)

Justice	Issues	+	-	%	Ideology
Mclachlin	37	17	20	44%	lib
Stevenson	2	1	1	50%	con
Iacobucci	24	9	15	38%	lib
Major	23	7	16	30%	con
Binnie	18	11	7	59%	lib
Bastarache	14	5	9	36%	con
Arbor	7	2	5	29%	mod
LeBel	13	6	7	42%	lib
Deschamps	9	6	3	63%	con
Fish	8	5	3	57%	lib
Abella	6	5	1	80%	lib
Charron	6	4	2	60%	lib
Rothstein	3	2	1	50%	con

Total Votes on Issues Decided = 313
Votes for Indian Legal Position = 118 (37%)
Votes Against Indian Legal Position = 195
[a] Sources: Charles Epp, *The Rights Revolution*, p. 169.

There are several interesting things to note about the voting patterns in Indian law cases. American courts resolved fewer issues in favor of Indian litigants, despite casting a slightly higher percentage of votes for them, which indicates the deep divisions over Indian law that exist in Indian law. Secondly, as table 4 indicates, these divisions run along ideological lines. Consider differences between the following conservatives (Thomas, Scalia, Rehnquist, Kennedy, O'Connor) and liberals (Breyer, Stevens, Souter, Ginsburg) from the Clinton-Bush era court: conservatives supported Indian litigants in 16% of the cases, compared with 34% liberal support of aboriginal positions.

Table 4: Individual Judicial Support for Indian Litigants: Supreme Court of the United States, 1985-2008

Justice	#	+	-	/	%	Ideology
White	36	9	27		25%	lib/con
Marshall	30	20	9	1	67%	Lib
Brennan	27	16	10	1	59%	Lib
Burger	12	5	7		42%	Con
Blackmun	38	22	15	1	58%	Lib
Powell	17	8	9		48%	Mod
Stevens	65	18	46	1	28%	Lib
Rehnquist	65	10	55		15%	Con
O'Connor	65	20	44	1	31%	Mod
Scalia	54	7	47		13%	Con
Kennedy	45	7	38		18%	Mod
Souter	38	15	23		39%	Lib
Thomas	35	2	33		6%	Con
Ginsburg	29	10	19		35%	Lib
Breyer	26	9	17		35%	Lib
Roberts	1		1		0%	Con

Total Votes in Favor of Indian Litigants = 178 (43%)
Total Votes against = 405 (57%)

Patterns of voting—in terms of the number of unanimous decisions versus the number of cases with dissenting opinions— also reveal some differences between Indian law in Canada and the United States. Tables five and six document the degree of unanimity in Canadian and American Supreme Court Indian law decisions. The higher levels of unanimity in the Canadian Supreme Court is consistent with its decision making patterns in other areas of law, and thus the differing levels of unanimity in the Canadian and American courts is not necessarily an effect of the specific Indian rights provisions of the

Canadian Constitution.[39] The overall level of support for aboriginal issues on the Canadian Supreme Court (37%), however, is only slightly higher than the level of support for aboriginal issues amongst Bush-Clinton era judicial liberals (e.g. Stevens, Breyer, Ginsburg, Souter.) Thus, one might well argue that the more limited scope of victories for Indian litigants in the U.S. Supreme Court is a consequence of the dominance of judicial conservatives in the post-1985 era. A further implication would be that, were liberal justices to achieve a majority on the American court, Indian jurisprudence in the United States would soon mirror the developments that have occurred in Canada since the adoption of the Constitution Act.

Table 5: Unanimity and Dissent in U.S. Supreme Court Indian Law Decisions, 1985-2008

Win-Unanimous	Loss-Unanimous	Win (1-2 in dissent)	Loss (1-2 in dissent)	Win (3-4 in dissent)	Loss (3-4 in dissent)
7 (11%)	22 (35%)	1 (1.5%)	9 (14%)	10 (16%)	14 (22%)

(% out of 63 legal issues decided; "win"= victory for Indian claimant)
% decided unanimously: 46%

Table 6: Unanimity and Dissent in Canadian Supreme Court Indian Law Decisions, 1985-2008

Win-Unanimous	Loss-Unanimous	Win (1-2 in dissent)	Loss (1-2 in dissent)	Win (3-4 in dissent)	Loss (3-4 in dissent)
14 (33%)	16 (38%)	3 (7%)	3 (7%)	2 (5%)	4 (10%)

(% out of total # of issues decided /42)
% decided unanimously: 71%

[39] Cynthia Ostberg and Matthew Wetstein, *Attitudinal Decision-Making in the Supreme Court of Canada.* Vancouver: UBC Press, 2007 p. 116. Out of all cases heard by the Canadian Supreme Court between 1984 and 2003, 24.2% were decided non-unanimously.

However, the divergence between Canadian and American jurisprudence can only be properly appreciated by considering the substance of the cases decided by the respective courts in the previous two decades. The Canadian Supreme Court has been a more consistent defender and promoter of the interest of aboriginal litigants than the "liberal bloc" on the American Supreme Court. Though the Court has not endorsed the entirety of the "aboriginal rights agenda," it has nevertheless used the opportunities created by the Constitution Act, in particular Section 35 (1) to advance the political status of First Nations. Yet it is also the case that the Supreme Court of Canada has not been simply "captured" by First Nations interest groups and their supporters.

Indian Law in Canada: Aboriginal Rights

In the following section, I will discuss those claims made by Indian litigants which are *not* based upon specific treaties or statutes, but instead are based upon un-enumerated "aboriginal rights"-- inherent rights of native peoples that cannot be traced to specific written commitments such as treaties or constitutions.[40] The first thing to note is that the development of aboriginal rights has been more prominent in Canada than in the United States, both in terms of the number and significance of the cases. The Canadian Supreme Court has not always endorsed views of "aboriginal rights" that coincide with those of aboriginal rights activists, however. The example of aboriginal rights jurisprudence thus provides significant but still limited support for those who argue that Canadian courts have become "the vanguard of the intelligentsia."[41] The development of aboriginal rights in Canada

[40] For the most thorough theoretical defense of aboriginal rights, see Patrick Macklem, *Indigenous difference and the Constitution of Canada.* Toronto: University of Toronto Press, 2001.

[41] The term "vanguard of the intelligentsia" is taken from F.L. Morton and Rainer Knopff, *The Charter Revolution and the Court Party.* Peterborough, Ontario: Broadview Press, 2000 p. 129 While Morton and Knopff are certainly correct about the tendency of the legal academy to support judicial activism, and the variety of ways the legal academy influences the Supreme Court, the case of aboriginal law shows that legal elites have only limited influence over Canadian law. For a discussion of the widespread support for aboriginal sovereignty in the legal academy, see Flanagan, *First Nations? Second Thoughts.* Montreal and Ithaca: McGill-Queen's University Press, 2000. pp 1-2.

over the past two decades is a clear case of "judicial activism," in the sense that the Supreme Court influenced important areas of public policy and has crafted novel doctrines while doing so. But it is not exactly a case in which courts have been captured by interest group litigants.

Secondly, the patterns of aboriginal law decisions in the American Supreme Court do not parallel Canadian developments. This is not merely because conservative majorities on the American Supreme Court have prevented a more robust conception of aboriginal rights. Liberal justices in the United States, particularly in the past two decades, have usually declined to articulate an ambitious conception of aboriginal rights, even in dissenting opinions. In fact, in some of the very few cases where the court has adopted novel approaches to the unenumerated, judicially-crafted rights of aboriginals, conservative judges have, on occasion, lent their support to certain race-based legal privileges. The divergence between American and Canadian aboriginal rights jurisprudence cannot be fully understand without taking into account the specific protections for aboriginal rights in the Canadian Constitution Act of 1982. Without the more robust protections for aboriginal rights found in this recently adopted "higher law" of Canadian politics, it is unlikely that there would have been a Canadian aboriginal rights revolution. This is not to say that, in supporting new interpretations of aboriginal rights the Canadian Supreme Court has been merely "following the law." The Supreme Court has been making the law, not interpreting it, because those who created the Constitution Act were themselves uncertain about the full scope of Section 35.[42] The law, however, provided a basis for aboriginal rights activism that is not available to American judges who might be politically inclined to support stronger versions of aboriginal rights.

In Canada, prior to the adoption of the Constitution Act of 1982, aboriginal rights were subject to the normal pressures of the political process. Some judges were willing to endorse some claims based on aboriginal rights.[43] But in general, parliamentary sovereignty was

---

[42] Douglas Sanders, "The Indian Lobby." in Keith Banting and Richard Simeon, ed. *Canada Notwithstanding: Federalism, Democracy, and the Constitution Act*. Toronto: Methuen Press, 1983. Pp 301-333.

[43] Canadian judges were already beginning to change their views on aboriginal rights before the Charter was born—before it was much more than a twinkle in

Pierre Eliot Trudeau's eye. This is shown in the case of *Calder v. Attorney General of British Columbia* 34 D.L.R. (3d) 145; 1973, one of the most important—in fact, one the only—pre-Charter cases that deal with the question of aboriginal title (the claim to a special kind of property right in land that is based upon traditional use and occupation of land by native peoples.). The importance of Calder lies not only in the influence it had on subsequent Indian-Government relations in Canada, but also in what it tells us about the nature of judicial politics in Canada.

The suit that was the basis of *Calder* was brought by members of the Nishga nation, which was comprised of four Indian bands from North Western British Columbia. The Nishga sought a declaration stating that their title to their ancestral land in British Columbia had never been lawfully extinguished. Their suit was dismissed at trial, as was their subsequent appeal to the British Columbia Court of Appeal. At the Supreme Court, the Nishga's appeal was dismissed in a closely divided vote. Three of the justices—Juson, Martland, and Ritchie—dismissed the appeal on its merits, while three others—Hall, Laskin, and Spence, voted to grant the Nishga their declaration. The deciding vote was cast by Justice Pigeon, who dismissed the appeal on jurisdictional grounds not directly related to aboriginal title.

Though the Nishga lost in court, the divided decision in *Calder* pushed the federal government to initiate a comprehensive land claims process to settle issues of aboriginal title regarding lands that had not been ceded by treaty. This represented part of the Trudeau government's retreat from its liberal—assimilationist aboriginal policy, articulated just four years earlier in the 1969 "White Paper." In many ways, the decision started to transform elite consensus on the status of Indians. The "progressive" position of the Liberal party once focused on the need for cultural adaptation and modernization; in the aftermath of Calder, the Liberal party very quickly moved to adopt a more "multi-cultural" perspective on aboriginal affairs, based upon the continued existence of distinct aboriginal communities, special aboriginal rights, and perhaps even a third-tier of government for native peoples. The *Calder* case, well before the establishment of Sec. 35 of the Canadian Charter, was able to influence aboriginal policy even though the decision itself was not a decisive victory for the Nishga.

This case provides evidence in support of the "court party" thesis of scholars such as Morton and Knopff, insofar as it shows that judges were willing to initiate part of the "rights revolution" without any direct impetus from the political branches of government or, more significantly, without any specific constitutional provisions to base their decisions on. One might object that the viewpoint of the dissenting justices, though "activist" in some sense, may nevertheless have been a legally correct recognition of Canada's unjust expropriation of aboriginal land, land which had been ceded to Indian peoples by actions of the imperial government. There was certainly some merit to the dissenters' position. Yet given the complexity and ambiguity of the evidence thought to trump treaty rights in those instances where the federal government found it necessary or convenient to do so. The Constitution Act revolutionized this political arrangement, despite the occasional attempts of Canadian politicians to foreclose broad readings of aboriginal rights.[44]

Though aboriginal rights were not initially a central concern of Trudeau's constitutional repatriation campaign, aboriginal groups exerted great pressure in order to get their concerns onto the constitutional agenda.[45] This effort was not in vain.

Of the two sections of the Constitution Act that were intended to protect the rights of First Nations, Section 25 has proven to be of lesser importance. Section 25 is primarily defensive in character; its purpose is to insure that the new rights established by the Charter do not undermine the special status of aboriginals. Indian leaders and spokespersons had worried that the individualistic thrust of Charter rights might be employed against the group-based rights of aboriginal communities, and Section 25 was intended to allay this fear. This section has been the subject of little judicial commentary since its inception.[46] Few cases have arisen in which individuals have challenged aboriginal practices on the basis of Charter rights and thus its impact has remained limited and largely unexplored.

---

presented, it was quite easy to make a plausible case either for or against the Nishga's claim. The dissenting justices, relying on centuries old legal documents, laid the basis for a massive change in public policy. Bora Laskin, a dissenter in Calder, even suggested in his constitutional law textbook that provincial laws were not applicable to native communities—a position entertained by no one before him, and very few afterwards. The Calder case and its impact are discussed in Thomas Flanagan, *First Nations? Second Thoughts*. Montreal and Ithaca: McGill-Queen's University Press, 2000 pp 123-126 and Alan Cairns, *Citizens Plus: Aboriginal Peoples and the Canadian State*. Vancouver: UBC Press, 2000.

[44] Sanders, "The Indian Lobby," pp 325-33.

[45] Cairns, *Citizens Plus*, pp 47-53.

[46] For a discussion of Section 25 and some of the possible ways it has been approached by Canadian courts, see Celeste Hutchinson, "Case Comment on *R. v. Kapp*: An Analytical Framework for Section 25 of the Charter."52 *McGill L.J.* 173 (2007)

Far more significant to both aboriginals and Canadians as a whole is Section 35 of the Constitution Act of 1982, which insulates aboriginal rights not from Charter claims but from parliamentary interference. The crucial clause of Section 35 reads as follows: "The existing aboriginal and treaty rights of the aboriginal peoples of Canada are hereby recognized and affirmed." Prior to the adoption of the Constituiton Act, the Canadian government had traditionally assumed the power to alter and amend all aspects of aboriginal rights.[47] The Canadian Supreme Court has interpreted Section 35 as an almost complete repudiation of parliament's ability to alter aboriginal and treaty rights. Yet this was only the starting point of the Court's interpretive work. The question of exactly what rights are protected by Section 35 is not answered within the Constitution Act itself; neither does the Constitution Act explain how the existence and scope of those protected rights are to be ascertained. Subsequent interpretations of "existing aboriginal and treaty rights" have illustrated the Supreme Court's deft ability to respect the letter of the constitutional text while maximizing the Court's power.

By failing to specify the scope of aboriginal rights, and by insulating those rights from the notwithstanding clause, the framers of the modern Canadian constitution delegated a large portion of responsibility for Indian policy to Canadian courts.[48] For example,

---

[47] For a challenge to the notion that Crown sovereignty vis a vis aboriginal peoples existed prior to the Constitution Act of 1982, see Bruce Clark, *Native Liberty, Crown Sovereignty: The Existing Aboriginal Right of Self Government in Canada.* Montreal and Kingston: McGill-Queen's University Press, 1990. Whatever the merits of this argument in theory, it certainly did not reflect the practices of post-Confederation Canadian governments, at least up until the adoption of the Constitution Act. See Alan Cairns' discussion of assimilation in Canadian Indian policy, *Citizens Plus*, pp 49-65.

[48] Some scholars have suggested that the expansive interpretation of Section 35 has led to illegitimate judicial activism, in the sense that courts have departed from the intentions of the framers when determining the scope and existence of aboriginal rights. (Gordon Gibson, *A New Look at Canadian Indian Policy.* Fraser Institute: Vancouver, 2009 pp 48-54) Following arguments made by James Kelly in regards to other aspects of judicial activism in the post-Charter era, I would suggest that the creative judicial activism in the development of aboriginal rights was an entirely predictable result of the wording of Section 35 and its protected place within the new constitutional order. (Kelly, *Governing with the Charter*, pp 89-95.) If the framers intended something different, then

aboriginal rights claimants were restricted by the language of Section 35 to those rights that were "existing" when the Constitution Act was adopted. Section 35 was not, on its face, meant to resurrect rights that had been extinguished by actions of the federal government since 1867. Within the context of this institutional constraint, the court still had the capacity to develop of vigorous aboriginal rights jurisprudence. To begin with, the question of whether or not a right had been extinguished in the pre-Constitution Act era was subject to controversy. The court eventually established a strict standard for determining if parliament had intended to extinguish a right.[49] This was not particularly controversial in itself; few people would object to the principle that a government should express its intentions clearly when abridging its previous commitments. More controversial was the question of what kinds of evidence Indian litigants could use to prove the existence of "existing rights," particularly when those rights were not traced to specific treaty commitments.

The first major development of aboriginal rights jurisprudence in the post-Constitution Act era was the case of *R. v. Sparrow*.[50] In this case, an Indian man was charged with violating the conditions of the fishing license that had been granted to his band. Sparrow's case was based on the claim that the regulations in question violated an aboriginal fishing right, a non-enumerated right that, despite not being based upon any specific treaty commitments, was nevertheless protected under Section 35 of the Constitution Act. According to the trial judge, no individual could claim an aboriginal right unless it was

---

they were extremely naïve. A more likely explanation of the framers' intent is that they were self-consciously abandoning a controversial policy field, in the hopes that courts would provide "cover" for policy decisions that would otherwise be difficult to defend before the voting public. For a discussion of this aspect of judicial power, see Malcolm Feeley and Edward Rubin, *Judicial Policy-Making and the Modern State.* Cambridge; New York: Cambridge University Press, 1998. pp 358-361

[49] For an explanation of why a strict interpretation of extinguishment is justified, given the historical circumstances of aboriginal treaty making, see Patrick Macklem, *Indigenous Difference and the Constitution of Canada.* Toronto: University of Toronto Press, 2001 pp 158-159, 180-184

[50] *R.v. Sparrow* 1 S.C.R. 1075 (1990)

supported by a special treaty, proclamation, contract, or other document, a position that had been established in pre-Constitution Act cases by the British Columbia Court of Appeal, in particular the case of *Calder v. Attorney General of British Columbia*[51] .

The British Columbia Court of Appeal took a slightly different perspective on the issues in *R. v. Sparrow*. The court ruled that Sparrow's claim did not need to be based upon any specific treaty commitments, and it rejected the Crown's argument that longstanding national fishing regulations had extinguished the right. However, the Court argued that the existence of the aboriginal right did not preclude national regulation. The right had not been extinguished, but Parliament's power to regulate the time, place and manner of fishing remained in place. In essence, the court ruled that the right encompassed fishing for "food purposes," liberally construed to allow fishing beyond subsistence needs, but not a right to determine how best to fish; that decision, for Indians and everyone else, would be made by the state. Due to Section 35, however, the court argued that aboriginal fishing rights entitled Indians to have priority over the interests of other groups.[52] Sparrow appealed this decision to the Supreme Court, arguing that aboriginal fishing rights should encompass immunity even from government regulations aimed at conservation. The Crown, in a cross-appeal, argued that the lower court had erred in holding that the aboriginal fishing right in question had not been "extinguished" prior to the adoption of the Constitution Act.[53]

The first question that the Supreme Court addressed was the meaning of "existing aboriginal rights" under Section 35 of the

---

[51] *Calder v. Attorney General of British Columbia* 8 D.L.R. (3d) 59 (1969)(BCCA)

[52] *R.v. Sparrow* 36 D.L.R. (4th) 246 (1986), (BCCA)

[53] The political and ideological stakes in this case were not clear cut. The national government (which was at this time controlled by the Progressive Conservative party) was supported not only by half a dozen provincial governments, but also by the British Columbia Wildlife Federation and the United Fisherman and Allied Workers' Union. The interests not only of governments, but also environmentalist and labor groups, were at odds with the claims of Sparrow and the First Nations organizations which supported him.

Constitution Act. In regards to fishing rights, at least, it was impossible to read Section 35 to mean that existing *regulations* of rights were "frozen" in their pre-1982 forms. This would constitutionalize an incredibly complex patchwork of regulations, regulations that differ not only between but within provinces. Were the court to adopt this interpretation, it would require the government to pursue constitutional amendments in order to adjust fishing regulations in response to changing technological and conservation needs.[54] As to whether or not the right existed at all, the Court stated that it was based upon the long existence of the Musqueam Indians as an organized society in the area of the Fraser River, and the fact that "the taking of salmon was an integral part of their lives, and remains so to this day."[55] As to whether this traditional right had been extinguished by government legislation, the central issue was whether or not the increasing intrusiveness of regulation since the 1870s had extinguished the right, despite the absence of a direct Parliamentary declaration that it intended to do so. The government's position was that the comprehensive regulations of the Fisheries Act had extinguished the aboriginal fishing rights claimed by Sparrow; the right did not "exist" in 1982, and was thus not protected under Section 35 of the Constitution Act.[56] The Court did not accept the Crown's argument that regulation equaled extinguishment, as the government's position was based upon the traditional notion that

---

[54] For a discussion of some of the complexities of Canadian fisheries policy see R. Quentin Grafton and Daniel E. Lane, "Canadian Fisheries Policy: Challenges and Choices" *Canadian Public Policy*. Vol. 24, No. 2 (June, 1998) pp 133-147.

[55] The significance of salmon, for the Musqueam, went beyond the "food purposes" referred to by the lower courts. According to Dr. Suttles, the anthropologist who provided expert evidence in the case, for the Musqueam people "The salmon were held to be a race of beings that had, in "myth times", established a bond with human beings requiring the salmon to come each year to give their bodies to the humans who, in turn, treated them with respect shown by performance of the proper ritual." The Court did not specify, in this case, whether the spiritual dimension of the Musqueam's fishing practices was essential to the aboriginal right claim. *R. v. Sparrow*, 1094-1095

[56] *St. Catherine's Milling and Lumber Co. v. The Queen* (1888), 14 A.C. 46; *Calder v. Attorney-General of British Columbia* (1973) S.C.R. 313.

common law rights—of which aboriginal rights were previously thought to be a part—were subordinate to the legislative power of parliament. Now, the Court argued that the extinguishment of aboriginal rights only occurred when Parliament directly expressed its intention to extinguish those rights. There were no such statements in the various iterations of the national Fisheries Act that had been in place since Canadian confederation in 1867.

Did the aboriginal right include the right to commercial fishing, as opposed to fishing for food and spiritual purposes? The Court recognized that this was the most serious question, in the sense that it was likely to have the most serious economic and environmental consequences. The Court did not rule directly on this broader issue, as Sparrow's claim dealt only with regulations that interfered with non-commercial fishing. The Court noted that the aboriginal fishing right could very well extend to commercial fishing:

> Government regulations governing the exercise of the Musqueam right to fish, as described above, have only recognized the right to fish for food for over a hundred years. This may have reflected the existing position. However, historical policy on the part of the Crown is not only incapable of extinguishing the existing aboriginal right without clear intention, but is also incapable of, in itself, delineating that right. The nature of government regulations cannot be determinative of the content and scope of an existing aboriginal right. Government policy can however regulate the exercise of that right, but such regulation must be in keeping with s. 35(1).[57]

In other words, this issue would be decided by Courts, not by Parliament.

In the *Sparrow* decision, the Canadian Supreme Court used Section 35 to carve out a new, more expansive role for Canadian courts in Canadian aboriginal policy, an outcome that was made possible by the text of the Constitution Act of 1982 but not one that was mandated by

---

[57] *R. v. Sparrow*, p. 1101

that text.[58] But it is also important to note that government power to regulate aboriginal rights was not eliminated by the Court. Instead, the Court argued that once conservation needs were taken into consideration, Indians would be entitled to a special claim on natural resources.

Proponents of aboriginal sovereignty—that is, those who argue that First Nations in Canada should exist as separate, self-governing nations—are, understandably, often critical of cases such as *Sparrow*. Some, such as Dan Russell, argue that the jurisprudence of the Canadian Supreme Court has not been affected by the aboriginal rights provisions of the Constitution Act. The *Sparrow* decision, in reaching the conclusion that aboriginal rights are not absolute, but are still subject in some instances to federal and provincial regulation, treated aboriginal rights with less deference than other rights protected by the Charter.[59] It is worth noting, however, that the Charter of Rights and Freedoms explicitly recommends a "balancing" approach to all rights contained in the Charter: "The Canadian Charter of Rights and Freedoms guarantees the rights and freedoms set out in it subject only to such reasonable limits prescribed by law as can be demonstrably justified in a free and democratic society."[60] Thus, the approach taken by Court in *Sparrow* cannot be said to be entirely without constitutional warrant. The fact that commentators such as Russell find fault with the Court's failure to promote aboriginal sovereignty does not undercut my claim that the courts were engaged in judicial activism. But it does serve to remind us of the relative modesty of that activism. The Canadian Supreme Court has been forced to address the issues raised by Section 35, and it has responded by fashioning new legal doctrines—but those doctrines are shaped by the broader, more deferential principles announced in the Charter, not necessarily by the theorists of aboriginal rights. The aboriginal rights revolution initiated

---

[58]Note the fact that the opinion makes no references to the "original understanding" of Section 35, or debates over the meaning of Section 35 during the re-patriation process. Numerous references are made, however, to academic interpretations of the significance of Section 35.

[59]Russell, *A People's Dream Aboriginal Self-Government in Canada*, Vancouver: UBC Press, 2000 pp 78-79.

[60] *Canadian Charter of Rights and Freedoms*, Section 1.

in *Sparrow*, as is befitting the actions of a Canadian court, was a quiet revolution.

The case of *R. v. Sparrow* helped to establish a new and more expansive understanding of aboriginal rights in Canadian law. In order to facilitate the further validation of aboriginal rights claims, the Supreme Court of Canada has changed the evidentiary standards that must be met in order to prove the existence of aboriginal rights. The justification offered by the court might seem bizarre in other legal contexts. The argument is as follows: in order to establish the existence of aboriginal rights (whether practices that are inherent to aboriginal culture— and therefore exempt from some aspects of government regulation— or claims to aboriginal title in land) evidence must often be drawn from times and cultures that did not employ written records. In the absence of such records, it is extremely difficult for aboriginal rights claimants to meet the evidentiary standards that are found in other areas of law such as torts, contracts, etc. Therefore, the rules of evidence must be relaxed if aboriginal groups are to have any of their claims validated in court. This conclusion may seem fair. But the rules of evidence developed in Anglo-American law have a logic of their own. Difficulties ensue when courts abandon those rules, even if it is in the pursuit of social justice.[61]

The role of evidentiary standards in evaluating aboriginal rights claims was dealt with most extensively in the case of *Delgamuukw v.British Columbia*, decided by the Supreme Court in 1997.[62] This case was based upon a claim to aboriginal title over 58,000 square kilometers in the interior of British Columbia, by the Gitskan and Wet'suwet'en peoples. The claim was based upon the historical use of the land by the Native Canadian tribes, as opposed to specific treaty commitments—it was, in other words, a claim to "aboriginal title."[63]

---

[61] For a discussion of the problems of evidence surrounding the practice of plea bargaining in the criminal process, see Hadley Arkes, *Beyond the Constitution*. Princeton: Princeton University Press, 1990. pp 173-206.

[62] *Delgamuukw v. British Columbia*, (1997) 3 S.C.R 1010

[63] See Dwight G. Newman, "Prior Occupation and Schismatic Principles: Toward a Normative Theorization of Aboriginal Title; Newman, Dwight G. *Alberta Law Review*, Volume 44, Issue 4, pp 779-802.

The court would not come to rule on the validity of this specific claim of the Gitskan and Wet'suwet'en, but it would explain the contours of aboriginal title, and what would be necessary (and allowed) in order to establish claims to aboriginal title.

Aboriginal title is described by the court and later commentators as "sui generis," alone of its kind, unlike property rights as usually understood in the common law. The claim to aboriginal title was a claim to far more than ownership, though in some ways aboriginal title is encumbered in ways that fee simple title is not.[64] The source of aboriginal title had been unclear from prior cases. In the *Delgamuukw* case, the court asserted that aboriginal title was rooted in the recognition of aboriginal title found in the Royal Proclamation of 1763, the common law notion of possession and occupation, and "systems of aboriginal law" which pre-dated contact and British sovereignty. The key to this assertion was the idea that the common law—with its notion of occupation as proof of possession—was only one possible source of proof of aboriginal title. Other forms of land use, not normally regarded as proof of possession in the common law, could also be used establish claims to aboriginal title. To demonstrate aboriginal title, it was necessary to show that the Indian tribe had exclusive occupancy of the land at the time when Crown sovereignty was first asserted. However, the Supreme Court had overturned the lower courts' ruling on this question, on the grounds that the trial and appellate courts had rejected the use of "oral histories" as evidence in determining the basis for aboriginal title.

The problem of using oral histories is similar to the problem of hearsay evidence. Hearsay evidence is limited in criminal cases for fairly obvious reasons. Such evidence is difficult to corroborate, easy to distort, and subject to misrepresentation without any ill-intention on the part of the witness. Similarly, the use of extrinsic sources in contract disputes is supposed to be confined, as much as possible, to those

---

[64] The basic characteristics of aboriginal title, as asserted by the Court in *Delgamuukw*, are as follows: 1) It is a right to exclusive use; that use does not need to be confined to traditional aboriginal practices, but uses must not be incompatible with traditional aboriginal practices. 2) It is inalienable to anyone except the Crown 3) It is held communally For a discussion of the some of the problematic economic consequences of aboriginal title, see Flanagan, *First Nations? Second Thoughts*, pp 185-186.

instances where the terms of the contract are unclear. This is because it is almost impossible to determine which extrinsic sources are relevant. Even if the relevant sources can be agreed upon, the evidence they provide is likely to be indeterminate and contradictory. And even more important is the fact that individuals, businesses, and organizations sign the terms of the contract alone— they do not reach any agreement about the meaning and relevance of the universe of extra-contractual information that might possibly reveal the true meaning of their agreements.65

The use of extrinsic sources has become routine in the area of statutory interpretation, particularly in the United States, and here the problems involved in moving beyond the text have been amply demonstrated.[66] Ambiguities in legislative debates, conflicting statements of intent, diverging media pronouncements, and even outright fraud usually obstruct judicial attempts to reconstruct the true intention of legislators. All of these evidentiary issues— in criminal law, contract law, and statutory interpretation— emerge out of conflicts where the relevant individuals are (usually) present, the relevant documents are available (and often recently drafted), and the relevant actions (a crime, the drafting of a contract, the enacting of a law) have occurred in the relatively recent past. This is rarely the case in questions involving aboriginal rights, and this is what makes the relaxation of evidentiary standards in aboriginal rights cases so contentious.

The Supreme Court did not actually resolve the issue— the worst possible outcome for all, according to some commentators.[67] Instead,

---

[65] Edmund Morgan, "Hearsay and Non-Hearsay." *Harvard Law Review*, Vol. 48, No. 7 (May, 1935), pp. 1138-1160; see also the discussion of evidence and formal rules of law in Walter Olson, *The Litigation Explosion.* Truman Talley Books: New York, 1991. pp 131-152

[66] E.g. Antonin Scalia, *A Matter of Interpretation.* Princeton: Princeton University Press, 1997.

[67] This is because property rights were left undefined in the area affected by the decision, making development impossible. Had the land and resource rights simply been assigned to the native community, this would not have been the case. See Owen Paul Lippert, *Beyond the Naas Valley: national implications of the Supreme Court's* Delgamuukw *decision.* Vancouver: Fraser Institute, 2000.

the Court decreed that a new round of litigation was required— though it also suggested that negotiation would be preferable— on the grounds that the trial judges had failed to properly interpret the oral evidence offered by the Indian tribes. The Court did not provide any detailed explanation of how this evidence—consisting of oral traditions, stories, and myths about land use in Northern B.C.—should be evaluated by the Court, except to say that it had to be placed on equal footing with official records and documentation. By laying down this interpretive principle, however, the court revolutionized—at least potentially—the scope of aboriginal title claims.

Yet despite the innovations in law introduced by the Canadian Supreme Court in its aboriginal rights jurisprudence, the Court has by no means endorsed the approach to aboriginal rights articulated by legal scholars and advocates for aboriginal rights.[68] This is important to note, because many critics of judicial activism in Canada have argued that the legal support structure of academics and public interest lawyers has become a transmission belt between the academy and the courts, which allows for the development of policies that would not be endorsed by elected officials. The Supreme Court of Canada has, on the basis of Section 35 of the Constitution Act, taken further steps in developing aboriginal rights than has the American Supreme Court. But in many ways it has still moved cautiously, much to the disappointment of the advocates of aboriginal rights.

In developing the jurisprudence of aboriginal rights, the Canadian Supreme Court has placed significant limits on the scope of those rights.[69] One significant limit that the Court has placed upon aboriginal rights protected by Section 35 is the idea that those rights must be

---

[68] E.g Patrick Macklem, *Indigenous Difference and the Constitution of Canada* Toronto: University of Toronto Press, 2001; John Borrows, *Recovering Canada: The Resurgence of Indigenous Law* Toronto, University of Toronto Press, 2002. According to some commentator, the Supreme Court of Canada has actually been less solicitous of the interests of Canadian Indians than the national government. (Jennifer E. Dalton, "Aboriginal Self-Determination in Canada: Protections Afforded by the Government and the Judiciary." *Canadian Journal of Law and Society*. Vol. 21, no. 1, 2006 pp. 11-37)

[69] Kent Roach, *The Supreme Court on Trial: Judicial Activism or Democratic Dialogue?* Toronto: Irwin Law, 2001. p. 172

related to the traditional culture and practices of native peoples[70]. The decision which announced this more restrictive aspect of Section 35 jurisprudence was *R. v. Van der Peet,*[71] another case based on a challenge to the legitimacy of Parliamentary fishing regulations. In evaluating the rights claim in this case, the court reiterated the position from *Sparrow* that while aboriginal rights could no longer be extinguished, they could still be subjected to regulation. The Court went beyond the *Sparrow* decision, however, in its description of what kinds of activities could be construed as aboriginal rights: "To be an aboriginal right an activity must be an element of a practice, custom or tradition integral to the distinctive culture of the aboriginal group claiming the right."[72] Two judges dissented from this opinion, arguing that the "frozen rights" approach to aboriginal rights would unduly constrain the freedom of native communities to adapt to changing economic circumstances. The majority opinion, according the Justice L'Heureux-Dube, treated aboriginal culture as if it was an artifact that had be preserved and isolated from the broader culture as a whole, as if the only purpose of aboriginal rights was to preserve native cultures as museum pieces. The majority decision in *Van der Peet* illustrates that, while the court has been willing to intervene into Canadian Indian policy, it has not used Section 35 of the Constitution Act to advance the claims of Indian litigants at every opportunity.

L'Heureux Dube and McLachlin, the dissenting justices in *Van Der Peet*, also dissented in the case of *R. v. NTC Smokehouse*, which dealt with the validity of federal fishing regulations.[73] The basis of their dissent was, as in *Van der Peet*, their objection to the restrictive or "frozen" conception of aboriginal rights advanced by the majority. In the final case in which L'Heureux Dube and McLachlin cast dissenting votes together, they found themselves voting against the aboriginal claimant. In *R. v. Nikal,* the majority overturned a conviction for

---

[70] In regards to aboriginal title, land use can depart from aboriginal practices, but must not be incompatible with traditional practices.

[71] *R. v. Van der Peet* (1996) 2 S.C.R. 507

[72] Ibid., at 549

[73] *R. v. NTC Smokehouse Ltd.* [1996] 2 S.C.R. 672

violation of fisheries regulations on the grounds that the regulations violated aboriginal rights.[74] L'Heureux Dube and McLachlin agreed that the regulations violated aboriginal rights, but they did not think that this gave individuals the right to refuse to apply for licenses which had many provisions that were perfectly valid. The dissents of L'Heureux Dube and McLachlin may well have been motivated by their policy preferences, but if so, those preferences do not reflect simple partisan divisions, or invariable preferences for certain categories of litigants. Despite their support for a very expansive, evolutionary conception of aboriginal rights, L'Heureux Dube and McLachlin were not led to subordinate all other legal considerations to the imperatives of Section 35.

There is also some indication that L'Heureux Dube and McLachlin were willing to accept the *Van der Peet* test as the law, despite their initial opposition to its approach to aboriginal rights. In the case of *R. v. Pamajewon*, a First Nations band in Ontario argued that, on the basis of the aboriginal right to self-government, it should be exempt from Ontario gaming regulations.[75] Under the *Van der Peet* test, this argument could not hold: casino gaming may be one of the most effective means of economic development for Indian tribes, but no anthropologist could convincingly demonstrate that it was an integral part of pre-contact aboriginal culture. L'Heureux Dube and McLachlin both joined the majority in this case, despite their initial rejection of the "frozen rights" approach to Section 35.

The connection that the Court has drawn between aboriginal rights and traditional aboriginal practices is the most serious limitation on the aboriginal rights revolution in Canadian law. Thus, in many instances, the victories won by aboriginal litigants are ambiguous. Consider the case of *R v. Bernard*, decided in 2005.[76] In this case, the Court ruled, in a unanimous decision, that Indians have the right to harvest wood on their traditional territory—that is, they have a right to harvest wood free from provincial regulation. The court has not simply immunized First Nations from resource regulations, however. Instead, the Court has

---

[74] *R. v. Nikal* [1996] 1 S.C.R. 1013

[75] *R. v. Pamajewon* (1996) 2 S.C.R. 821

[76] *R. v. Bernard* (2005) 2 S.C.R. 220

displaced provincial governments as the overseers of natural resource policy. This is because the Court has empowered itself to determine whether the exercise of aboriginal rights are in fact compatible with traditional aboriginal culture. In *R v. Bernard*, the court implied that the right to harvest wood would not extend as far as the right to conduct commercial wood harvesting (or the power to license wood harvesting.) The right to harvest wood for personal uses, free from provincial regulation, is not inconsiderable. But it nevertheless falls fall short of the full goals of Indian litigants. The Court, while endorsing some expansive understandings of aboriginal rights, has not been captured by the aboriginal rights community; instead, it has asserted judicial control over issues once left to the process of political negotiation and compromise.

This assertion of judicial control over aboriginal affairs, through the device of connecting aboriginal rights claims to traditional aboriginal culture, is in some ways the worst of all possible outcomes, regardless of one's general political perspective on aboriginal self-government. The court's decision manages to run counter to the logic of both liberal multiculturalism and classical liberal economic rationality. Most proponents of multiculturalism would reject the notion that Courts should determine the meaning of aboriginal culture, especially if courts conceive of culture as an unchanging thing as opposed to an ongoing process.[77] From the perspective of economic rationality, it is entirely possible that the collective interest of Canadian society as a whole would actually be better served by granting aboriginal groups more clearly defined rights over natural resources. This is because the benefits (e.g. employment in resource extraction and transportation) that come from development (e.g. mining, logging, etc.) exist whether the underlying resources are owned by provinces or by aboriginal tribes.[78]

While cases such as *R. v Sparrow* indicate that the Court is willing to play a revolutionary role in aboriginal rights cases, and cases such as

---

[77] E.g. Dimitrios Panagos, "The Plurality of Meanings Shouldered by the Term "Aboriginality." *Canadian Journal of Political Science.* Volume 40, Issue 3, September 2007 pp591-613

[78] Owen Lippert, ed. *Beyond the Nass Valley : National implications of the Supreme Court's Delgamuukw decision* Vancouver : Fraser Institute, 2000

Delgamuukw suggest that Court is not afraid to court political controversy when dealing with the claims of First Nations, it would be wrong to exaggerate the scope and successes of aboriginal rights litigation in Canadian Courts. The program announced in *Sparrow* was sharply curtailed by *Van der Peet*, and the Court—usually in unanimous decisions—has not been willing to push forward novel understandings of aboriginal rights, or expand the notion of aboriginal rights to include the right to self-government or sovereignty. But while the development of aboriginal rights in Canada has been modest compared to the utopian speculations of academic theorists,[79] Canadian courts have been more receptive to aboriginal rights claims than have American courts. Interestingly, this is not only a consequence of the power and influence of right-wing conservatives on the American court.

Aboriginal Rights in the United States and the Limits of the Hidden Law: Tribal Sovereign Immunity, Civil and Criminal Jurisdiction, Taxation and Regulatory Powers

There are few parallel cases from the American Supreme Court which deal with the question of "aboriginal rights" in the sense of un-enumerated rights and powers of Native Americans. Yet while litigation by Indian tribes in the United States is dominated by questions of treaty and statutory interpretation, the issue of aboriginal rights is not entirely absent; it often arises in the context of disputes over the position of Native American tribes in the American constitutional order as a whole. American courts have also entertained the idea that Indian tribes have common law rights that, while ultimately subordinate to federal sovereignty, may in some circumstances help to determine the scope of tribal power in areas such as the jurisdiction of courts, tax immunity, and the taxation powers of Indian tribes.[80] Thus while the American Constitution does not give explicit recognition to the existence of aboriginal rights, there are

---

[79] E.g. Patrick Macklem, "First Nations Self-Government and the Borders of the Canadian Legal Imagination." *McGill Law Journal*, Vol. 36, No. 2 pp 382-435.

[80] F. Cohen, *Handbook of Federal Indian Law*. Washington, D.C.: US Government Printing, 1982. pp 486-493.

American equivalents to the Canadian cases that deal with the existence and scope of the "hidden law" of Indian peoples.

In the absence of explicit Constitutional protections for this hidden law, however, the American Supreme Court has taken only limited steps to expand the scope of aboriginal rights. According to some scholars, the absence of an American revolution in aboriginal rights can be traced to political sources: the rise of conservative justices on the Supreme Court is the main, and perhaps the only, obstacle to a transformation in American Indian law that would parallel the transformations that have occurred in Canada and Australia.[81] I will argue that the absence of an aboriginal rights revolution in American jurisprudence cannot be traced to the prominence of conservative justices on the Supreme Court. While there are divisions amongst Supreme Court justices on the scope of aboriginal rights, those divisions do not follow any clear political pattern. American and Canadian Indian law have developed in different directions as a consequence of the differing status of aboriginal rights and aboriginal peoples in their written constitutions.

Consider the example of tribal sovereign immunity. This is a court developed doctrine, first articulated in the early 20th century, based upon the implications of the semi-sovereign status of American Indian tribes recognized by state constitutions.[82] It is roughly analogous to the doctrine of state sovereign immunity, with the notable exception that tribal sovereign immunity can be altered and abridged by federal law. American Supreme Court cases dealing with sovereign immunity reveal some interesting divisions amongst the justices, divisions that do not fall along the assumed political fault lines that so often divide the Court.

---

[81] E.g. Robert A. Williams, Jr. *Like a Loaded Weapon: The Rehnquist Court, Indian Rights, and the Legal History of Racism in America.*Minneapolis: University of Minnesota Press, 2005.

[82] For a discussion of tribal sovereign immunity, see Kirsten Matoy Carlson, "Towards Tribal Sovereignty and Judicial Efficiency: Ordering the Defenses of Tribal Sovereign Immunity and Exhaustion of Tribal Remedies." *Michigan Law Review.* Vol. 101, No. 2 (Nov., 2002) pp 569-601.

Kiowa Tribe of Oklahoma v. Manufacturing Technologies Inc.,[83] decided in 1998, is the only case since 1985 in which Native American litigants achieved success at the Supreme Court level on the basis of an aboriginal rights claim. In this case, the majority of the court (consisting of Kennedy, O'Connor, Breyer, Rehnquist, Scalia, and Souter) ruled that the Kiowa Tribe had immunity from breach of contract suits in state courts, even regarding off- reservation business. The court did not deny the power of Congress to extinguish or alter the tribe's legal immunity from suits in state court, but still concluded that Congress had not clearly extinguished this aspect of tribal sovereignty. Justice Stevens, joined by Ginsburg and Thomas in dissent, argued that the extension of tribal immunity had never been applied in the context of off-reservation activity, and the court should refrain from extending the doctrine of tribal sovereign immunity to such circumstances.

The justices' votes in *Kiowa* do not seem to follow any clear political pattern. It is worthwhile to consider the substance of the arguments in *Kiowa*, in order to assess the legal sources of disagreement that created such an unusual voting coalition on the court. The suit emerged from disagreements between the Kiowa and Manufacturing Technologies over the sale of stock; the tribe, having defaulted on payment for the stock, was sued in an Oklahoma state court. The tribe moved to have the case dismissed for lack of jurisdiction, but both the trial and appellate court found that the Kiowa did not enjoy immunity from suit for breaches of contract involving off-reservation commercial conduct. According to the Oklahoma Court of Appeals, the decision to exercise jurisdiction by Oklahoma over other sovereigns, whether Indian tribes or sister states, was a matter of comity; because the state holds itself open to breach of contract suits, it may allow its citizens to sue other sovereigns acting within the state. According to Kennedy, this argument was invalid because it was based upon the assumption that state sovereign immunity was co-extensive with the sovereign immunity of Indian tribes: "In *Blatchford*, we distinguished state sovereign immunity from tribal sovereign immunity, as tribes were not at the Constitutional Convention. They were thus not parties to the 'mutuality of concession' that 'makes the States' surrender of immunity from suit by sister States plausible.'"[84] Thus

---

[83] *Kiowa Tribe of Oklahoma v. Manufacturing Technologies*, 523 U.S. 751

[84] *Kiowa Tribe of Oklahoma v. Manufacturing Technologies*, p 756.

tribal immunity is a matter of federal law, and is not subject to diminution by the States. Kennedy paused to note that there was "reason to doubt the wisdom of perpetuating the doctrine" of tribal sovereign immunity, as the economic activities of Native American tribes had become more intertwined with society as a whole.85 Yet he still argued that judicial assessments of the proper place of Indian tribes in the modern American economy could not justify limitations on tribal sovereign immunity.

Stevens began his opinion with a forceful rejection of the majority's premise that tribal sovereign immunity can exist absent specific statutory or treaty commitments:

> There is no federal statute or treaty that provides petitioner, the Kiowa Tribe of Oklahoma, any immunity from the application of Oklahoma law to its off-reservation commercial activities. Nor, in my opinion, should this Court extend the judge-made doctrine of sovereign immunity to pre-empt the authority of the state courts to decide for themselves whether to accord such immunity to Indian tribes.[86]

The courts had not merely declined to act, but had extended the doctrine of sovereign immunity by allowing it to cover off-reservation activity—a conclusion even more troubling by the fact that the Court had ruled in some cases that sovereign immunity did not even extend to on-reservation activity.[87]

The key thing to note about the politics of the *Kiowa* decision is that they are distinctively legal politics, that is, disputes about the meaning and implications of law. From a political perspective, the issue turns on questions of economic rationality and economic fairness (for those who make contracts with Native American tribes), and questions about the justification for the unique status of Native American tribes in

---

85 Ibid., p. 758

[86] *Kiowa Tribe v. Manufacturing Technologies Inc.* p. 760 (Stevens, dissenting.)

[87] E.g. *Puyallup Tribe, Inc. v. Department of Game of Washington* 433 U.S. 165

light of their particular historical experiences. As we will see, Justice Stevens will not hesitate to endorse Indian claims based upon statutes and treaties—cases where the bottom-line "policy issues" are more or less identical as in the *Kiowa* case. And this is the crucial point to note: the votes of justices, and the outcomes of Indian law cases, shift in response to the various ways in which *Congress* has recognized, restricted, or extinguished Indian rights. This is not to say that there are no political differences over the meaning of Native American rights in the Supreme Court. But the scope of judicial politics is shaped not simply by judicial preferences regarding the advantages and disadvantages of Indian sovereignty.

The United States Supreme Court has only rarely crafted expansive interpretations of tribal civil jurisdiction, or tribal immunity from the civil jurisdiction of state courts. Between 1985 and 2008, the United States Supreme Court decided 8 cases which addressed the civil jurisdiction of tribal courts and tribal sovereign immunity from civil claims in state courts. The court ruled in favor of tribal claims in 2 out of 8 of the cases. In the six cases in which the court ruled against tribal claims, not a single justice voted against the outcome of the case.88

Again, this is not to suggest that there are no political fault-lines on the court in regards to the scope of tribal sovereign immunity—though in some cases, those fault lines are only apparent in the reasoning used by various justices, not in the outcome of the specific questions before the court. In the case of *Nevada v. Hicks*, for instance, the court was divided not over the outcome of the case, but over the broader question of tribal civil jurisdiction over non-members (including state law enforcement officials).[89] The case dealt with a civil action against a state official, who obtained tribal and state search warrants in order to investigate the house of a tribe member suspected of off-reservation

---

88 The cases: *Iowa Mutual Insurance v. LaPlante et al* (1987), *Ok. Tax Commission v. Graham*, (1989) *Ok. Tax Commission v. Citizen Band Potatwatomi*, (1991) *Strate v. A-1 Contractors*, (1997) *Kiowa Tribe v. Manufacturing Technologies*, (1998) *El Paso Natural Gas Company v. Laura Neztsosie et al*, (1999) *C & L Enterprises, Inc. v. Citizen Band Potawatomi Indian Tribe* (2001) *Nevada et al v. Floyd Hicks et al* (2001), *Inyo County, California v. Paiute-Shoshone Indians* (2003)

[89] *Nevada v. Hicks* 533 U.S. 353 (2001)

hunting violations. The tribe member brought an action in tribal court against Nevada games wardens for trespass, abuse of process, and violations of civil rights. In response, the state brought an action in the District Court, seeking a declaratory judgment that the tribal court lacked jurisdiction. The District Court granted summary judgment for the tribe member, and the decision was upheld on appeal to the 9th circuit court. On subsequent appeal, the Supreme Court ruled that the tribal court did not have jurisdiction in the case. But the five separate opinions written in the decision reveal some of the fissures that exist on the court regarding questions of tribal sovereignty.

Justice Scalia, joined by Rehnquist, Kennedy, Souter, Thomas, and Ginsburg, argued that the general principle in adjudicating questions of tribal jurisdiction is that, with only a narrow range of exceptions, Indian tribes lack jurisdiction over non-members. Tribal sovereignty is not connected to territory, and though the allegedly tortious activity took place on tribal lands, this did not necessarily establish tribal jurisdiction. While Indian tribes have the right to create laws for tribal governance insofar as this affects the relationships amongst tribe members, this does not give the tribe jurisdiction over state officials who are acting to enforce state laws that apply to tribal members. Just as federal enforcement of legitimate federal laws does not impair state governments, state enforcement of legitimate state laws does not impair the capacity of tribes to govern themselves.

In a concurring opinion, Justices Souter, Thomas, and Kennedy laid down an even more restrictive interpretation of tribal civil jurisdiction, arguing that tribal civil jurisdiction never extends to non-members. The justification for this narrow reading of tribal jurisdiction lay in both the complexity of tribal law and the questionable independence (in some circumstances) of tribal courts.[90] Souter's opinion went beyond the narrow question presented to the court—the question of tribal court jurisdiction over state officers enforcing state law-- and imposed an even more stringent understanding of tribal court jurisdiction.

[90] For a particularly harsh criticism of this aspect of Souter's opinion, see Robert A. Williams, Jr. *Like a Loaded Weapon: The Rehnquist Court, Indian Rights, and the Legal History of Racism in America.* Minneapolis: University of Minnesota Press, 2005 p. 143.

Ginsberg and O'Connor thought the broader issue should be left undecided, while Breyer and Stevens wished to adopt a more lenient interpretation. Stevens had also voted in dissent in the two cases where a majority of the court had voted in favor of a more expansive interpretation of tribal sovereign immunity and civil jurisdiction, which raises a further obstacle to any purely political interpretation of the Court's decision in these cases. What guided Stevens' opinions in both the *Hicks* and *Kiowa* cases was a territorial conception of tribal sovereignty, not a preference or aversion for the interests of Indian tribes.

The Court's decision in *Kiowa* is an exception to the general rule that the American Supreme Court justices have been hesitant to expand the scope of aboriginal rights, especially in regards to court-crafted doctrines regarding tribal sovereign immunity and civil jurisdiction. The divergent development of aboriginal rights jurisprudence in Canada and the United States supports the thesis that constitutional language can have a significant impact on judicial decision-making. The debate over aboriginal rights in Canadian courts takes place on an entirely different constitutional playing field, not because of the political preferences of a majority of Canadian judges, but because Section 35 of the Constitution Act of 1982 provided a basis for a re-thinking of the relationship between aboriginal rights, the doctrine of extinguishment, and the power of Parliament. There has been no parallel development in American law, but this is not because of the triumph of "the new right" in American courts, as even liberal appointees have declined to develop a doctrine of aboriginal rights in dissent. In the few cases which advanced and developed the aboriginal right to sovereign immunity, conservative justices on the American Supreme Court have in some instances endorsed expansive interpretations of aboriginal rights. In declining to connect tribal sovereign immunity to traditional Indian lands or traditional Indian practices, Scalia and Rehnquist endorsed a position rejected by the liberal majority on the Canadian Supreme Court. In general, the Canadian Supreme Court has been more willing to interpret broadly the unwritten rights of First Nations; the greater reticence of the American Supreme Court to endorse similar rights is not merely a consequence of the political balance of power on the court, but rather result of differences in constitutional law.

Interpreting Indian Treaties

Treaty interpretation in Canada, much like the interpretation of aboriginal rights, is an exercise in constitutional interpretation. Treaty rights have the status of higher law, and cannot be altered through recourse to the "notwithstanding clause" which allows both provincial and federal parliaments to limit the impact of Charter rights. Treaty interpretation in the United States is more akin to statutory interpretation. Any interpretation of Indian treaties by American courts can be altered by the national government—though Congressional reaction to judicial statutory and treaty interpretation is much more complicated in the American context due to the complexity of the American legislative process.

Since the adoption of the Constitution Act of 1982, The Canadian Supreme Court has ruled on nine cases that deal with the interpretation of treaties between Native Canadians and the Crown. All nine of these address the application of hunting, fishing, or logging regulations. The court ruled in favor of Indian litigants in 5 of these cases, and all but 3 of the cases were decided unanimously. The questions that emerge in cases dealing with treaty rights are similar to those that deal with aboriginal rights, as both treaty rights and aboriginal rights are accorded constitutional protections under Section 35. However, only those aboriginal and treaty rights that were "existing" at the time of the adoption of the Constitution Act are afforded the protections of Section 35. Therefore, in ruling on these claims, courts must determine not only what rights are at stake, but also whether those rights have been extinguished.

One might imagine that determining the nature of aboriginal rights would be a more complex, more contested, and more subjective endeavor than determining the meaning of treaty rights, as the latter are actually based upon written agreements. This turns out not to be the case. Just as Canadian courts re-shaped the law of evidence in dealing with aboriginal rights claims, so too have the courts re-shaped the law of evidence in dealing with treaty claims. In fleshing out the meaning of Section 35 of the Constitution Act, the Canadian courts have created a novel approach to treaty interpretation that has few parallels in American jurisprudence.

In interpreting how Section 35 should be applied to Indian treaty rights in Canada, the court has adopted what might be called an evolutionary approach, a mode of interpretation that treats the constitution as a "living tree,"[91] as opposed to dead paper. Under this approach, the meaning of treaties cannot be understood solely in relation to the specific terms or understandings that were held at the time that they were signed. Rather, the scope of treaty rights must be evaluated in light of evolving historical circumstances. For instance, in the case of *R. v. Sioui*, the court ruled that the descendants of Huron Indians had the right to camp, cut trees, and make fires for ceremonial purposes in the provincial parks of Quebec.[92] The "treaty" in this case was a one-paragraph "note of safe conduct" issued to a band of Hurons by an English General in 1760.[93]

The case of *R. v Marshall* exemplifies the Court's approach to treaty interpretation; it is also a treaty case that attracted a large amount of public attention, due to its potential effects on the regulation of fisheries in the Maritimes[94]. Marshall was charged with selling 463 pounds of eels without a license. The only question was whether or not he possessed a treaty right to catch and sell eels, according to the terms of the treaties signed in 1760 and 1761 between the Mik-Maq Indians and the British crown. The treaties contained no explicit reference to any right to trade free from regulation, and as a consequence the trial court and the Nova Scotia Court of Appeal ruled against Marshall. The Supreme Court, in a 5-2 decision, ruled that the lower courts had erred in not taking into account extrinsic evidence in interpreting the terms of the treaty. In particular, the lower courts had not properly considered the oral terms of the agreement that had shaped the Mik Maq people's understanding of the treaties. Justice Binnie, in his opinion for the majority, indicated that the Supreme Court would take a broader perspective on the meaning and content of the treaties:

---

[91] See the discussion of Alan C. Cairns, "The Judicial Committee and its Critics." *Canadian Journal of Political Science*. Vol. 4, No. 3 (Sept., 1971) pp 301-345.

[92] *R. v. Sioui* (1990) 1 S.C.R. 1025

[93] Flanagan, *First Nations? Second Thoughts* Montreal and Ithaca: Queen's-McGill University Press, 2000. p. 137.

[94] *R. v. Marshall* (1999) 3 S.C.R. 456

> It seems clear that the words of the March 10, 1760 document, standing in isolation, do not support the appellant's argument. The question is whether the underlying negotiations produced a broader agreement between the British and the Mik Maq, memorialized only in part by the Treaty of Peace and Friendship, that would protect the appellant's activities that are the subject of the prosecution.[95]

In order to interpret the scope of Mik Maq treaty rights, therefore, it was necessary not only to interpret the treaty, but also to interpret how the Mik Maq people had understood the terms of the treaty and the negotiations that lay, somehow, underneath the treaty.

The lower courts had rejected the use of extrinsic evidence in treaty interpretation. Justice Binnie found three reasons to object to that decision. First, he argued that even in a modern commercial context, extrinsic evidence can be used to show that written contracts do not necessarily contain all of the terms of the contract.[96] Secondly, while in the commercial context, extrinsic evidence is admissible in order to resolve textual ambiguities in the written contract, the same rules do not apply to treaty interpretation, where historical and cultural context can be used "even absent any ambiguity on the face of the treaty."[97] Finally, the treaty had been concluded verbally, but only afterwards written up the Crown. As a consequence, it was neither necessary nor fair to regard the written terms of the treaties as conclusive. The majority accepted the position of Marshall, on the basis of the extrinsic provided by academic historians, anthropologists, and the oral traditions and folk tales of the Mik Maq.

In dissent, Justice McLachlin (joined by Justice Gonthier) argued that the trade clauses of the 1760-1761 treaties did not confer a general right to trade. The dissenting justices did not reject the liberal approach to treaty interpretation that had been the general practice in Canadian

---

[95] *R. v. Marshall* 472

[96] Binnie did not address the problems that emerge, even in contemporary cases, from the use of extrinsic evidence in interpreting commercial contracts.

[97] *R. v. Marshall*, 474

(and American) law—they accepted that doubtful or ambiguous provisions of treaties should be interpreted in favor of the aboriginal signatories.[98] Nor did they reject categorically the use of extrinsic evidence in treaty interpretation. Yet as the specific trading clause of the 1760 treaties only established an obligation for the Mik Maq to trade exclusively with the British, it was impossible to establish a general right to trade regardless of the historical and cultural context. It was unlikely that the Mik Maq had failed to understand the terms of the treaty as written. Though the European language they were most fluent in was French, the British negotiators had employed French missionaries as translators, missionaries who had deep familiarity with the Mik Maq.[99] What made the majority's decision even more difficult to understand was that the Mik Maq, in agreeing to trade exclusively with the British, actually surrendered their trading autonomy in signing the treaties. That an agreement in 1760 to trade only with the Crown could be converted into immunity from federal regulation in 1999 was difficult to accept.

The 1999 *Marshall* decision showed that a majority of the Court was willing to creatively re-construct treaty rights. Later cases would illustrate, however, that there would be limits to judicial creativity. In 2005, in the consolidated cases of *R. v. Bernard/R v. Marshall*, individual members of the Mik Maq tribes of New Brunswick claimed that the treaties which conferred immunity from fishing regulations also conferred immunity from logging regulations.[100] The Court ruled, in a unanimous opinion, that the claims to immunity from logging regulations were not a "logical evolution" of the traditional trading practices of the Mik Maq. The distinction between the claim to immunity from logging regulations and the claim to treaty immunity from fishing regulations was that the Mik Maq had not engaged in commercial timber harvesting in the 1760s. While the Court had been

---

[98] Peter S. Heineke, "Chevron and the Canon Favoring Indians" *University of Chicago Law Review*. Vol. 60, No. 3/4 (Summer, 1993) pp 1015-1042.

[99] See the discussion of the education of the Mik Maq in Harold E. L. Prims, *The Mi'Kmaq: Resistance, Accommodation, and Cultural Survival*. Harcourt Publishers: Fort Worth, 1996. pp 74-75.

[100] *R v. Marshall; R. v. Bernard* 2 S.C.R. 220 (2005)

willing to transform a several hundred year old treaty agreement into immunity against modern fishing regulations, it still relied on a theory of treaty rights that limited the scope of judicial creativity. The "living tree" of treaty rights would be cultivated and pruned by the Court, not by the Mik Maq, who would only be allowed to make claims based upon traditional economic practices.

The Canadian Supreme Court, in interpreting Indian treaties, has occupied the middle ground between the critics and the proponents of aboriginal sovereignty. Critics of aboriginal sovereignty have argued against the expansive "evolutionary" approach to treaty rights, suggesting that this allows courts to essentially invent new privileges for Indian tribes.[101] Conversely, the supporters of aboriginal sovereignty have argued that the treaties adopted by the Crown provide support to the claim that aboriginal communities should be treated as separate, self-governing nations.[102] The courts have followed neither the critics nor supporters of aboriginal sovereignty. For better or worse, the Court has been guided by the implications of Section 35 of the Constitution, and the broader regime change that came about as a consequence of adopting the Charter of Rights and Freedoms. While there were no clear signals from the ratifying debates over what the participants expected from the aboriginal rights provisions of the Constitution Act, those provisions had to mean something—and in the absence of any clear original intent, the Courts had to assume the role of creators of constitutional meaning. Conservative critics of the Canadian Supreme Court may well be right that this is a disastrous way to make law and policy. But it is also important to remember that, in relation to the Court's interpretation of aboriginal and treaty rights, the Canadian Supreme Court has not served as the vanguard of the aboriginal rights intelligentsia. The Court has clearly engaged in activism in developing its treaty interpretation jurisprudence, but that activism was promoted by the terms of the Constitution Act and the relative silence of its framers on the meaning of Section 35. While many particulars of that jurisprudence may be theoretically unconvincing, it is difficult to argue that the Court's willingness to

---

[101] See Gibson, *A New Look at Canadian Indian Policy*, pp 153-199 and Flanagan, *First Nations? Second Thoughts* (2008) pp 134-166

[102] Macklem, *Indigenous Difference and the Constitution of Canada*, pp 132-160.

shape the content of Section 35 is illegitimate. The Court has resisted the much broader claims of aboriginal rights activists, and placed reasonable limits on the scope of aboriginal treaty claims, and in doing so it has found a way to respect the text of the Constitution Act without unduly infringing on the traditional powers of Parliament and the Provinces.

The power of Canadian courts in Indian policy can be traced not only to the ideological dispositions of the justices themselves, or to the effectiveness of interest group litigation, but rather to the decisions made and language used by the framers of the present day Canadian constitution. Section 35 of the Canadian Constitution Act is a result of a decision to judicialize part of public policy, just as surely as the entrenchment of Charter rights reflected the framer's willingness to increase the power of courts.

While Canadian courts were empowered by the Canadian constitution to play a leading role in issues related to Indian policy, the experience of American courts has been different. Due to the differing language of the American constitution, treaties between Native American tribes and the American federal government do not have the special protections provided by Canadian constitutional law. The differences between the Canadian and American approaches to treaty interpretation help to illuminate the constraints that constitutional language places upon judicial power. Between 1985 and 2008, the American Supreme Court decided seven cases which raised eight separate issues related to treaty interpretation. The Court ruled in favor of Indian treaty claims on 3 of those issues.[103] Yet during this period, there is no American equivalent to the *Marshall* case: that is, there is no case which established new approaches to the use of evidence in interpreting treaties. Does constitutional language fully account for this divergence between Canadian and American jurisprudence? The United States Supreme Court's treaty interpretation cases yield a somewhat mixed answer to this question. Unlike the cases dealing with tribal sovereign immunity and the jurisdiction of tribal courts, treaty interpretation cases have produced clearer ideological divisions on the

---

[103] *Oregon v. Klamath* (1985), *United States v. Dion* (1985) *United States v. Cherokee Nation of Oklahoma* (1987) *South Dakota v. Bourland* (1993) *Oklahoma Tax Commission v. Chickasaw Nation*(1995) ,*Minnesota v. Mille Lac Band of Chippewa Indians* (1997) *State of Arizona v. State of California* (2001)

American Supreme Court. But even so, the shifting votes of American Supreme Court justices indicate that judges are motivated not merely by underlying policy issues, such as whether the powers of tribal governments should be extended vis a vis state and national governments. The legal issues that arise in treaty interpretation-- such as the degree of ambiguity in the terms of the treaties, or the question of whether Congress has acted to abrogate treaty rights—guide the decisions of the American Supreme in ways that cannot be reduced to the political preferences or ideological affinities of individual justices.

The central principle of Native American treaty interpretation in American law is that ambiguous issues should be resolved in favor of Indian tribes.[104] Differences amongst justices emerge, unsurprisingly, over what issues are in fact ambiguous. For example, in *Oregon v. Klamath Indian Tribe,*[105] the Klamath tribe argued that, based upon the terms of the treaty that established its original reservation, it continued to possess the right to fish and hunt free from state regulations on lands that it had ceded to the United States in 1901. Writing for the majority, Justice Stevens (joined by Burger, White, Blackmun, Rehnquist, and O'Connor) ruled that, because the 1864 treaty did not establish any special hunting and fishing rights outside the boundaries of the reservations, no such rights continued to exist in the lands that were ceded in 1901. The absence of any explicit discussion of hunting and fishing rights in the 1901 agreement could not be interpreted as a sign that the parties did not intend to extinguish hunting and fishing rights; the presumption was that, when the land was transferred, the rights were extinguished. The essential weakness of the tribe's position, according to Stevens, was that it assumed that hunting and fishing rights were somehow separate from the reservation itself. Though the court was willing to consult the historical record of negotiations in order to evaluate how the tribe had understood the treaty, it was not willing to adopt the evolutionary approach to treaty interpretation that

---

[104] Francis Prucha, *American Indian Treaties: The History of a Political Anomaly*. Berkeley: University of California Press, 1994. p. 386.

[105] *Oregon v. Klamath* 473 U.S. 753 (1985).

was on display in Canadian cases such as *R v. Sioui* and *R. v. Marshall.*[106]

In a dissenting opinion, Justice Marshall (joined by Justice Brennan) argued that the majority opinion, while consistent with the "boilerplate" language of the 1864 Treaty and 1901 Agreement, discarded one of the central facets of Indian treaty cases: Indian treaties should be interpreted as they were understood by the tribe and, when in doubt, ambiguities in treaty law should be resolved in favor of Indians. The cession of land in 1901 contained no record of any negotiations regarding hunting and fishing rights, and thus it was reasonable to conclude, with the Klamath, that the tribe had not intended to surrender those rights. The central difficulty with Marshall's argument is that, like the majority of the Canadian Supreme Court in *Marshall* case, it was based on the presumption that the Indian tribes in question were not capable of articulating and defending their interests in negotiations with governments. The Klamath in the early 20th century were much more likely than the Mik Maq in the late 18th to understand their legal interests: they were English speakers, they had long experience with the treaty process and government negotiation, and they had access to legal counsel (and not merely French Canadian missionaries like the Mik Maq.)[107] Based on the "silence" of the 1901 text regarding off-reservation hunting rights, Marshall wanted to read those rights into existence close to 100 hundred years after the initial agreement and transfer of land had taken place. In support of his position, Marshall suggested that the payment received by the tribe for the land ceded in 1901 had to be interpreted as compensation—compensation for the failure of the government to prevent incursions by settlers, hunters, and trappers into land that was part of the initial reservation established in 1864. While the tribe accepted that it formally transferred title to those lands in accepting compensation, they continued to hunt, trap, and fish on the land free from state regulation. The actions of the Klamath suggested that they understood the 1901 Agreement to involve a transfer of land, but not an extinguishment of their hunting and fishing rights.

---

106 Francis Prucha, *American Indian Treaties: The History of a Political Anomaly*. Berkeley: University of California Press, 1994 p. 407.

107 See Theodore Stern, *The Klamath Tribe: A People and Their Reservation*. Seattle: University of Washington Press, 1965.

Marshall's position was not entirely unprecedented in American constitutional law. The court had always recognized that hunting and fishing rights—in particular, the right to special protections from state regulation for Indian tribes—could exist independently from claims to land.[108] But in most cases, this was thought to depend upon specific treaty provisions, or upon specific actions by Congress. There was one precedent that stood for the proposition that rights could survive by implication, even when a reservation was fully terminated: the case of *Menominee Tribe of Indians v. United States*.[109] The Menominee Tribe had been granted a reservation in the 1854 Treaty of Wolf River, a reservation that included hunting and fishing rights. By the 1950s, the tribe was subjected to a new round of federal termination policy, which was to bring to an end their traditional status (and exemption from state regulations) by 1961.110 The question in this case was whether the termination of the reservation had also extinguished hunting and fishing rights that had been recognized in the 1854 Treaty of Wolf River. The Termination Act of 1954, which had led to the creation of a tribal corporation to manage tribal property, as well as the creation of a new county government in Wisconsin that coincided with the boundaries of the reservation, also provided that "the laws of the several States shall apply to the tribe and its members in the same manner as they apply to other citizens or persons within their jurisdiction."111 Thus the state argued that its hunting and fishing regulations should apply to tribal members.

A majority of the Court argued that the Termination Act had not extinguished the hunting and fishing rights of the Menominee, on account of Public Law 280 which had been passed by the same Congress that passed the Termination Act of 1954. Public Law 280,

---

[108] E.g. Mary Pearson " Hunting Rights: Retention of Treaty Rights after Termination." *American Indian Law Review* , Vol. 4, No. 1 (1976), pp. 121-133

[109] *Menominee Tribe of Indians v. United States.* 391 U.S. 404 (1968)

110 David Wilikins, *American Indian Sovereignty and the U.S. Supreme Court.* Austin: University of Texas Press, 1997 pp 166-167

111 MenomineeTermination Act of 1954 (68 Stat. 250 (1954))

which created procedures for the extension of state jurisdiction over Native American tribes, also stated that "Nothing in this section . . . shall deprive any Indian or any Indian tribe, band, or community of any right, privilege, or immunity afforded under Federal treaty, agreement, or statute with respect to hunting, trapping, or fishing or the control, licensing, or regulation thereof."[112] The Court concluded that Public Law 280 protected the existing treaty rights to hunting and fishing, notwithstanding the Termination Act. In dissent, Justices Stewart and Black—representatives, according to some, of the emerging styles of conservatism on the Court[113]—argued that the language of the Termination Act had to govern the Court decision. That Act had explicitly terminated the special status of the Menominee, including their hunting and fishing rights, and Public Law 280 was not intended to qualify this expression of the government's termination policy; Public Law 280 was meant to deal with state jurisdiction in Indian country, while in this case the "Indian Country" in question was no longer in existence.

The contrasting cases of *Klamath* and *Menominee* suggest a plausible, political explanation for the evolution of the American Court's approach to treaty interpretation: that is, liberal justices in the Warren Era, who were willing to adopt expansive understandings of aboriginal treaty rights, were gradually replaced by Justices modeled on the likes of Frankfurter, Stewart, and Black— justices who placed a higher premium on either deference to Congress and state governments, or fidelity to the explicit terms of Congressional treaties. It is important to remember, however, that a preference for one mode of treaty interpretation over another is still a legal rationale, one that cannot be reduced to a policy preference for greater Native American autonomy.

The *Klamath* case is certainly an example of the unwillingness of the American Supreme Court, in marked contrast to the Canadian Supreme Court, to depart from the text of treaties in deference to claims regarding the intentions of those who made the treaties. The breakdown

---

[112] David Wilkins and K. Lomawaima, *Uneven Ground: American Indian Sovereignty and Federal Law.* Norman: University of Oklahoma Press, 2001. p. 132-133.

[113] Thomas Keck, *The Most Activist Supreme Court in History*. (Chicago: University of Chicago Press, 2004) pp 102-103.

of voting in that case—with holdovers from the Warren Era opposed to the new appointees of the Rehnquist and Burger Era—suggests a political or "attitudinal" interpretation of the outcome. But it is important to note the limits that liberal dissenters placed upon their support for aboriginal interests. Even justices who advocated expansive interpretations of treaty rights, such as Marshall and Brennan in the *Klamath* case, did not see fit to "constitutionalize" Indian treaty rights by immunizing them from extinguishment by federal action. In interpreting treaties, justices are not infinitely flexible in their attempts to endorse either Native American interests or the prerogatives of state and federal governments.

For instance, in the case of *United States v. Dion,*[114] Marshall authored an opinion, for a unanimous court, which upheld the conviction of several Native Americans for the killing of golden eagles in violation of the Endangered Species Act. This decision overturned the ruling by the Court of Appeals that the hunting of golden eagles by Yankton Sioux Indians was protected by an 1858 Treaty. In another unanimous case, *United States v. Cherokee Nation of Oklahoma,* [115] the court ruled that the Cherokee's treaty rights to riverbed mineral deposits did not entitle them to compensation for damages caused by a federal navigational improvement project. These cases illustrate some of the complexities involved in interpreting the outcomes of legal cases: in a conflict between the cultural rights of Native Americans and the desire to protect threatened wildlife, it is difficult to determine what it means for an opinion to be "liberal" or "conservative." Or consider the *Cherokee Nation* case: would an opinion that endorsed the Cherokee's claim to compensation have been a "liberal" outcome, if it implied an expansive understanding of the protections for property rights and compensation entitlements under the Fifth Amendment? These cases show that the interpretive principles advocated by Marshall and Brennan were just that—principles that were meant to guide approaches to treaties, not rhetoric designed to help advance a specific conception of "Indian policy."

While some issues in treaty interpretation produce voting coalitions rooted in the familiar ideological divisions of the court, other

---

[114] *United States v. Dion* 476 U.S. 734 (1986).

[115] *United States v. Cherokee Nation of Oklahoma* 480 U.S. 700 (1987)

issues are not so predictable, even when the political stakes are just as evident. In *Oklahoma Tax Commission v. Chickasaw Nation,*[116] the Court unanimously agreed with the Chickasaw's claim, based upon federal treaties, to an exemption from an Oklahoma motor fuels tax. The Court split 5-4 over whether the same treaties prohibited Oklahoma from imposing income taxes on Indians who worked but did not reside on reservation. The majority opinion, joined by Justices Thomas, Scalia, Kennedy, and Rehnquist, was written by Justice Ginsburg. The case illustrates that, contrary to some claims, the Rehnquist Era court (and Rehnquist-era conservatives) have not usurped the policy-making role of Congress—the court has simply maintained a "geographic" approach to the problem of state-tribal relations, tying the rights of Indian individuals to territory and place of residents, not their status as Indians. This may well be the preferred policy position of the majority: neither too much protection from state taxation from the tribes, nor too little. But the position adopted by the court is not part of a crusade to eliminate the special status of the tribes, or to enforce assimilation and uniform citizenship rights—however attractive those policies might be to those of a conservative or libertarian bent.

There are instances in which majorities on the American Supreme Court adopt "Canadian" approaches to treaty interpretation, in the sense that they adopt interpretations of treaty rights that undermine long settled legal expectations regarding the scope of state power and tribal sovereignty. This is not a consequence—or rather, not only a consequence—of the desire of some justices to empower Native American tribes. The case of *Minnesota vs. Mille Lac Band of Chippewa Indians*[117] illustrates that treaty cases depend on the ambiguities of treaty language, and the ambiguities of federal actions and laws held to have abrogated Indian treaties. In this case, the court endorsed the Chippewa's claim to possess hunting, fishing, and gathering rights in lands that had been ceded to the United States in an 1837 Treaty. There were three hurdles to the Chippewa's claims, that is, three possible actions by the federal government which undercut the

---

[116] *Oklahoma Tax Commission v. Chickasaw Nation* 515 U.S. 450 (1995)

[117] *Minnesota vs. Mille Lac Band of Chippewa Indians* 526 U.S. 172 (1999)

Chippewa's claim to usufructuary118 rights on off-reservation land. First, there was an executive order from 1850 that (amongst other things) claimed to revoke those rights. Secondly, an 1855 treaty between the Chippewa and the federal government stated that the Chippewa relinquished "any and all right, title and interest, of whatsoever nature" in the land in the question. Finally, the government of Minnesota argued that the admission of Minnesota as a state extinguished the claims of the Chippewa.

Writing for the majority, O'Connor, joined by Stevens, Souter, Ginsburg, and Breyer, argued that the 1850 executive order was not authorized by Congress or by any inherent executive authority. In addition, the history of negotiations surrounding the 1855 Treaty revealed that Congress did not intend to annul the rights in question. In regards to the final objection, O'Connor concluded that the admission of Minnesota did not annul the rights of the Chippewa, as there was no explicit discussion of extinguishment of those rights in the Congressional enabling act, and as the rights were reconcilable with state sovereignty.

Political divisions certainly exist in this case, but this is not only because of its underlying policy dimensions (should Native American tribes be granted more power or less?) but because of the constitutional issues it raises. At root, where the (liberal) majority saw much ambiguity in the treaty of 1837, the (conservative) dissenters saw very little. Thomas, joined by Scalia, Rehnquist, and Kennedy, argued that the executive order, subsequent treaty, and admission of Minnesota into the Union all had the effect of extinguishing the rights claimed by the Chippewa bands of Milles Lac. The majority had argued that the executive order lacked Congressional authorization, and thus had no effect on earlier treaty rights. Thomas, in upholding the validity of the order, did not point to inherent executive authority, but rather to the relevant terms of the treaty: "The privilege of hunting, fishing, and gathering the wild rice, upon the lands, the rivers and the lakes included in the territory ceded, is guaranteed to the Indians, during the pleasure of the President of the United States."[119] Thus, in contrast with the

118 Usufructurary rights are rights to use property that belongs to another.

[119] Justice Thomas, dissenting opinion, *Minnesota vs. Mille Lac Band of Chippewa Indians (*1999) 226.

majority, Thomas accepted that treaties themselves can be the basis of Presidential power.120

In denying that treaties can be a basis for Presidential power—an interpretive move that Rehnquist correctly identified as an error in his dissent-- the majority mobilized its creative power in order to uphold the Chippewa's claims. But Milles Lac is in many ways the exception that proves the rule. Creative mis-reading in treaty interpretation is not on display in every treaty case; neither is the conservative-liberal split in voting. In *Milles Lac*, the majority placed a great deal of emphasis upon the split between Presidential action and Congressional authorization—but this is an interpretive move that is only useful, in the context of treaty interpretation, when Congress has not made its intentions explicit. Political divisions on the court regarding the scope of Indian sovereignty can only be expressed in some circumstances, circumstances that are circumscribed by law.

In Canada, the limits of treaty interpretation are very different. The judicial interpretation of Indian treaties in Canada has undergone a revolution, initiated by Section 35 of the Constitution Act. The privileges accorded by treaties between Parliament and Native Canadians are, under the Canadian Constitution, of a more exalted status than the rights protected by the Charter. Under the protection of Section 35, the Court has adopted an innovative approach to treaty interpretation, allowing for the use of "oral histories" to determine the content and scope of treaties. This has led to some important victories for Native Canadians, and to some serious policy consequences in many parts of the country. But the new approach to treaty interpretation has not led the court to act as the vanguard of the Indian rights intelligentsia. As in the case of aboriginal rights, the courts have assumed the power to not only determine the meaning of treaties, but also to ascertain how the protections afforded by treaties evolve over time. As the superintendents of evolving treaty rights, the courts have not always served Indian interests; but they have consistently endorsed judicial supremacy in aboriginal affairs.

In the United States, the courts have rejected judicial supremacy in treaty interpretation. There has been no attempt, in American Indian law, to challenge the basic presumptions regarding Congressional

---

120 For a discussion of how treaties can serve as the basis of Presidential power, see Michael D. Ramsey, *The Constitution's Text in Foreign Affairs*. Cambridge, Mass.: Harvard University Press, 2007.pp 163-164

sovereignty that have governed the relationships between Native Americans and American society since the 18th century. In other words, the constitutional negotiations that led to Section 35 of the Constitution Act created a different institutional environment for Canadian Courts, one more conducive to the advancement of aboriginal interests. The significance of Constitutional amendments, or failed amendments, is not obvious, and it is certainly not invariant.[121] But in the case of aboriginal rights, the differing constitutional frameworks of Canada and the United States have led Canada to experience a more robust, court-led revolution in aboriginal treaty rights.

Indian Law and Statutory Interpretation: Land Claims, Taxation, Regulation

The central hypothesis that I have advanced thus far is that the patterns of Indian law decisions in Canada and the United States cannot be explained simply on the basis of the political preferences of the Court's members. Section 35 of the Constitution Act 1982 provided a textual basis for judicial activism in Canada that is not available for American judges, even for those who might be inclined to support the interests of aboriginal peoples.[122] What this means in practice is that the decisions of Canadian courts, when interpreting aboriginal and treaty rights, are effectively insulated from challenges by national or provincial governments—something which is not true for many of the rights protected under the Canadian Charter of Rights and Freedoms.

There are several reasons to suspect that the differences between Canadian and American courts will extend to issues in statutory interpretation that affect Native peoples. In general, American courts are more capable of "statutory activism" than are courts in Parliamentary systems of government. Parliamentary governments have

---

[121] E.g. F.L. Morton, "The Supreme Court's Promotion of Sexual Education: A Case Study of Institutional Capacity." *Polity*. Vol. 16, No. 3 (Spring, 1984) pp 467-483.

[122] This does not mean that the particular patterns of post-1982 aboriginal rights activism in Canadian courts can be traced to the "Framers" of the Constitution Act. Rather, Section 35 provided a general pre-text for judicial activism, both by recognizing aboriginal and treaty rights AND by insulating those rights from the "notwithstanding clause."

the capacity to respond to adverse statutory decisions with relative ease. The American political system, in general, favors inaction. In addition, the American legislative process is more likely to produce ambiguous laws, which provides another pretext for the exercise of judicial power. Thus, just as Canadian courts are empowered by Section 35 when interpreting aboriginal and treaty rights, American courts have reasons to be emboldened when engaged in statutory interpretation.

When interpreting statutes that affect the interests of Indian tribes, the American Supreme Court has exhibited some of the creativity that the Canadian Supreme Court has displayed in interpreting aboriginal rights and treaty rights. The Canadian Supreme Court decided 14 cases between 1985 and 2008 that dealt with statutory rights claims of aboriginal litigants; the Supreme Court of the United States decided 42 cases that dealt with the statutory claims by Native Americans. Indian litigants in Canada won 4 out 14 cases, while Native Americans won 13 out of 42 cases. In terms of the policy consequences, the statutory victories for aboriginal litigants in Canada were not as significant as cases such as *Delgamuukw* and *Marshall.*[123]In the United States, judicial activism in Indian policy has more often been channeled through statutory interpretation.

If there has been an aboriginal rights revolution in the United States, it has occurred in statutory interpretation. Whereas the development of aboriginal rights and treaty rights in the United States has been modest—the Court has not adopted the framework for the use of evidence or interpretation of treaties that was adopted in Canada—claims based on statutory rights have in some instances led the American Supreme Court to adopt new approaches to several legal issues, such as the use of historical evidence, the problem of long-dormant legal claims, and the interpretation of statutes of limitation.

---

[123] The *Delgamuukw* and *Marshall* cases a) affected the rights of non-native groups that were not parties to the cases b) introduced new legal standards (in regards to the use of evidence and standards of treaty interpretation, for example). The statutory victories for aboriginal litigants in Canada came in cases dealing with the garnishment of "on reservation" property for the non-payment of fees (*Mitchell v. Peguis Indian Band*,1990), the exemption of unemployment benefits from taxation (*Williams v. Canada* , 1992),, the scope of tribal taxation powers (*Canadian Pacific Ltd. v. Matsqui Indian Band*, 1995) and the fiduciary duty of the national government regarding transfers of native land.

American courts have not been empowered to provide special constitutional protections to the rights of Native American tribes. Yet because many legal claims of Native Americans are based on the application and interpretation of statutes, American courts can still play a considerable role in shaping policies that affect American Indians. In American Indian law, courts are more constrained at the constitutional level than at the statutory level.

The case of *County of Oneida vs. Oneida Indian Nation*[124] illustrates how judicial activism in American Indian law can emerge in the context of statutory interpretation. In this case, the Oneida Indian Nation claimed that a land transfer between the Oneida and the state had violated federal Indian law (specifically, the Non-Intercourse Act of 1790.) The problem was that this violation was alleged to have occurred in the 1790s. In many ways, the case is similar to the major aboriginal and treaty rights cases in Canada, such as *Delgamuukw* and *Marshall*, cases which were legally significant because the courts adopted novel approaches to the use of evidence and treaty interpretation, and politically significant because they affected a broad range of economic interests. A similar dynamic was on display *County of Oneida v. Oneida Indian Nation*. In order to endorse the claims of aboriginal litigants, the court had to adopt a variety of novel approaches to legal interpretation.

The County of Oneida had appealed the initial district court decision, in which the court declared that the Non-Intercourse Act had been violated by the improper transfer of land in the 1790s. The County did not dispute this ruling, but it did suggest that further barriers stood in the way of the Oneida's claim. The County argued that the Oneidas could not maintain a private cause of action for violations of the Non-Intercourse Act; in other words, the Oneida had no private right to enforce a public law.[125] More importantly, they argued that the action was time-barred (that is, prohibited by the relevant state statute of limitations), that any cause of action had abated, and that the United States had ratified the conveyance. The tribe had existed as an

---

[124] *County of Oneida vs. Oneida Indian Nation* 470 U.S. 226 (1985).

[125] For a discussion of the concept of private attorneys general, see Trevor W. Morrison, " Private Attorneys General and the First Amendment." *Michigan Law Review*, Vol. 103, No. 4, (Feb., 2005), pp. 589-675

organized entity for the entire period of time, and its leaders were educated and politically astute; thus the Oneida had been fully capable of challenging the transfer of land had they thought it invalid. Even if the Non-Intercourse Act had been violated, the passage of 200 years should have ratified the transaction. The Second Circuit court of appeals rejected the County's arguments, with one judge dissenting.[126]

In a 5-4 decision, the Supreme Court affirmed the lower court's ruling.[127] The first issue addressed by Justice Powell in his majority opinion was whether the tribe could in fact bring the case at all. Lawyers for the County of Oneida argued that the Oneida were attempting to enforce a public law—the Non-Intercourse Act—which had pre-empted whatever federal common law rights they might have had to contest the conveyance of the land. The District Court and the Court of Appeals had ruled that the Oneida had both a federal common law right of action and an implied statutory cause of action under the Non-Intercourse Act. Powell wisely declined to address the second issue—the practice of creating private attorneys general had not been common in the 1790s. But it was not made clear why the federal common law rights of the Indians had not been pre-empted by the Non-Intercourse Act itself. It was this law that had made the transfer of land to New York illegal in the first place. Powell argued that the Non-Intercourse Act was not meant to provide a comprehensive scheme for dealing with the transfer and sale of Indian land, on the grounds that the law itself contained no explicit remedial provisions. Furthermore, Powell argued that subsequent Congressional actions showed that the national government did not wish to pre-empt suits by Indian tribes asserting their property rights: "Nothing in the statutory formulation of this rule suggests that the Indians' right to pursue common-law remedies was thereby pre-empted."[128] What Powell left entirely unclear was the purpose of the statute. The government of the 1790s, apparently, had found it necessary to codify the procedures for

---

[126] *Oneida Indian Nation v. County of Oneida* 719 F.2d 525 (1983)

[127] Powell was joined by O'Connor, Blackmun, and (in the relevant portion) by Marshall and Brennan. Stevens, in dissent, was joined by Rehnquist, White, and Chief Justice Burger.

[128] *County of Oneida vs. Oneida Indian Nation* 470 U.S. 240 (1985)

purchasing Indian land, a law that presumably the national government would have the responsibility to enforce. In Powell's argument, the statute was not necessary: "the Non-Intercourse simply put in statutory form what was or came to be the accepted rule—that the extinguishment of Indian title required the consent of the United States."[129] By simply ignoring the fact that it was a public law at stake, Powell could argue that the Oneida had the right to enforce the requirement for consent.

Having determined that the Oneidas had a federal common law right to bring their claim, Powell quickly dispensed with other objections made by the County. While in most situations the absence of a federal statute of limitations would lead to the application of an analogous state statute of limitations, Powell argued that this could only be done if it was consistent with the underlying federal policy, and the evidence in this case suggested that Congress wished to impose no limitations on Indian land claims. The passage of subsequent laws addressing the transfer of Indian land did not affect the Oneida's claim, and subsequent national treaties had not explicitly recognized the unlawful 1795 transfers of land. Perhaps the most interesting claim made by the petitioners was that the case was non-justiciable, in the sense that responsibility for Indian relations was an example of "a textually demonstrable constitutional commitment of (an) issue to a co-ordinate political department."[130] But Powell rejected this claim as well; questions related to Indian affairs were not rendered non-justiciable by virtue of Congress' plenary power in this field. In conclusion, Powell observed, almost in surprise, that "one would have thought that claims dating back for more than a century and a half would have been barred long ago." [131] But there was in his opinion no insuperable legal barrier to the Oneida's claim.

The dissent, penned by Justice Stephens and joined by Burger, White, and Rehnquist, argued that barriers to this action either did exist, or had to be created immediately. The first paragraph summarizes the major objections of the dissenters:

---

[129] *County of Oneida vs. Oneida Indian Nation* 470 U.S. 240 (1985)

[130] *Baker v. Carr* 369 U.S. 186 (1962)

[131] *County of Oneida v. Oneida Indian Nation* 470 U.S.253 (1985)

> In 1790, the President of the United States notified Cornplanter, the Chief of the Senecas, that federal law would securely protect Seneca lands from acquisition by any State or person: "If . . . you have any just cause of complaint against [a purchaser] and can make satisfactory proof thereof, the federal courts will be open to you for redress, as to all other persons" . . . The elders of the Oneida Indian Nation received comparable notice of their capacity to maintain the federal claim that is at issue in this litigation... They made no attempt to assert the claim, and their successors in interest waited 175 years before bringing suit to avoid a 1795 conveyance that the Tribe freely made, for a valuable consideration. The absence of any evidence of deception, concealment, or interference with the Tribe's right to assert a claim, together with the societal interests that always underlie statutes of repose—particularly when title to real property is at stake—convince me that this claim is barred by the extraordinary passage of time. It is worthy of emphasis that this claim arose when George Washington was the President of the United States.[132]

The central focus of Stevens' dissent was the majority's refusal to apply any time bar to the Oneida's claim, on the grounds that it would be inconsistent with federal policy. While the majority may have been correct in its judgment that federal policy aimed, on the whole, to err on the side of protecting the interests of Native American tribes, it failed to consider the effects that the decision would have upon the broader community. If resolving legal ambiguities in favor of Indian tribes was a general federal policy, so too was protecting the stability and integrity of land titles. Given the fact that there had been no legal impediment to the tribe's actions since 1795, the decision of the majority appeared even more suspect.

Stevens also argued that there was a certain degree of paternalism in the majority's reasoning. Powell's argument was based on the premise that the Oneida should not be held to the same standards as other peoples, despite the fact that the group had received formal education since the 1790s, had a sophisticated form of government, and

---

[132] *County of Oneida vs. Oneida Indian Nation* 470 U.S. 255 (1985)

had demonstrated their capacity to petition the government for their grievances. As the tribe was self-governing and fully capable of utilizing the legal system, the delay in pursuing their claim was inexplicable.

The Oneida's argument that various congressional statutes (supported by legislative histories) since the 1950s supported their claim was rejected by the dissenters, on the grounds that a) the statutes only referred to actions brought by the United States, and b) there was no indication that the statutes were meant to revive claims that had already been barred. Given the lack of clarity regarding Congressional intent, Stevens argued that it made little sense to assume that Congress wished to remove all limitations. Chief Justice Marshall, speaking on the same issue more than one hundred years earlier, argued that "it deserves some consideration, that in the absence of an applicable limitation, those actions might, in many cases, be brought at any distance of time. This would be utterly repugnant to the genius of our laws."[133]

In the same case, Marshall wrote that in a country where not even treason can be prosecuted after three year, "it could scarcely be supposed that an individual would remain forever liable to a pecuniary forfeiture."[134] One could argue, along with some theorists of multiculturalism, that it might make sense to hold settler societies as a whole responsible for historical injustices against minority groups, especially in regards to indigenous people who were conquered and Africans who were enslaved in the new world.135 But it was not the political community that would, in this instance, be paying the costs for righting ancient wrongs. It would be specific landowners who would be punished for legal violations that had occurred centuries before their birth. In endorsing the interests of Indian tribes in this case, the majority had evaded both the restraints of the common law and the idea of collective responsibility for historical wrongs. It is, however, one of

[133] *Adams v. Woods* 6 U.S. 336 (1805)

[134] *Adams v. Woods* 6 U.S. 342 (1805)

[135] E.g. Lawrie Balfour, "Reparations after Identity Politics." *Political Theory*, Vol. 33, No. 6 (Dec., 2005), pp. 786-811

the very few cases in which the Supreme Court of the United States adopted novel approaches to the law in order to endorse the claim of Native American litigants.

The Non-Intercourse Act of the 1790s was a law much honored in the breach; or at least, this was the opinion of a number of additional litigants after the decision of the Supreme Court decision in *County of Oneida v. Oneida*. But the outcome in County of Oneida was not always repeated. The Supreme Court's willingness to advance the interests of Indian tribes through "statutory activism" was limited by various legal factors, most notably by the impact of 20th century federal Indian policies. In cases where the underlying policy dimensions were the same, the court would reach different conclusions based upon the presence (or absence) of distinctively legal factors.

The case of *South Carolina v. Catawba Indian Tribe*[136], for instance, bore many similarities to *County of Oneida*. The Catawba claimed that land, which they held by virtue of the 1763 Treaty of Fort Augusta with the English Crown, had been improperly conveyed to South Carolina in 1840s, in violation of the Non-Intercourse Act. The tribe, in an action initiated in 1980, laid claim to a fifteen mile tract of land in South Carolina, as the federal government had never properly consented to the transfer of land to South Carolina. The underlying policy dimensions were essentially identical to County of Oneida: in both cases, an Indian tribe sought restitution for a violation of federal law, in a situation where rectifying that violation would involve disrupting many thousands of present day land owners.

The outcome was different in this case because the validity of the Catawba's claim, unlike the Oneida's, had been altered by federal Indian policy in the 1950s and 1960s, the "termination era" of federal Indian policy in which the national government attempted to normalize the relationship between Indians and state governments.[137] The Catawba Act of 1962[138] had revoked the tribe's constitution, and

---

[136] *South Carolina v. Catawba Indian Tribe* 476 U.S. 498 (1986).

[137] George Pierre Castile, *Taking Charge: Native American Self-Determination and Federal Indian Policy, 1975-1993.* Tucson: University of Arizona Press, 2006. pp 10-12.

[138] 25 U.S.C. § 931-38 (1976)

established (according to the majority) that special federal services and statutory protections for Indians were no longer applicable to the Catawba; they would be subject to state laws in precisely the same manner as other citizens of South Carolina. The significance of this is that, if the special federal laws dealing with state-tribal relations were no longer applicable to the Catawba, the tribe and its members could not raise claims under the Non-Intercourse Act for violations that had occurred in the 19th century. Such claims would have been precluded by state statutes of limitation.

The lower courts had ruled that the provisions dealing with the applicability of state laws applied only to the individual Catawba tribe members, not to the tribe itself. The majority did not reject the general principle that ambiguous provisions in Indian law should be resolved in favor of Indian tribes, but they did not agree that Congressional intent was ambiguous in this case. Congress had made it clear that the Catawba Act was to revoke both the tribal constitution and special protections for individual tribe members, and the Court could not ignore the express language of Congress in favor of a convoluted grammatical construction of certain provisions of the law. As Justice Stevens wrote, "it would be most incongruous to preserve special protections for a tribe whose constitution has been revoked while withdrawing protection for individual members of that tribe."[139] Thus while the underlying political question was the same in the *County of Oneida* and *Catawba* cases—should courts act to rectify centuries-old violations of the Non-Intercourse Act?—the fact that the Catawba tribe has been subjected to federal termination policy in the 1960s placed them in a weaker legal position. At least, this would seem to explain the shift in votes by Justices Powell and Brennan, both of whom had supported the Oneida's claim but found themselves voting against the claims of the Catawba.

Justice Blackmun, joined by Justice Marshall and O'Connor, authored the dissenting opinion in the case. Blackmun thought that the Court's traditional approach to interpreting statutes regulating Indian affairs mandated a ruling in favor of the Catawba. That traditional approach—resolving ambiguities in treaties and statutes in favor of Indian tribes—was itself justified by the fraud and abuse that had

---

[139] Justice Stevens, majority opinion, *South Carolina v. Catawba Indian Tribe* 476 U.S. 507 (1986).

characterized the relationship between Indian tribes and settler societies. In the estimation of Blackmun, the Catawba Act did not clearly foreclose the tribe's claim, because it was not clear that the law applied South Carolina's statute of limitations to claims that originated prior to the adoption of the Catawba Act. The court, in subjecting the federal law claims of the Catawba to South Carolina's statute of limitations, was straining to implement an assimilationist policy that Congress had since rejected.

Blackmun's opinion in this case shows that, to some extent, how judges view the significance of the early history of American-Indian relations affects their decisions in cases which address the interests of Native Americans. But as a comparison of the *Oneida* and *Catawba* cases illustrate, judicial interpretations of the Non-Intercourse Act are sensitive to the facts on the ground, not necessarily driven by the desire of judges to rectify the unfair deals between states and Indian tribes in the 18th and 19th centuries. Other cases dealing with the Non-Intercourse Act illustrate this pattern.

The case of *Mountain States Telephone and Telegraph Co. v. Pueblo of Santa Ana*[140] also illustrates the complexities that emerged from the application, or non-application, of the Non-Intercourse Act to Indian tribes. It also illustrates the shifting votes of some justices in cases that raise identical issues of policy. This case dealt with the question of whether the Non-Intercourse Act applied to transactions between the Pueblo and private parties, a question made complex because, for most of the 19th century, the Pueblo were not recognized as a Native American tribe under the Non-Intercourse act. In the absence of such recognition, the Pueblo were entitled to alienate their lands without the need for special federal supervision. The Pueblo received recognition under federal law as a Native American Indian tribe in the early 20th century, thus placing a cloud over the title of the thousands of non-Indians who had purchased parcels of land from them.[141]Congress enacted the Pueblo Lands Act of 1924 in order to address the problem, the stated purpose of which was to "settle the complicated questions of title and to secure for the Indians all of the lands to which they are

---

[140] *Mountain States Telephone and Telegraph Co. v. Pueblo of Santa Ana* 472 U.S. 237 (1985).

[141] Under the New Mexico Enabling Act of 1910. 36 Stat. 557

equitably entitled."142 In this case, the court had to address whether the grant of an easement for a telephone line, prior to the 1924 Act, had been in violation of the Non-Intercourse Act, thereby entitling the Pueblo to trespass damages.

The question turned upon whether Congress had intended to apply the Non-Intercourse Act to the Pueblo, in which case approval of alienation of land would have had to come from Congress instead of the Secretary of the Interior. The majority argued that Congress, in taking into account the peculiar history of the Pueblo, had not stated that the conditions of the Non-Intercourse Act applied to the Pueblo. The dissenting justices (Blackmun, Brennan, and Marshall) argued that the canons of federal Indian law construction dictated a different outcome. First, the majority's opinion rested on the argument that Congress wanted to create, for the Pueblo, a statutory arrangement that was not applied to any other Indian tribe (that is, alienation of unallotted Indian lands, subject only to the supervision of the Secretary of the Interior). While the awkward and obscure provisions of the Pueblo Land Act permitted this construction, it did not dictate it. Given the ambiguity of the statutory language, the dissenters argued that the Court should have assumed that Congress wanted to apply the same legal standards to the Pueblo which, under the Non-Intercourse Act, it applied to all other Indian tribes.

The *Oneida*, *Catawba*, and *Pueblo* cases illustrate several interesting aspects of American Indian law, and American judicial politics. Some of the innovative developments in Canadian aboriginal rights and treaty interpretation are mirrored in statutory interpretations of American Indian law, as shown by the Court's treatment of violations of the Non-Intercourse Act. But the scope of the "statutory aboriginal rights" revolution has been constricted, not simply by the presence of a consistently "anti-aboriginal" voting bloc on the court, but rather by the differing statutory issues surrounding the specific cases. The *policy* imposed in the Oneida case—the potential expansion of Native American land claims—was rejected by the very same court, when faced with the very different circumstances created by the Pueblo Land Act of 1924 and Congressional termination policy in the 1950s and 1960s. This is not to deny the political or ideological dimensions to these cases. For instance, Marshall and Blackmun consistently upheld

142 Pueblo Land Act, 1924 43 Stat. 641

aboriginal claims in these cases, on the grounds that ambiguities in federal Indian law should always be resolved in favor of Native Americans—and in American law, such ambiguities are not difficult to find. However, this interpretive principle did not dictate the votes of all liberal justices—most notably Justice Brennan, who joined the majority in rejecting the Native American claims in the Catawba case. These cases, and others dealing with the statutory rights of Native Americans, also illustrate an important difference between Canadian and American judicial politics: the way in which legislative politics in the United States creates greater opportunities for judicial activism. This ultimately helps to explain why the Canadian court, which has engaged in a transformation of Indian law since the adoption of the Constitution Act, has been unwilling to endorse the substantive claims of environmentalist interest groups.

The legal or Constitutional sources of the American Supreme Court's Indian law decisions are also reflected in cases dealing with the taxation and regulatory powers of Indian tribes, issues that also turn for the most part on questions of statutory interpretation. Between 1985 and 2008, the American Supreme Court decided twenty cases dealing with the taxation and regulatory powers of Indian tribes under federal law. In eight of those cases, the Supreme Court granted either a complete or partial victory for the claims made by Native American tribes; in ten of those cases, the claims were rejected entirely. While these cases are few in number, they are not lacking in significance. The cases raise crucial questions about the potential for tribes to maintain and expand their governing powers, and questions about the relative value of "assimilation" versus "separation and preservation" in Indian policy. The political dimensions of the cases, however, do not seem to have determined the votes of the justices.

For instance, in cases such as *Cass County v. Leech Lake Band of Chippewa*[143] and the *City of Sherill v. Oneida Indian Nation,*[144] the Supreme Court refused to correct for federal assimilationist policies that have reduced the political power of Native American organizations. In these cases, Native American governments claimed sovereignty (and thus immunity to local and state taxes) over land that,

[143] *Cass County v. Leech Lake Band of Chippewa* 524 U.S. 103 (1998).

[144] *City of Sherill v. Oneida Indian Nation* 544 U.S. 197 (2005).

while part of reservations in the past, had been sold in accordance with federal assimilationist strategies and later re-purchased by the tribes. Only one dissenting vote was cast in these cases, by Justice Stevens.[145] In other words, the attempt by tribes to overcome the consequences of assimilationist policies aimed at eliminating reservations, policies now repudiated by the federal government, were rebuffed by a broad coalition of justices. The forced allotment and assimilation policies of the national government are generally considered one of the more unjust acts of the federal government against Native American peoples.146 Yet the court—and the majority of its liberal justices—has not allowed itself to be a forum for the correction of this historical injustice.

While the American Supreme Court was unwilling to extend tax immunities of Indian tribes in novel situations, it has been willing to maintain more traditional aspects of Indian tax immunity. Again, the shifting outcomes in these cases show that the decisions of the court are not guided by the underlying policy issue of whether or not Indian tribes should be afforded *any* tax immunities. The taxation and regulatory cases revolve around a series of related questions. Do rights to tax exemptions inhere in Indians as individuals, or are those rights inherent in the territorial sovereignty (or, more accurately, "domestic dependent nation status') of Indian tribes? How can the scope of Indian territory be determined? How should courts assess the regulatory jurisdiction of tribes over non-Indian individuals and businesses on reservations? 147

The obstacles to any revolution in aboriginal sovereignty can be best observed in the cases that the court decided unanimously. 12 of 23 taxation and regulatory decisions made by the Court between 1985 and

---

[145] Stevens argued that all land owned by the tribe in its historical tribal reservation qualified as "Indian Country," and thus could not be taxed without Congressional consent.

[146] E.g. Deborah A. Rosen, *American Indians and State Law*. Lincoln: University of Nebraska Press, 2007. Pp 215-217

[147] The Court dealt with twenty three taxation and regulatory issues related to Indian tribes during this period; seven of the issues were resolved in favor of the Indian tribes.

2008 were unanimous. The *Cass County* case (as well as the *City of Sherill* case, in which Justice Stevens was the lone dissenter) limited the ability of Indian tribes to expand their territorial sovereignty through the re-purchase of previously alienated lands. The court has also, in unanimous decisions, rejected the following claims regarding the taxation and regulatory powers and immunities of Indian tribes:

i) limited the power of Indian tribes to tax non-members within their territorial boundaries[148]

ii) refused to extend tax exemptions to Indian-owned companies for work done off of their reservations[149]

iii) rejected tribal claims to maintain governing authority over alienated lands[150]

iv) rejected expansive interpretations of "Indian country" thereby limiting the taxation power of certain tribes[151]

v) accepted state regulation of on-reservation sales to non-members[152]

Thus some of the most promising avenues for the expansion of Native American sovereignty, and the privileges of Native American individuals and businesses, have been entirely rejected by almost all of the recent members of the Supreme Court, regardless of their political disposition or orientation.

On the other hand, the court remains committed to certain core aspects of tribal regulatory and taxation powers and immunities, as can be seen in cases in which Native American claims regarding these issues have been upheld unanimously:

i) Indian tribes can impose taxes on mineral lessees without approval of the Secretary of the Interior[153]

---

[148] *Atkinson Trading Company v. Shirley*, 532 U.S. 645 (2001.)

[149] *Arizona Department of Revenue v. Blaze Construction*, 526 U.S. 32 (1999).

[150] *South Dakota v. Yankton Sioux Tribe*, 522 U.S. 329 (1998).

[151] *Alaska v. Native Village of Venetie*, 522 U.S. 520 (1998).

[152] *New York v. Millhelm, Attea, and Bros.* 512 U.S. 61 (1994); *Oklahoma Tax Commission v. Citizen Band Potawatomi* 498 U.S. 505 (1991).

[153] *Kerr McGee Corp. v. Navajo Tribe of Indians* 471 U.S. 195 (1985).

ii) States cannot impose excise taxes on the sale of lands within Indian reservations[154]

iii) An Indian does not have to live on reservation for the presumption against state taxation to be applied in assessing state taxes[155]

iv) States cannot tax fuel sold on reservation.[156]

The thread that connects the most important of these decisions is the attempt by state governments to tax on-reservation activities without explicit federal approval. This issue affects the core of tribal sovereignty. Differences amongst the justices emerge—and clearer political divisions as well—over what constitutes "on reservation activity," and what constitutes federal abrogation of tribal sovereignty. The question is whether the resolution of more ambiguous issues surrounding the taxation and regulatory powers of Indian falls into clear political patterns. For Indian litigants, the unfortunate news is that conservative and moderate judges tend to be more uniformly opposed to expansive interpretations of tribal taxation and regulatory powers than their liberal counterparts, who are less united in their support of aboriginal litigants. The following non-unanimous taxation and regulatory cases yielded victories for aboriginal litigants:

i) States cannot impose royalty taxes on on-reservation mineral lessees (Rehnquist, Stevens, White, dissenting).[157]

ii) States and counties are not authorized by Public Law 280 to impose gaming regulations on Indian casinos (Stevens, O'Connor, Scalia dissenting).[158]

iii)The Yakima Indian tribe has zoning authority over fee land owned by non-members in the "closed" section of their reservation (White, Rehnquist, Scalia, Kennedy dissenting).[159]

---

[154] *County of Yakima v. Yakima Indian Nation* 502 U.S. 251 (1992.

[155] *Oklahoma Tax Commission v. Sac and Fox Nation* 508 U.S. 114 (1993).

[156] *Oklahoma Tax Commission v. Chickasaw Nation* 515 U.S. 450 (1995).

[157] *Montana v. Blackfoot Indian Tribe* 471 U.S. 759 (1985).

[158] *California v. Cabazon Band of Mission Indians* 480 U.S. 202 (1987).

[159] *Brendale v. Yakima Indian Nation* 492 U.S. 408 (1989).

While it is difficult to make generalizations based on these few cases, it is apparent that opposition to Indian litigants comes from conservative and moderate justices. Yet even so, the shifting votes of conservatives and moderates indicates that individual decisions are dictated not so much by the underlying policy dimensions of the case (e.g. scope of state taxation jurisdiction vis a vis tribes) as by the central legal issue (whether or not national laws have authorized state regulations or taxation.) So, for instance, Rehnquist and O'Connor took opposite positions on the questions of state taxation of on-reservation mineral lessees (O'Connor opposed the state tax, Rehnquist supported it is dissent) and the application of state gaming laws to tribal casinos (Rehnquist opposed the application of the laws, O'Connor supported them in dissent.) *Oklahoma v. Citizen Band Potawatomi,* decided in 1991, is particularly interesting in this regards, because the Court unanimously upheld tribal claims regarding sovereign immunity at a time when many elected officials were beginning to question the wisdom of the doctrine.[160]

The court rejected Native American claims in the following non-unanimous cases:

i) New Mexico can impose a severance tax on non-Indian on oil and gas facilities located on reservation (Blackmun, Brennan, and Marshall dissenting).[161]

ii) The Yakima Indian Nation does not have zoning authority over fee lands owned by non-members in the "open" section of their reservation (Blackmun, Brennan, Marshall, dissenting).[162]

iii) The state can impose an ad valorem tax on the sale of on-reservation land (Blackmun dissenting).[163]

---

[160] E.g. David E. Wilkins and K. Tsianina Lomawaima, *Uneven Ground: American Indian Sovereignty and Federal Law*. Norman, Okla.: University of Oklahoma Press, 2001 pp 216-220, which discusses the efforts of Republican Senator Slate Gorton to limit tribal sovereign immunity on a wide range of issues.

[161] *Cotton Petroleum Corp v. New Mexico* 490 U.S. 163 (1989).

[162] *Brendale v. Yakima Indian Nation* 492 U.S. 408 (1989).

[163] *County of Yakima v. Yakima Indian Nation* 502 U.S. 251 (1992).

iv) Tribes cannot regulate hunting and fishing of non-members in disputed territory. (Blackmun and Souter dissenting).[164]

v) States can impose taxes on the wages of tribe members who live off-reservation (Breyer, Stevens, O'Connor, Souter dissenting).[165]

vi) The Crow Tribe cannot receive restitution for taxes imposed by state government on a mining company that had leased tribal land (Souter and O'Connor dissenting).[166]

vii) A state government can impose taxes on a Native American tribe's gasoline suppliers (Ginsburg and Kennedy, dissenting).[167]

Justice Blackmun was the most consistent supporter of Native American claims during this period, voting for an expansive interpretation of tribal regulatory and taxation powers in all of the decisions he participated in. His approach to these cases may well have been determined by a predisposition to support Indian interests, buttressed by the long-standing rule of interpretation that ambiguities in law and treaties should be resolved in favor of Native American tribes. But Blackmun's expansive understanding of ambiguity was mostly expressed in dissent. The pro-Native American voting bloc that he formed with Brennan and Marshall was replaced by a cohort of liberal and moderate justices (Stevens, O'Connor, Souter, Kennedy, Breyer, and Ginsburg) whose support for Native American claims was much less consistent. This is not to say that their legal reasoning was inconsistent; on the contrary, it seems as if the voting of liberal and moderate justices in these cases was determined by a different assessment of the "ambiguities" in federal Indian law. It is not possible to reject the "attitudinal" explanation for the decreased support for Native American taxation and regulatory claims that developed over the course of the 1990s. But it is possible to see that the obstacles to an American rights revolution do not come solely from judges that are regarded as conservative or right-wing. Liberal and moderate justices on the American Supreme Court have not followed their Canadian

---

[164] *South Dakota v. Bourland* 508 U.S. 679 (1993).

[165] *Oklahoma Tax Commission v. Chickasaw Nation*, 515 U.S. 450 (1995).

[166] *Montana v. Crow Tribe of Indians*, 524 U.S. 968 (1998).

[167] *Wagnon v.Prairie Band of Potawatomi*, 546 U.S. 1072 (2005).

counterparts regarding the scope of aboriginal sovereignty and self-government. One does not need to deny the presence of political considerations to agree that the different legal and Constitutional regimes in Canada and the United States structure the ways judges of similar ideological predispositions approach Native American legal claims.

The Limits of Indian Rights: American Constitutionalism, Tribal Sovereignty, and the Post-New Deal Constitutional Order

The limited support for Indian claims amongst moderate and related justices on the American Supreme Court may be related to broader developments in the "progressive" conception of constitutional law.168 The progressive constitutional order can be considered from the perspective of the substantive political commitments of its proponents (the expansion of state power, coupled with the expansion of a new sphere of "human rights" that limit the power of the state) as well as the interpretive "moves" deployed in order to facilitate these commitments (e.g. an expansive interpretation of the commerce clause, a progressive or evolutionary approach to questions of rights.)[169] It may be the case that the construction of the post-New Deal liberal order as a whole is incompatible, or at least in tension with, some of the legal claims of Indian tribes in the United States.

The modern progressive approach to constitutional law was constructed to accommodate the power of the modern state to regulate the national economy. Subsequently, progressive jurisprudence has produced a network of individual rights to restrain the now expanded

---

[168] The common denominator of the various strains of early 20th century American progressivism is the belief that older standards of rights and constitutionalism must be adjusted, so as to permit the modern administrative state to address the complexities of modern economic conditions. See Thomas West, "Progressivism and the Transformation of American Government." In Marini and Masugi, editors, *The Progressive Revolution in Politics and Political Science: Transforming the American Regime.* Lanham, Md.: Rowman and Littlefield, 2005. pp 13-35

[169] Ken I. Kersch, *Constructing Civil Liberties: Discontinuities in the Development of American Constitutional Law.* Cambridge: Cambridge University Press, 2004. p. 338

power of the national state.[170] The claims of Indian tribes are difficult for liberal justices to endorse in practice, because those claims are not readily incorporated into this edifice of modern progressive constitutionalism: their claims are not simply analogous to those of other subordinated groups, and in addition, their claims can be in tension with the expansion of national power. As Sidney Harring has noted, "The doctrines of Indian law have been kept far removed from civil rights law, and the legal struggles of Indian people have involved different cases and distinct legal issues from the legal struggles of other racial minorities. "[171] If we wish to understand the institutional constraints on Indian rights in the United States, it is necessary to consider why the project of Indian sovereignty may be difficult to reconcile with the project of progressive constitutionalism.

In contrast with many other interest group litigants, the constitutional and legal aspirations of Indian tribes are not phrased in the language of progress or "living constitutionalism."[172] Their claims often rest on appeals to the past—promises enshrined in treaties, principles that were implicit in the Constitution and elaborated by the Supreme Court in the early part of the 19th century. The Supreme Court of the 19th century—particularly the late 19th century--- hardly offered a consistent defense of the constitutional and legal claims of Indian tribes. Yet unlike the proponents of modern commerce clause jurisprudence or "new rights," Indian tribes are often able to look to the principles and practices of the past in order to find a basis for their present day aspirations.[173] Proponents of tribal sovereignty might also find some unsuspected allies on the contemporary Supreme Court.

---

[170] Howard Gillman, *The Constitution Besieged.* pp 202-204

[171] Sidney Harring, *Crow Dog's Case: American Indian Sovereignty, Tribal Law, and United States Law in the Nineteenth Century.* Cambridge University Press: Cambridge, 1994. p. 12

[172] See the discussion in N. Bruce Duthu, *American Indians and the Law.* New York: The Penguin Group, 2008 pp xxi-xxx

[173] It is important to note that some commentators argue that past American Indian law decisions offer few resources for present day Native Americans; according to this argument, American Indian law needs to be re-constituted in its entirety (Williams, *Like a Loaded Weapon*, pp xx-xxvii).

A look at some recent cases on tribal sovereignty reveals the difficulty of reconciling an "Indian rights revolution" with the progressive, post-New Deal constitutional narrative. The case of *U.S. v. Lara*[174], for instance, illustrates the limits of even "pro-Indian" progressive jurisprudence within the American context. Lara, who had been prohibited from entering the Spirit Lake Tribe's reservation, assaulted a federal officer who was in the process of removing him. Having pleaded guilty to assault in Tribal Court, Lara was subsequently charged by the federal government. The key question in this case was whether the federal prosecution constituted "double jeopardy" under the fifth amendment. According to established interpretations of the fifth amendment, states and the national government can prosecute the same individual for the same actions without running afoul of the double jeopardy clause. The issue here was whether the same rule would apply to consecutive prosecutions by a tribal government and the federal government.

The question turned upon whether the power of Indian tribes to prosecute non-members was an inherent aspect of tribal sovereignty, or whether it was based upon delegated federal power; if tribal prosecutorial power was delegated federal power, then the prosecutions in this case would run afoul of the fifth amendment. Lara certainly had reason to believe that, under existing doctrine, tribal prosecutorial power had to be regarded as a delegated federal power. In the 1990 case of *Duro v. Reina*[175,] the court had ruled that Indian tribes lacked criminal jurisdiction over non-member Indians. Congress, in response to vigorous lobbying by Indian tribes, altered the Indian Civil Rights Act to establish "the inherent power of Indian tribes… to exercise criminal jurisdiction over Indians."[176] But did it made sense to speak of an "inherent power" that could be shaped and constrained by a superior government? If the federal government controlled the criminal jurisdiction of Indian tribes, how could the tribes be sovereign?

Stephen Breyer, writing for the majority, ruled that Mr. Lara could not avail himself of the fifth amendment's provisions regarding "double jeopardy", as Indian tribes and the federal government are "separate

---

[174] *U.S. v. Lara* 541 U.S. 193 (2004)

[175] *Duro v. Reina* 495 U.S. 676 (1990)

[176] 25 U.S.C. 1301(2) amended by Act of Oct. 28, 1991, 105 Stat. 646

sovereigns." The central problem with Breyer's argument was that he also argued that that the "Indian Commerce Clause" gave Congress plenary legislative power over Indian tribes; tribes were "sovereign," except for the fact that their powers were entirely dependent upon the actions of Congress. The tribes were sovereign, but not sovereign. Justice Thomas, in his concurring opinion, observed that Breyer's opinion reflected the "schizophrenic" character of American Indian law--- that is, he argued American Indian law has the tendency to assert incompatible things. Thomas agreed that "double jeopardy" did not apply in this case, and that this was because the prosecutions were conducted by separate sovereigns. However, he also argued that the two sovereigns in questions could not really be separate if the jurisdiction of one—the Indian tribe— could be altered by the other. If the double jeopardy clause did not apply to Lara's case, it could only be because the powers of the tribe were neither created nor directly controlled by Congress. The logic of the case led to the conclusion that Congress lacked plenary power over Indian tribes.

The differences between Breyer and Thomas in this instance illustrate how doctrine might play an independent role in shaping judicial-decision making in American Indian law. The approaches of these two jurists to Indian sovereignty and the Indian commerce clause are shaped by their broader reading of Congressional commerce clause power. Breyer reads the "Indian commerce clause" as establishing Congressional plenary power over Indian affairs, because he also believes that the commerce clause gives Congress the power to make laws regarding any subject matter connected "commerce," understood as economic activity or actions that might in some way affect economic activity. Thomas does not think that the commerce clause can be construed so as to confer such expansive powers on Congress in regards to either economic issues or Indian affairs. To put it in slightly different terms, the conclusions that Thomas and Breyer reach in this case about the scope of Indian sovereignty are dictated by their respective interpretations of the commerce clause and American federalism.

As illustrated by Breyer's opinion in *U.S. v. Lara*, the construction of the post-New Deal constitutional order places limits on the ability of progressive jurists to endorse the claim of Indian tribes to be exempt from the general legislative power of Congress. Any limits on Congressional power under the Indian commerce clause implies a general limitation on Congress' commerce powers. Yet the progressive jurisprudence of the 20th century is in many ways built on the idea that courts should not impose limits on this aspect of Congressional power.[177] Doctrines invented to facilitate the liberal state-building project of the mid-20th century may well be incompatible with post-liberal attempts to re-establish tribal sovereignty.

The issues of federal power under the "Indian Commerce Clause" and tribal sovereign immunity indicate that doctrine plays an independent role in shaping Indian law.[178] Doctrines that were created in broader struggles over American federalism and the scope of national power prove to have unanticipated implications for Indian law. Surprisingly, the objectives of Indian litigants may in some instances be better served by the activism of the "new right" than by the commitments of legal liberalism. This is because, in many ways, the goals of Indian litigants—the protection of the jurisdiction and sovereignty of territorially based communities—are at odds with expansive conceptions of national power, one of the central tenets of legal liberalism. In contrast, the Canadian Constitution Act, by providing a clearer separation between aboriginal issues and issues of federalism, may allow Canadian jurists to develop a jurisprudence of aboriginal sovereignty that does not have any implications for the scope of national power in other areas.

Conclusion

Since the adoption of the Constitution Act and the Charter of Rights and Freedoms, the Canadian Supreme Court has emulated developments in American Constitutional law in areas such as criminal law, abortion rights, and the rights of women. But in regards to the rights of Native Canadians, Canadian jurisprudence has diverged from American, and this divergence is a sign of the importance of constitutional language in shaping judicial power. In its aboriginal

---

[177] I do not mean to imply that Thomas' construction of the commerce clause is correct . For an interesting discussion of some of the problems of trying to establish a theory of federalism based on the commerce clause, see Ralph Rossum *Federalism, the Supreme Court, and the Seventeenth Amendment.* Lanham, Md.: Lexington Books, 2001.

[178] Gerald Baier, *Courts and Federalism: Judicial Doctrine in the United States, Australia, and Canada.* UBC Press: Vancouver, 2006.

rights jurisprudence, the Canadian Supreme Court has upheld the claims of First Nations litigants more often than has its American counterpart, and more importantly, the Court has handed down a few key decisions that have provided a strong basis for future litigation. Looked at in terms of the overall number of votes for Indian legal claims, and the patterns of those votes on the Canadian and American courts, it cannot be denied that the differences between Canadian and American Indian law over the past two decades is connected to the liberalism of Canadian justices, ultimately rooted in the liberalism of Canada's governing regime. But the patterns of American Indian law, in relation to issues such as tribal sovereign immunity, tribal court jurisdiction, treaty interpretation, and tribal land claims, cannot be explained through politics alone. In American Indian law, the rights of Indian tribes are ultimately subordinate to the plenary power of the national government. Canada's post-modern Constitution created a process in which Canadian courts would become the ultimate arbiters of Indian legal claims, and the scope of aboriginal sovereignty. Differences between Canadian and American Indian law cannot be fully understood without taking into account how constitutional language has shaped judicial decision-making, and constrained judicial politics.

CHAPTER FOUR: THE LIMITS OF ENVIRONMENTAL LAW IN CANADA AND THE UNITED STATES

The case of the *Nuclear Energy Institute v. EPA,*[1] decided by the D.C. Circuit Court of Appeals in 2004, dealt with the selection of the Yucca Mountains as a depository site for the nation's nuclear waste. A whole host of regulatory bodies working in conjunction with Congress and the President had cooperated in reaching the decision on the site location. An additional host of environmental groups and localities joined the state of Nevada in challenging the final decision to locate the depository in the Yucca Mountains. The environmental petitioners argued that the waste storage site would lead to the contamination of the groundwater in nearby communities. Ed Goedhart, a member of Citizen Alert and Nuclear Information, was granted standing to bring the case. According to the court, "although radionuclides escaping from the Yucca repository may not reach Goedhart's community for *thousands of years*, his injury is 'actual or imminent,' for he lives adjacent to the land where the Government plans to bury 70,000 metric tons of radioactive waste—a sufficient harm in and of itself."[2] This construal of "actual or imminent harm" was somewhat unusual.

Nuclear waste remains deadly for literally millions of years. It boggles the lay mind to imagine how, in the present day, human engineers could aspire to design a storage site that would remain safe over such an extended period of time. Yet that is the task that Congress asked executive branch agencies, including the EPA and the Department of Energy, to undertake in regards to the Yucca mountain project. The EPA decided to construct a storage facility that could be anticipated to safely contain the material for 10,000 years. While the courts were unwilling to endorse all the various procedural objections made against the decision to locate the waste dump at Yucca Mountain, it did overturn the EPA's decision to set its safety target at a mere ten millennia. Instead, the court argued that the EPA was required, by statute, to devise a storage site that would be safe not only ten thousand years from now, but into the unimaginably distant future. And that was

[1] *Nuclear Energy Institute v. EPA*, 373 F.3d 1251 (2004).

[2] Ibid., at 1266

exactly what the statute seemed to demand, or rather, the political process created by the statute led to that conclusion.

Congress did not directly determine that the EPA take a million-year, cosmic perspective on the fate of nuclear waste in the Yucca mountains. Instead, Congress asked the EPA to make regulations that were "based upon and consistent" with the recommendations of the National Association of Scientists (NAS), which had been given resources to analyze the problem of long-term nuclear waste storage.[3] The EPA argued that the language of the statute did not simply turn the agency into the servant of the NAS, but rather was meant to allow for a certain degree of flexibility in interpreting the findings of the NAS experts. The decision on how to regulate radioactive materials raised policy questions that lay outside the specific expertise of the NAS scientists, and thus the EPA should be allowed considerable discretion as to how make their regulations "based upon" and "consistent" with the NAS recommendations. While the court unanimously rejected all other petitions made by environmental groups in this case, they were not willing to allow the EPA to depart from the statutory language of the Energy Policy Act. Indeed, you would have to depart from the ordinary understanding of the English language to argue that the EPA's determination of the proper time-horizon for the Yucca mountain site was "consistent" with the recommendations of the NAS. In one sense of the term, the court was engaged in the very worst kind of judicial activism: intervening into policy disputes so complex that not even four

---

[3] The relevant portion of the 1992 Energy Policy Act reads as follows:

> "The [EPA] Administrator shall, based upon and consistent with the findings and recommendations of the National Academy of Sciences, promulgate, by rule, public health and safety standards for protection of the public from releases from radioactive materials stored or disposed of in the repository at the Yucca Mountain site. Such standards shall prescribe the maximum annual effective dose equivalent to individual members of the public from releases to the accessible environment from radioactive materials stored or disposed of in the repository. The standards shall be promulgated not later than 1 year after the Administrator receives the findings and recommendations of the National Academy of Sciences . . . and shall be the only such standards applicable to the Yucca Mountain site." (EnPA § 801(a)(1))

years of law school could prepare you to evaluate them. But while the court was actively exercising power against other branches of government, this judicial activism had been authorized by Congress.

This case illustrates some of the reasons why American courts end up being drawn into the details of the environmental policy-process. Canadian courts and Canadian judges—despite their evident progressive proclivities in other areas, such as Indian law—have been hesitant to enter into the details of environmental policy. This chapter will attempt to assess why this is the case, and how the differing constitutional architecture of the Canadian and American political systems place differing constraints on environmental jurisprudence.

One can better understand the significance of the differences between Indian law in Canada and the United States by comparing those decisions with developments in environmental law. Looked at in isolation, it is difficult to determine whether the divergence between Canadian and American approaches to aboriginal rights and the powers of Indian tribes are a consequence of constitutional differences, or a consequence of judicial ideology. The advocates of the attitudinal model of judicial behavior, for instance, would hypothesize that the transformation of Indian law in Canada can be understood as a consequence of changing judicial ideologies, ultimately rooted in the "progressive" understanding of Indian rights that began to take hold of Canadian elites during this period. From this perspective, there appears to be no institutional features of the American constitutional system which might prevent a Canadian-style revolution in Indian rights. Such a revolution simply awaits the appointment of more sympathetic judges. My argument is that the constraints imposed by constitutional architecture can best be seen by comparing aboriginal rights jurisprudence with environmental law jurisprudence in Canada and the United States. This comparison will not reveal the absence of politics in environmental jurisprudence, but it will illustrate that a parliamentary system of government presents very different opportunities for the judicialization of public policy than does a system based upon the separation of powers. As the attitudinal model would predict, the progressivism or liberalism that is evident in Canadian aboriginal rights decisions is also evident, to some extent, in environmental law decisions. But the very nature of parliamentary government prevents Canadian courts from playing more than a limited role in environmental policy. To summarize: in the USA, a progressive judiciary has tended and will tend to produce a pro-environment jurisprudence; in Canada, a "progressive" judiciary will, in matters of environmental policy, be much more deferential to the decisions of national policy-makers.

Most commentators in the United States have acknowledged that courts have played a major role in the development of environmental policy.[4] In Canada, the role played by judges in environmental policy has been far less prominent, though it has also been subject to much less study. The key to understanding the differences between the role of Canadian and American courts in environmental policy is to reflect on the difference between "judicial activism" and "judicialization." While these two words have been used in a variety of different ways, I will use them to refer to two distinct modes of judicial power. Judicial activism occurs whenever judges trump the decisions of other government actors; hence, it makes sense to speak of legitimate or illegitimate acts of judicial activism. Judicialization refers to a narrow range of judicial activism, in which judges do not merely overrule government decisions based upon the dictates of federalism, or fundamental rights, but rather to decisions which override the statutory interpretations and even scientific determinations of executive officials. Judicial activism is usually exercised to prevent governments from acting; "judicialization" has the potential to involve courts in the detailed control of vast ranges of public policy.[5] My argument is that, while both Canadian and American courts have engaged in "judicial activism" in environmental policy (particularly in regards to issues of

---

[4] E.g. Melnick, *Regulation and the Courts: The Case of the Clean Air Act.* Brookings Institution: Washington, 1984 pp 4, 387; Susan Rose-Ackermann. *Controlling Environmental Policy: The Limits of Public Law in Germany and the United States.* New Haven: Yale University Press, 1995.; Bruce A. Ackerman and William T. Hassler, *Clean Coal/Dirty Air.* New Haven: Yale University Press, 1981.

[5] For examples of judicialization in the United States, see Ross Sandler and David Schoenbrod, *Democracy by Decree: What Happens When Courts Run Government.* New Haven: Yale University Press, 2003; Malcolm Feeley and Edward Rubin, *Judicial Policy-Making and the Modern State.* Cambridge: Cambridge University Press, 1998. Phillip J. Cooper, *Hard Judicial Choices: federal district court judges and state and local officials.* New York and Oxford: Oxford University Press, 1988.

federalism) the Canadian courts have refrained from "judicializing" environmental policy.

This chapter will consider why the Canadian courts, despite the generally "progressive" nature of the Canadian judiciary, have not attempted to judicialize environmental policy. I will proceed by examining the constitutional and statutory framework of Canadian environmental policy, the question of legal standing in the Canadian judicial system, and the relationship between courts and administrators within this legal and political structure. At the same time, I will attempt to explain the connection, in the American system, between changes in legal doctrine (the law of standing), the separation of powers, and the judicialization of environmental policy.

The Canadian political system has presented some crucial opportunities for courts to play a role in environmental policy. Canadian courts have developed a pro-environmental jurisprudence that mirrors the jurisprudence of liberal American judges in two crucial ways. First, the Canadian courts have given an extremely broad reading of federal jurisdiction in environmental policy. Secondly, they have made it easier for aggrieved individuals and environmental groups to raise their claims in court. But the environmental revolution in Canadian law appears to come to an end—for the most part—with changes in jurisdiction and changes in the law of standing. Canadian courts have played a limited role in the development of the substance of environmental policy, whether looked at in terms of rulings that shape the meaning of statutory law or decisions that determine the fate of development projects. Despite the court's willingness to engage the demands of post-materialist litigants in other contexts[6], the Canadian Supreme Court is constrained by the institutions of parliamentary from "judicializing" environmental policy.

My main conclusion is that the parliamentary system inhibits judicial statutory activism, in contrast with the American separation of powers, because the Canadian judiciary cannot seriously claim to be the sole effective restraint on an executive branch that desires to evade the law and the will of the legislative branch. Or, to put it differently, the problem of executive-legislative conflict does not exist as a constitutional problem in parliamentary governments. As David Smith

---

[6] Ian Brodie, *Friends of the Court: The privileging of interest group litigants in Canada*. Albany, N.Y.: State University of New York Press, 2002. pp 49-75.

puts it, "Government in Canada does more than execute political decisions; it determines them ."[7] For a court to claim that "the Crown" is not following Parliamentary will, it must, in a sense, accuse the governing party of false consciousness.[8] The clear and direct link between the legislature and the government is the key to understanding the deferential approach of Canadian courts to statutory interpretation. The Canadian parliamentary system of government has not foreclosed all opportunities for judicial influence on environmental policy. Nevertheless, Canadian judges have retained a norm of deference towards government decision-makers that often leads them to resist the claims of environmental rights activists.

This chapter will begin by examining some of the similarities between Canadian and American environmental law jurisprudence in the areas of jurisdiction and justiciability. It will then proceed to examine how their approaches to statutory interpretation and bureaucratic decision-making differentiate the judiciaries of Canada and the United States. First, it is necessary to consider some of the problems involved in assessing and comparing environmental law jurisprudence.

The Problems of Comparisons in Environmental Law

The great difficulty in analyzing environmental policy lies in assessing the significance of cases. As some scholars have pointed out, the attempt to quantify the significance of environmental law decisions so as to permit statistical inference is undercut by the inherently subjective nature of any attempt to quantify the significance of environmental decisions.[9] It is even more difficult to evaluate whether or not the

---

[7] David Smith, *The Invisible Crown : The First Principle of Canadian Government*. Toronto: University of Toronto Press, 1995. P. 65

[8] cf. S.L. Sutherland, "Responsible Government and Ministerial Responsibility: Every Reform its Own Problem." *Canadian Journal of Political Science*. Volume 24, Number 1, pp 91-120. Sutherland argues that responses to the problem of bureaucratic government tend to undermine the capacity of cabinet ministers to control administrative discretion.

[9] R. Shep Melnick, "Environmental Litigation and Institutional Analysis: Wenner and Ackerman & Hassler." *American Bar Foundation Research Journal*. Vol. 8, No. 3 (Summer, 1983) pp 740-751.

claims of environmental groups will actually help to improve environmental protection.

In order to assess the relationship between Canadian and American courts in environmental policy, it is necessary to classify the various ways in which courts can affect the environmental policy process. There are three general ways in which courts exercise their power in the environmental policy process:

1. Constitutional Activism[10]

Constitutional activism in Canadian and American environmental policy typically involves decisions regarding federalism; that is, courts can play a role in determining which level of government plays what kind of role in shaping environmental regulation. Theoretically, courts could engage in constitutional activism through the creation of fundamental rights related to environmental quality, though this is an option that has not been taken in either the USA or Canada. However, there are other dimensions of fundamental rights that can place limits on the scope of environmental policy.

2. Legal-Procedural Activism

Legal-Procedural activism refers not to judicial constructions of government powers and individual rights, but rather to the ways in which judges interpret the meaning of legal cases—in other words, judges exercise power in environmental policy by shaping the doctrine of justiciability.[11] In environmental law, the most crucial questions regarding justiciability relate to standing—that is, who can bring an environmental policy related claim to court, and under what circumstances.

3. Statutory Activism

---

[10] I use the term "activism" in a "value-neutral" sense; it is not meant to imply that the exercise of judicial power in environmental decisions are incorrect, but rather is meant to imply that, correct or not, courts can exercise power in environmental policy through these four modes of decision-making.

[11] For a discussion of justiciability and its development in 20th century American law, see Mark Silverstein, *Judicious Choices: The New Politics of Supreme Court Confirmations*. New York: W.W. Norton and Co., 1994.

Statutory activism refers to judicial rulings which overturn the interpretations of law made by executive officials. Here, activism refers to decisions to challenge the interpretations of statutory law made by executive branch officials and bureaucrats.

Differences in the constitutional architecture of the Canadian and American political systems create differing opportunities to exercise these forms of judicial activism. In the American context, environmental law decisions are more contentious, and judicial votes more divided, than is the case in Canada. But this is not to say that Canadian courts have played no role in shaping environmental policy. Canadian courts have shaped environmental policy primarily through constitutional and legal activism. Statutory activism is far more attenuated. Political structures, in other words, shape the ability of courts to judicialize public policy; in a Parliamentary system, the opportunity to judicialize environmental policy is much more attenuated than in a system based upon the separation of powers.

Differences in environmental policy-making in Canada and the United States makes comparisons of their environmental jurisprudence somewhat complicated. The Canadian Supreme Court has decided relatively few cases addressing environmental issues, which is a result of the relative paucity of national environmental laws in Canada.[12] Some scholars argue that Canadian regionalism (and, in the case of Quebec, nationalism and separatism)[13] combined with the resource intensive nature of the Canadian economy, have led provinces to jealousy guard against national regulatory initiatives that might have disparate impacts on different parts of the country. As a consequence, Canadian federal courts have had fewer opportunities to influence national environmental policies. Therefore, while a comparison of Canadian and American Supreme Court decisions might tell us

---

[12] Melody Hessing, Michael Howlett, and Tracy Summerville. *Canadian Natural Resource and Environmental Policy*. Vancouver: UBC Press, 2005 pp 60-64

[13] Grace Skogstad and P. Kopas, "Environmental Policy in a federal system: Ottawa and the provinces." In *Canadian Environmental Policy: Ecosystems, politics, and process*. Ed. R. Boardman. Toronto: Oxford University Press, 1992.

something about how those courts have addressed some of the issues raised by environmental law cases, it is difficult to draw conclusions because of the relative paucity of comparable cases.

However, if we look at the lower federal appeals courts in the United States, and lower federal appeals courts and provincial courts of appeal in Canada, it is easier to find cases that are comparable. This is because these courts, particularly in the United States, deal with an immense number of cases addressing issues related to the environmental assessment of specific construction, development, and resource extraction projects. The stakes in these cases, in other words, are broadly similar. As we will see, however, Canadian and American courts have very different patterns of decision-making in these cases, patterns which I will argue cannot be explained on the basis of political ideology alone.

Constitutional Activism in Canadian and American Environmental Law

Both Canadian and American courts have refrained from establishing "environmental rights" that could act as judicial trump cards in environmental policy making.[14] Yet judicial constructions of constitutional law, particularly in regards to federalism, have had a major impact on environmental policy in both nations. These federalism decisions can be readily interpreted through a political framework. As we would expect, American judges and justices are more likely to disagree about the scope of national government power in matters related to the environment. The more ideologically homogenous Canadian judiciary has, at least in recent decades, been a consistent supporter of national regulatory power, thereby providing a good illustration of the "centralization thesis" developed by scholars such as Martin Shapiro and Andre Bzdera.[15] who both argue that high

---

[14] For a typical indication of the constitutional aspirations that accompanied the rise of the environmental movement in the United States, see J.Y.P. Jr., "Toward a Constitutionally Protected Environment." *Virginia Law Review*. Vol. 56, No. 3, (April, 1970.) pp 458-486.

[15] Andre Bzdera, "Comparative Analysis of Federal High Courts: A Political Theory of Judicial Review." *Canadian Journal of Political Science*. Volume

courts tend to act as agents of the central governments which establish and staff them.

The American Supreme Court initially laid the groundwork for national environmental regulation through its post-New Deal jurisprudence, which eased or eliminated previous constitutional limits on the scope of national government regulation. The case of *Hodel v. Virginia Surface Mining and Reclamation Association,*[16] in which a group of oil companies and landowners challenged the Surface Mining Control and Reclamation Act of 1977 is an example of the court's typical approach to national environmental regulation in the post-war era. The court ruled that Congress' determination that there was a relationship between surface mining and interstate commerce had to be accorded deference, and determined that the act was not unconstitutional on other grounds. Congress' goal of preventing competition between states on the basis of environmental standards was ruled to be a legitimate basis for national legislation under the commerce clause. The "rational relationship/reasonable basis" test gave Congress almost complete jurisdiction over all aspects of pollution and the natural environment.[17] However, this expansive interpretation of the commerce clause has been challenged by many conservative jurists.[18] Environmental law decisions in the American Supreme Court often illustrate these continuing divisions in the American court over the scope of national power under the commerce clause.

26, Number 3 (January, 1993) pp 3-29; Martin Shapiro, *Courts: A Comparative and Political Analysis*. Chicago: University of Chicago Press, 1981.

[16] *Hodel v. Virginia Surface Mining and Reclamation Association* 452 U.S. 264 (1981.)

[17] For a discussion and critique of the court's post-New Deal approach to federal jurisdiction over environmental issues, see Jonathan H. Adler, "Wetlands, Waterfowl, and the Menace of Mr. Wilson: Commerce Clause Jurisprudence and the Limits of Federal Wetland Regulation. " *Environmental Law*, Vol. 29, No. 1 (Spring, 1999).

[18] Richard H. Fallon, Jr. "The 'Conservative' Paths of the Rehnquist Court's Federalism Decisions." *University of Chicago Law Review*. Vol. 69, No. 2 (Spring, 2002) pp 429-494.

Rapanos v. United States (2006)[19] is one of the few instances in recent decades in which the court has challenged a national environmental regulation on the grounds that it exceeded the powers of Congress under the commerce clause. The case dealt with objections by several developers whose projects had been halted by the EPA due to violations of the Clean Water Act. The court ruled that, contrary to the interpretations of national regulators, certain wetlands located entirely within state boundaries were not subject to national regulations, as they were not part of inter-state commerce. Four justices (Chief Justice Roberts, and Justices Scalia, Thomas and Alito) rested their decision on commerce clause grounds. The fifth justice in the majority, Justice Kennedy, agreed that the interpretation of the Clean Water Act by the U.S. Army Corps of Engineers in this case was inadequate, but he did not agree with other members of the majority regarding the precise scope of national regulatory power over in-state waters. The dissenting justices—Stevens, Souter, Breyer, and Ginsburg—essentially held to the post-New Deal line that had been established in *Hodel v. Viriginia*. The *Rapanos* decision reveals the deep divisions in the court between those who adhere to the post-New Deal precedents which established a broad basis for federal jurisdiction over environmental issues, and those more conservative justices who wish to return to a more restrictive understanding of the commerce power. However, divisions over the precise scope of the commerce clause in regards to environmental issues are not always drawn along simple "liberal" and "conservative" ideological lines.

In five other instances between 1985 and 2008, the court has been willing to use the commerce clause to limit the regulatory power of state governments. These cases all rested upon interpretations of the "dormant commerce clause" doctrine, according to which the court can invalidate state regulations that aim to restrict interstate commerce by penalizing out-of-state businesses.[20] According to dormant commerce clause doctrine, states cannot pass laws that interfere with interstate

---

[19] *Rapanos v.United States*, 547 U.S. 715 (2006).

[20] For a discussion and critique of the "dormant commerce clause" jurisprudence, see Matin A. Redish and Shane Nugent, "The Dormant Commerce Clause and the Constitutional Balance of Federalism." *Duke Law Journal*, Volume 1987, No. 4 (Sept. 1987) pp 569-617.

commerce, as the Constitution granted that power to Congress; thus, even when "dormant" (not actively being used by Congress) the commerce power can invalidate certain state laws. For instance, in the case of *Fort Gratiot Sanitary Landfill v. Michigan Department of Natural Resources*[21] the court ruled that Michigan's attempt to limit the importation of waste across state and county lines was in violation of the commerce clause. But unlike the *Rapanos* case, the political dimensions of the Fort Gratiot case were not so apparent in the votes of the justices.

The majority opinion in *Fort Gratiot* was joined by Stevens, White, O'Connor, Scalia, Kennedy, Souter, and Thomas, with dissents by Rehnquist and Blackmun. The majority opinion focused upon the ways in which the regulations discriminated against out-of-state commerce, thereby traversing the lines of the "dormant commerce clause," whereas the dissenters thought that the state could defend the restrictions as legitimate environmental safety regulations, even if they might have some impact on trade between the states. Similarly, in the case of *Chemical Waste Management v. Hunt,*[22] the court ruled that Alabama's fees on out-of-state waster were impermissible under the commerce clause; Rehnquist was joined in dissent by Justice Blackmun. The case of *Oregon Waste Systems v. Oregon,*[23] which raised the same issues as the *Chemical Waste Management* case, also saw Rehnquist and Blackmun join together in dissent. In *C & A Carbone Inc. v. Town of Clarkstown*[24] (1994), the court dealt with a town ordinance which required that all non-recyclable, non-hazardous waste moving in or out of the town had to be processed at a designated transfer station. Once again, the voting patterns in the case do not reveal any clear political divisions. The majority, consisting of Kennedy, Stevens, Scalia, Thomas, Ginsburg, and joined in a concurring opinion by O'Connor, ruled that the town ordinance was in

---

[21] *Fort Gratiot Sanitary Landfill v. Michigan Department of Natural Resources*, 504 U.S. 353 (1992.)

[22] *Chemical Waste Management v. Hunt*, 504 U.S. 334 (1992.)

[23] *Oregon Waste Systems v. Oregon*, 511 U.S. 93 (1994)

[24] *C & A Carbone Inc. v. Town of Clarkstown*, 511 U.S. 383 (1994)

violation of the commerce clause. In dissent, Souter, Rehnquist, and Blackmun argued that the ordinance had not been shown to discriminate against out of state business, and that it served a clear public purpose. The final case dealing with dormant clause doctrine and its relationship with environmental regulations is *United Haulers Association v. Oneida-Herkimer Solid Waster Management Authority*[25] (2007), in which the court ruled in favor of a local ordinance that directed all solid-waste generated within the county had to be processed at a local, public processing facility. The majority opinion, written by Chief Justice Roberts and joined by Souter, Ginsburg, Breyer, Scalia, and Thomas, ruled that the regulation was valid as, unlike the cases discussed above, the law did not differentiate between in-state and out-of-state businesses, and thus could be sustained as a legitimate exercise of the state's police power. In dissent, Justices Alito, Kennedy, and Stevens suggested that this ordinance was in violation of the dormant commerce clause, as it discriminated in favor of a state-owned monopoly.

What these cases illustrate is the differing degrees of "politicization" in American commerce clause jurisprudence insofar as it influences environmental policy. *Rapanos* offers a clear example of the conflict between differing conceptions of the scope of national government power, with the justices falling into clear political "blocs" in their voting. The "dormant commerce clause" cases are more difficult to interpret, because the political dimensions are not so clear. This is because the policy objectives of the regulations in question are ambiguous: are the states and towns aiming to promote environmental health and safety, or are they engaged in a protectionist racket? One could very well argue that, questions of law aside, the votes in each case illustrate whether the justices are more concerned with problems of environmental pollution, or more concerned with the problem of state protectionism. Yet there is no clear liberal or conservative position in the three cases dealing with state and local regulation of out-of-state waste; in terms of the question of the scope of national power over the environment, as in the case of many other federalism issues, the

---

[25] *United Haulers Association v. Oneida-Herkimer Solid Waste Management Authority* 550 U.S. 330 (2007)

political divisions are clearer.[26] The role played by the American Supreme Court in determining the scope of state and federal jurisdiction over environmental policy reveals that the court is divided along political lines when dealing with the scope of national power; in regards to the scope of state power, the court is both less divided, and less divided into clearly opposed ideological camps. Stated somewhat differently, the environmental law decisions of the American Supreme Court that deal with the commerce clause (whether dormant or awake) do not seem to revolve around judicial assessments of environmentalism. Conservative justices who were willing to strike down national environmental regulations in one context (*Rapanos*) were willing to uphold state environmental regulations (*United Haulers*); liberal justices could be found arguing for extensive national regulatory power in the *Rapanos*' dissent, but they could also be found arguing against state environmental regulations in *Chemical Waste Management*, *Carbone*, and *United Haulers*. The commerce clause decisions in environmental law do not seem to follow a political logic based upon underlying policy preferences; rather, the divisions seem to emerge from legal disagreements over the scope of state and national jurisdiction under the commerce clause.[27]

Over the past two decades the Canadian Supreme Court has tended to support a broad interpretation of federal government jurisdiction, much like the American Court in the immediate post-Ned Deal era. In regards to environmental policy, the Canadian Supreme Court has interpreted the ambiguous division of powers in the Constitution Act in a manner that consistently favors the national government. On paper, environmental policy in Canada is a shared jurisdiction of the federal

---

[26] For a discussion of how the Rehnquist court's federalism jurisprudence relates to broader debates over Constitutional interpretation, see Richard A. Brisbin, Jr. "The Reconstitution of American Federalism? The Rehnquist Court and Federal-State Relations." *Publius*, Vol.28, No. 1 (Winter, 1998) pp 189-215.

[27] The environmental law-commerce clause cases illustrate the broader point that federalism decisions are often the best indicator of the independent impact of legal reasoning as opposed to political preferences in the judicial process. See Gerald Baier, *Courts and Federalism: Judicial Doctrine in the United States, Australia, and Canada*. Vancouver and Toronto: UBC Press, 2006.

and provincial governments.[28] For a wide range of environmental issues, both the provinces and the federal government can make plausible claims to be the responsible authority. As a result, Canadian courts have had the opportunity to influence environmental policy through their ability to decide who will decide.

The Canadian Constitution Act 1982 makes no reference to the environment itself, but environmental subject matters are intertwined amidst the powers delegated to the federal and provincial governments. Section 91 lists various federal powers that deal with the environment: sea coasts and inland fisheries, navigation and shipping, and federally-owned land and waters all fall under federal jurisdiction. An even broader general power to deal with environmental issues has been discerned in the "peace, order, and good government" clause of section 91. In contrast to the text of the American constitution, power over unenumerated matters in Canada devolves to the federal government (at least in regards to matters that are not "local" in nature.)[29] Federal authority over the environment can also be asserted through the treaty making powers, at least theoretically. Thus, through the POGG clause, federal paramountcy, the enumerated section 91 powers, and through treaties, the federal government has the potential to assert authority over a broad range of environmental subjects.[30]

---

[28] Melody Hessing and Michael Howlett, *Canadian Natural Resource and Environmental Policy: Political Economy and Public Policy*. (Vancouver: UBC Press, 1997) pp 56-60.

[29] The "centralizing" intentions of the framers of the British North America Act of 1867 (Canada's first constitution) were often stymied by the pro-provincial decisions of the British Judicial Committee of the Privy Council (the highest court of appeal in the Canadian legal system prior to the 1930s) during the first century of Canada's existence. See Peter Russell, *Constitutional Odyssey*. Toronto: University of Toronto Press, 1993 pp 41-48; for a defense of the "provincialist" or de-centralized conception of Canadian federalism that first emerged in the late 19th century in response to the political forces promoting centralization under the British North America Act of 1867, see Robert Vipond, *Liberty and Community: Canadian Federalism and the Failure of the Constitution* (Albany: State University of New York Press, 1991).

[30] For a discussion of the environmental provisions of Constitution Act, the scope of national regulatory power, and Canada's political economy, see Marsha A. Chandler, "Constitutional Change and Public Policy: The Impact of

Proponents of provincial jurisdiction over the environment can find considerable support in the British North America Act as well, however.[31] Section 92 grants provinces control over local waters and undertakings, property and civil rights, local and private undertakings, and provincial lands and resources. Section 92a grants the provinces exclusive jurisdiction over non-renewable resources, a privilege which is jealously guarded by those provincial politicians who fear that national control might be used to "correct" the uneven distribution of natural resources through the various provinces.[32] Yet despite the textual (and political) reasons for a de-centralized conception of environmental jurisdiction, the Canadian Supreme Court has, over time, tended to favor the federal government in disputes over environmental jurisdiction.

In the 1980s, the Canadian Supreme Court enacted a partial revolution in federalism, a revolution that had occurred in American law around the time of the New Deal. In Canada, a fairly restrictive interpretation of the national government's powers survived the Great Depression, and the courts continued to place significant limits on national regulatory power for several decades afterwards.33 While the national government had several enumerated powers in the British North America Act that were relevant to environmental policy, by the 1980s it still seemed as if the scope of the Canadian federal government's power to regulate the environment were constrained by federalism, as developed and enforced by the courts. Few had ever argued that the British North America act granted the federal

---

the Resource Amendment (Section 92a)" *The Canadian Journal of Political Science*. Volume 19, Number 1, pp 103-126.

[31] For an analysis of provincial-level environmental policy-making, see Mark Winfield, "The Ultimate Horizontal Issue: The Environmental Policy Experiences of Alberta and Ontario, 1971-1993." *The Canadian Journal of Political Science*. Volume 27, Number 1, 1994. pp 129-152.

[32] Robert D. Cairns, "Natural Resources and Canadian Federalism: Decentralization, Recurring Conflict, and Resolution." *Publius*, Vol. 22, No. 1 (Winter, 1992) pp 55-70.

33 Milton J. Esman. "Federalism and Modernization: Canada and the United States." *Publius*, Vol. 14, No. 1 (Winter, 1984), pp. 21-38

government a general regulatory power over "the environment." Judges in Canada, as well the Judicial Committee of the Privy Council, had also ruled that international treaties, should they address matters of environmental concern or, indeed, any matter at all, had to respect the federal-provincial balance of power established by the British North America Act.34 In addition, the "POGG" powers of the national government were given a narrow interpretation. Certain subjects were held to meet the so-called "national dimensions test," and were therefore valid under Section 91; the court also allowed Section 91 to be invoked on the basis of national emergencies.[35] But neither the national dimensions test nor the emergency powers interpretation of the "POGG" powers conferred a general power to regulate the environment on the national government. At least, that was how the Court had interpreted Canadian Federalism prior to the late 1980s.

The case of *R. v Crown Zellerbach Canada*[36] initiated an important change in the Court's approach to national government power over environmental regulation. This case dealt with the applicability of the federal Ocean Dumping Control Act to a paper company whose operation affected provincial sea-waters. The national government argued that, although water pollution associated with pulp and paper mills had traditionally been seen as part of provincial jurisdiction, the national dimensions of environmental problems justified a new, more expansive interpretation of federal regulatory powers under the POGG clause. A majority of four on the court, against vigorous protests by the governments of British Columbia and Quebec, upheld the Ocean Dumping and Control Act. In doing so, the Supreme Court endorsed a "provincial inability" test that would have the potential to legitimize a wide range of federal environmental policies.

---

[34] *AG Canada v. AG Ontario (Labour Conventions)* 1 DLR 673 (1937)

[35] See the discussion in David Schneiderman, "Harold Laski, Viscount Haldane, and the Law of the Canadian Constitution in the Early Twentieth Century." *The University of Toronto Law Journal*, Vol. 48, No. 4 (Autumn, 1998) pp 525-529

[36] *R. v. Crown Zellerbach*, (1988) CanLII 63 (S.C.C.).

In regards to questions of federal jurisdiction, the environmental law decisions of the Canadian and American courts have followed similar trajectories. In Canada, the courts have acted to expand national jurisdiction in the post-Charter era, much as Roosevelt appointees on the American Supreme Court expanded federal jurisdiction through their re-interpretations of the commerce clause. While it is certainly the case that the presence of greater ideological diversity in the American Supreme Courts leads to greater contention over the scope of federal jurisdiction, the court's environmental law/commerce clause decisions do not produce neat political divisions in judicial voting. Nevertheless, one pattern is relatively consistent: liberal constitutional activism, in both Canada and the United States, tends to favor increased national regulatory power over the environment. Similarities between liberal approaches to environmental law in Canada and the United States also appear when we consider the issue of legal standing.

The Greening of Justiciability: Expanding the Scope of Standing in Canada and the United States

The development of environmental law in Canada and United States has also been shaped by changing interpretations of the law of standing. Standing is an aspect of the law of justiciability, that part of the judicial process in which courts attempt to determine whether or not an "issue" or conflict is in fact a legal "case." For example, an issue is not justiciable if a judicial decision cannot affect the outcome; the case is "moot." Similarly, under the rules of justiciability, courts have typically demanded that the parties to a case have a genuine conflict of interest—this is referred to as the doctrine of adverseness. "Standing" refers to the question of whether or not an individual, group, or organization has a right to assert specific legal claims. Historically, this has meant that, in order to have "standing" to raise a legal claim, an individual must have suffered (or be about to suffer) a concrete and particularized injury to their own rights. The doctrine of standing, in Anglo-American jurisprudence, was meant to limit or prevent abstract or hypothetical claims from overwhelming the legal system. As Maxwell Stearns has observed, the requirements of standing are rooted in the pragmatic recognition of the costs of litigation; given the real costs of litigating, it makes sense that individuals should only be able to invoke the judicial system to protect their own rights, to and prevent or redress real, concrete injuries.[37]

In practice this means, or rather has meant, that no individual has an abstract right to the enforcement of law, if the enforcement or non-enforcement of law does not affect them. For instance, in the early twentieth century case of *Frothingham v. Mellon,*[38] the U.S. Supreme Court ruled that an individual did not have the power to challenge a federal spending program merely because they objected to it on constitutional grounds. Only if the law affected them directly would they have a "case or controversy" in law, and the indirect effect upon their tax bill occasioned by an individual spending program was not sufficient to establish a case or controversy in law, The change in the courts approach to standing is most evident in the case of *Flast v. Cohen.*[39] In this case, the Warren court granted standing to a party to that wished to contest aspects of state spending, on the grounds that spending itself directly violated the First Amendment. Since that time, Congress has taken upon itself the duty of altering the laws of standing, particularly in relationship to environmental laws and regulations. Members of Congress, though most typically Congressional Democrats, have thought that the participation of citizen groups as "private attorneys general" would be useful in supporting environmental regulation against potentially recalcitrant bureaucrats and executive officials.[40] However, under the Rehnquist court, the rules of standing became a source of considerable controversy in American law. Many of those controversies have dealt with standing in the context of environmental law.

---

[37] Maxwell L. Stearns, "Standing Back from the Forest: Justiciability and Social Choice." *California Law Review.* Vol. 83, No. 6 (Dec., 1995) pp 1309-1413.

[38] *Frothingham v. Mellon*, 262 U.S. 447 (1923)

[39] *Flast v. Cohen*, 392 U.S. 83 (1968)

[40] For a discussion of the rise of "private attorneys general," see Jeremy Rabkin, "The Secret Life of the Private Attorney General." *Law and Contemporary Problems* Vol. 61, No. 1 (Winter, 1998) pp 179-203.

The development of the law of standing in the American Supreme Court parallels the development of commerce clause jurisprudence. Just as the courts of Rehnquist and Roberts divided over the scope of national government power, so too have thy divided over the meaning of standing—which is to say, the court is often divided over what it means for some conflict to be a legal case. In *Lujan v. Defenders of Wildlife,*[41] for example, Justice Scalia re-asserted the idea that, in order to challenge government actions, individuals had to suffer concrete and particularized harms. The harms had to be traceable to government action, and amenable to a judicial remedy. Not surprisingly, this new precedent did not settle the issue. Some commentators suggested that the *Lujan* decision had the potential to undermine all of the various "citizen suit" provisions that are part of most major national environmental statutes.[42] This has not yet come to pass, though the issue of standing continues to be a source of conflict in federal courts. It is not necessarily the case that this is only a consequence of differing political preferences of federal judges. Since the *Lujan* decision, there has been no case in which the Supreme Court has struck down citizen suit provisions of environmental law, which indicates that while *Lujan* might potentially limit Congressional control over the law of standing, its "zone of interests" test is not particularly restrictive.

The U.S. Supreme Court has decided three environmental law cases in which standing was the central issue since 1992, and in each case the outcome was very different. In *Bennet v. Spears,*[43] the court ruled unanimously that a group of land-owners had standing under the Endangered Species Act to challenge lake-level regulations that were intended to protect two varieties of endangered fish. In *Chicago Steel*

---

[41] *Lujan v. Defenders of Wildlife*, 504 U.S. 555 (1992)

[42] E.g. "Read for all it is worth, the decision (Lujan) invalidates the large number of statutes in which Congress has attempted to use the 'citizen-suit' device as a mechanism for controlling unlawfully inadequate enforcement of law." Cass R. Sunstein "What's Standing after Lujan? Of Citizen Suits, 'Injuries,' and Article III." *Michigan Law Review*. Vol. 91, No. 2 (Nov. 1992) pp 163-236 (p. 165).

[43] *Bennett v. Spear*, 520 U.S. 154 (1997)

and Pickling Co. v. Citizens for a Better Environment,[44] another unanimous decision, the court ruled that an environmental group could not be granted standing, where the relief they sought was unrelated to any alleged injury. Environmentalists might point out that the clearest pattern in these few cases is the fact that environmentalist groups lost on the question of standing, while private land owners and state agencies were granted standing. Yet the *Lujan* decision has not led to complete administrative autonomy for national environmental policy-makers, though this may well be because those who might apply the decision with a ruthless consistency do not yet hold a majority on the court.[45] The expansion of standing continues to influence American environmental law and environmental policy, though the scope of standing is still contested.

Within the American political system, the transformation of standing has greater ramifications than in the parliamentary systems of government, because the tensions between the separation of the executive and legislative branches invariably produces more occasions to claim that "the rule of law" has been violated by executive discretion. Insofar as American courts adopt an illegitimate role in environmental policy, it is because they attempt to uphold a rigid conception of the rule of law. Particularly within the American system of separated powers, the post-1960 conception of standing allows legalism to trump political prudence. The traditional rules of standing, in contrast, allowed courts to limit abstract legalism without endorsing executive lawlessness. If the rules of standing are abandoned, then this creates the space for courts to substitute their own discretion for that of the executive branch, despite claims that this is done in the name of Congressional supremacy or the "rule of law."

---

[44] *Chicago Steel and Pickling Co. v. Citizens for a Better Environment* 523 U.S. 83 (1998)

[45] For a thorough-going critique of "citizen suit" provisions on the grounds of their incompatibility with the Constitutional separation of powers, see Charles S. Abell, "Ignoring the Trees for the Forests: How the Citizen Suit Provision of the Clean Water Act violates the Constitution's Separation of Powers Principle." *Virginia Law Review*, Vol. 81, No. 7 (Oct., 1995) pp 1957-1987.

A key example of this is the case of *Massachusetts v. EPA,*[46] heard by the DC Circuit court of appeals in 2005 and by the United States Supreme Court in the spring of 2007. In this case, an assortment of states and environmental interest groups petitioned the courts in the hopes of forcing the EPA to adopt more stringent regulations of carbon dioxide emissions from new motor vehicles. The EPA argued that it lacked statutory authority to regulate carbon dioxide emissions from motor vehicles. Secondly, even if it did possess the authority to do so, the EPA claimed it possessed discretion to not promulgate regulations, due to the uncertainties regarding the environmental effects of carbon dioxide and other green house gases. In other words, Congressional authorization to regulate green house gasses did not require the EPA to exercise that power in this instance. From the perspective of the environmental interest groups and state attorneys general bringing this petition, however, the EPA's decision to not promulgate regulations was not just a disastrous policy choice: it was an illegal violation of Congressional intention as expressed in the Clear Air Act and its subsequent amendments.

The first question that had to be addressed by the U.S. Supreme Court in *Massachusetts v. EPA* was whether any of the petitioners had standing to bring the case at all. In an opinion written by Justice Stevens, the majority argued that the state of Massachusetts met the requirements of standing. Like all states, Massachusetts possessed an interest in protecting its territory, and the state claimed that its territory which was threatened by global warming. In terms of the legal requirements for standing, Massachusetts claimed to be facing a threat of imminent injury. Could this imminent injury be traced to the inaction of the EPA ? In a sense it could. The decision to not regulate carbon dioxide could contribute to the injury, even if it was impossible specify the scope of the effect; a "causal nexus" existed between the EPA decision and the anticipated injury. Perhaps most difficult to assess was the final requirement of the rule of standing: redressability. As the term "global warming" implies, the problem of carbon dioxide emissions exists at a global level. No regulatory decision by the EPA alone, particularly a decision that would only affect carbon dioxide emissions

---

[46] *Massachusetts v. EPA* 367 U.S. App. D.C. 282 (2005) *Massachusetts v. EPA*, 127 S. Ct. 1438 (2007)

for new motor vehicles, could eliminate the threat of global warming. Yet, as in regards to the criterion of causation, the majority argued that even the limited impact of the EPA decision could provide some "redress" for the effects of global warming. Despite the complexities of the issue, the speculative nature of the actual injuries that were suffered by Massachusetts, and the admittedly limited impact that any EPA regulation would have on that injury, the majority argued that Massachusetts had met the requirements of standing.

The dissenting opinion of Justice Roberts (joined by Alito, Scalia, and Thomas) reflected a much more traditional—and much narrower—conception of what constitutes a case in law. Roberts rejected the majority's claim that the requirements of standing should be loosened because one of the petitioners was a state. Perhaps more importantly, Roberts argued that all of the claims regarding the elements of standing—injury, causation, and redressability—were absent in this case. The injuries were not imminent in any normal sense of the word, and the impact of EPA decisions on global warming was minuscule, if not non-existent. Thus, whether or not the EPA was acting in accordance with its statutory requirements, the court could only grant standing to Massachusetts by a wholesale reformation of the law of standing; in order to treat this as a legal case, the court would have to redefine what it meant for a conflict to be a "case or controversy" in law.

The liberalization of the law of standing has been one of the major goals of the Canadian environmental movement, who have long envied the ability of American environmentalists to play a role in the enforcement of environmental law.[47] Americans have had long experience with "private attorneys general," and advocates of increased environmental regulation in Canada have, unsurprisingly, regarded this policy device as key to environmental protection in Canada.[48] For some commentators, as long as the government alone is responsible for

---

[47] S. Elgie "Environmental Groups and the Courts: 1970-1992." in G. Thompson, M. McConnell, and L. Huestis, editors. *Environmental Law and Business in Canada.* (Toronto: Canada Law Books, 1993.); Hessing and Howlett, *Canadian Natural Resource and Environmental Policy*, pp 203-204.

[48] Boyd, *Unnatural Law*, pp 232-233.

enforcing environmental law, environmental law will never be enforced responsibly. Yet it was far from clear whether the emergence of judicial activism in other areas of Canadian policy would lead to the "greening" of justiciability. In his 1994 article on environmental litigation in Canada, Michael Howlett found that Canadian courts have not followed the lead of their American counterparts in regards to questions of legal standing.[49] Howlett argued that the constitutional transformations of the 1980s had simply not given courts any mandate to rearrange the processes of Canadian environmental law and policy. The Constitution Act and the Charter itself did not address the law of standing in regards to environmental matters. Furthermore, Canadian courts have been unwilling to read Section 7 of the Charter as if it contained an implied right to a clean environment.[50] The courts have also ruled that the Charter only applies to relations between citizens and government (i.e. it does not apply to the relations between citizens and, say, a polluting company).[51]Thus, while the Constitution Act and the Charter were likely to transform many aspects of law, it was unlikely to "judicialize" Canadian environmental policy.

Yet over the past three decades Canadian citizens have expanded their ability to raise public or quasi-public claims through the courts, even in cases that are not based on the Charter or Constitution Act. Traditionally, the general rule for civil cases involving the public interest was that individuals could only pursue a case relating to a public grievance if they were "exceptionally prejudiced by the wrongful act."[52] In 1986, the Supreme Court of Canada offered further clarification regarding the prerequisites for private individuals to raise public interest claims in the courts: the issue must be "justiciable" (that is, it must be amenable to a court's decision), it must not be "trivial" or

---

[49] Howlett, "The Judicialization of Canadian Environmental Policy 1980-1990A Test of the Canada-United States Convergence Thesis." *Canadian Journal of Political Science*. Vol. 27, No. 1 (March, 1994) pp 99-127.

[50] Section 7 of the Charter: Security of the Person

[51] Thomas M.J. Bateman, "Rights Application Doctrine and the Clash of Constitutionalisms in Canada." *Canadian Journal of Political Science*. Vol. 31, No. 1, (March, 1998) pp 3-29.

[52] *Smith v. Attorney General of Ontario*, [1924] S.C.R. 331 at pp. 337-338

"speculative," the individual must have either a strong personal interest in the case or a strong interest based on involvement in the policy process, and there must be no other reasonable means by which the action could be brought before the courts.[53] As Howlett observes, these rules leave judges a great deal of discretion as to whether they will grant standing or withhold it. However, he interprets the discretionary aspects of the Canadian law of standing as an indication that environmental policy is less judicialized in Canada than in America, where litigants are often empowered by broad statutory provisions for standing.[54] The real question, however, is whether Canadian judges have used their discretion so as to emulate the American law of standing. And here, Howlett's prediction has been disproved by Canadian judicial practice over the course of the 1990s.

In environmental law decisions during the 1990s, Canadian courts enacted a veritable revolution in the law of standing. Despite the fact that the Canadian parliament has not attached specific "citizen suit" provisions to environmental legislation, Canadian courts have been quite willing to allow private groups to contest government action.[55] The Supreme Court of Canada has consistently adhered to broad understanding of the scope of standing in the post-Charter era.[56] Canadian courts have liberalized standing laws to such an extent that there are few substantive barriers to standing for Canadian environmental interest groups.

---

[53] *Finlay v. Canada (Minister of Finance)*, [1986] 2 S.C.R. 607 See also W.A. Bogart, "Understanding Standing, Chapter IV: *Minister of Finance v. Finlay*," *Supreme Court Law Review*, Volume 10, 1988. pp 377-97.

[54] E.g. Joseph L. Smith, "Congress Opens the Courthouse Door: Statutory Changes to Judicial Review Under the Clean Air Act." *Political Research Quarterly*. Volume 58, Number 1, 2005. pp 139-149.

[55] See the comparison of Canadian and American environmental regulation in Kathryn Harrison "Is Cooperation the Answer? Canadian Environmental Enforcement in Comparative Context." *Journal of Policy Analysis and Management*, Vol. 14, No. 2 (Spring, 1995), pp. 221-244

[56] Rainer Knopff and J.E. Glen, "Courts, Tribunals, and the Environment in Canada. In Kenneth Holland et al, editors, *Federalism and the Environment: Environmental Policymaking in Australia, Canada, and the United States*. Greenwood Press: Westport, Conn., 1996.

One might object that the fact that federal courts tend overwhelmingly to grant standing to public interest groups in environmental policy does not necessarily mean that the rules of standing have been liberalized in Canada. Perhaps dozens of potential public litigants are dissuaded from even attempting to have their day in court by rigid rules of standing, rules which insure that only those with a concrete right at stake will be able to challenge the decisions of elected officials and expert bureaucrats. According to some researchers, for instance, Canadian environmental groups devote most of their resources towards non-litigation based political strategies, such as public education.[57] Perhaps this indicates that the law of standing is less lax than it first appears.

A few examples will illustrate that this is probably not the case. The bar for standing in Canadian environmental law has been set very low, and even the most abstract claims made against administrative agencies have an excellent chance of being heard by Canadian courts. A litigant need not face the threat of having her farmland covered by an artificial lake in order to contest dam-building permits. She need only show an authentic sense of aesthetic disapproval for dams; it might help if she can show that there was a minor procedural error in the permit-granting process. The crucial point is that Canadian courts are willing to hear cases on the basis of policy objections. These policy objections need to be cloaked in the rhetoric of "rights talk," or based on semi-plausible readings of obscure statutory passages, but these are of course simple operations for any moderately skilled practitioner of the legal arts.

The case of *Canadian Environmental Law Association v. Canada-Minister of Environment,*[58] is probably the most interesting example of the complete erosion of the rules of standing, at least insofar as those rules relate to environmental policy. In this case, CELA raised a challenge to a half-dozen federal-provincial environmental policy

---

[57] Jeremy Wilson, "Continuity and Change in the Canadian Environmental Movement: Assessing the Effects of Institutionalization." in Debora L. VanNijnatten and Robert Boardman, editors, *Canadian Environmental Policy: Context and Cases.* (Oxford: Oxford University Press, 2002) pp 46-65.

[58] *Canadian Environmental Law Association v. Canada (Minister of the Environment)* (1999) 3 F.C. 564

agreements. CELA wanted the courts to declare these agreements invalid, due to the fact that they seemed to place restrictions on the discretionary power of federal ministers in several areas related to environmental policy. It is important to note that CELA was challenging *agreements* in this case. No actual actions had been taken on the basis of those agreements. CELA's case for the illegality of the agreements was based on an assortment of hypothetical scenarios. It is also crucial to remember that the Canadian Constitution makes federal-provincial agreements of this kind a practical necessity, due to that document's imprecise delimitation of environmental jurisdiction.[59] CELA's case was based on nothing more than its distaste for the particular modus vivendi that had emerged from the process of federal-provincial diplomacy. Given the absence of any clearly relevant constitutional right, and given the absence of any actual government actions, why should CELA have been allowed to voice its objections in a federal court? The federal-provincial agreements seemed to be no business of CELA. Were its members apprehensive about the possible consequences of such agreements, they could of course vote against federal politicians who foolishly deign to compromise and cooperate with their provincial counterparts.

The trial judge in this case was unmoved by, if not unaware of, these objections to CELA's claims. Judge Reed assumed that the business of Canada is CELA's business as well, and proceeded to address the substantive issues of the case (e.g. did the federal minister of the environment fetter her own discretion and the discretion of other ministers in an unconstitutional manner?) And indeed, aside from the issue of standing, not everything would go CELA's way. In fact, CELA was not able convince the judge to overturn the agreements or declare sections of them unconstitutional. As is often the case in Canadian environmental law, litigants with no concrete stake in a case are granted standing only to have their application dismissed.

---

[59] Thus Canadian political scientists commonly refer to "federal-provincial" diplomacy (e.g. Richard Simeon. *Federal-Provincial Diplomacy: The Making of Recent Policy in Canada*. Toronto: University of Toronto Press, 1972) as the process of hammering out agreements over jurisdiction, resources, transfer payments, national policy, etc.

Friends of the Island (FOTI) v. Canada[60] also illustrates how the rules of standing have been gutted in Canadian law. *FOTI v. Canada* is an amusing example, as it contains a peculiar application of strict construction in legal interpretation. The Canadian government, in conjunction with the government of Prince Edward Island, intended to construct a bridge connecting PEI with mainland Canada. According to the then-existing rule dealing with environmental issues related to federally approved projects—the Environmental Assessment and Review Process Guidelines Order (EARPGO)—the Minister of Public Works had to assess environmental impact when approving a bridge of this kind.[61] Due to the high level of public concern, the Minister of Public Works asked the Minister of the Environment to refer the details of the project to an environmental assessment panel. The panel concluded that the possible environmental damage caused by the bridge was too great to allow for construction to continue, though it was willing to consider the development of an underground tunnel. The Minister of the Environment, presumably after considering the relative costs of tunnels and bridges, felt that it would be possible for the final bridge plan to mitigate the environmental problems addressed by the panel. By January of 1993, eight years after the initial plan for the bridge had begun, Strait Crossing Incorporated was given the construction contract.

The "Friends of the Island" group (FOTI) challenged the bridge construction project on two grounds. First, FOTI argued that the EARPGO had not been fully complied with in the project review and assessment stage. Secondly, the group claimed that the decision to replace the PEI ferry with a bridge constituted a violation of the Prince Edward Island terms of Union. The PEI Terms of Union state that the Dominion Government (Canada) is required to maintain an "an

---

[60] *Friends of the Island v. Canada (Minister of Public Works)* (1993) 2 F.C. 229

[61] For a discussion of the Canadian environmental assessment process, see Marcia Valiant, "The Legal Foundations of Canadian Environmental Policy." Debora L. VanNijnatten and Robert Boardman, editors. *Canadian Environmental Policy: Context and Cases.* Oxford: Oxford University Press, 2002. pp 17-19.

efficient steam service" between PEI and mainland Canada.[62] As the Canadian Federal Court reporter helpfully points out, "a bridge is not an efficient steam service."[63] Clearly, a legal violation of considerable magnitude was at stake.

One might well wonder whether a right to ferry service is so fundamental as to deserve judicial protection, especially in an era when so many reject the notion of "frozen rights" in favor of a progressive, ever-changing, "living tree" conception of rights. The government's lawyers certainly did their best to argue for a flexible interpretation of the terms of union. Yet even if Judge Reed felt compelled to adopt Protestant interpretative principles in this case,[64] he was still faced with a problem: the right to ferry service had not yet been abridged. True, the government had shown a clear intention to neglect its traditional responsibility for efficient steam service. The people of PEI (or at least their self-chosen spokespersons), ever jealous of incursions on their sacred liberties, were not about to ignore the federal government's clear intention to violate their right to a three-hour boat ride. Yet as the government lawyers also observed, there was no way to show how FOTI had an interest in the case, an interest that might distinguish them from the general public. The PEI terms of agreement actually specified that it was the right of the provincial *government* to challenge violations of the agreement in court. The trial court judge was not impressed by these considerations. FOTI were granted standing, despite the fact that no right had been violated, and despite the fact that they were not the most likely possessor of the relevant rights. Unlike the case of *CELA v. Canada*, FOTI was granted more than standing; the judge granted them a stay against the permit for bridge construction, thereby insuring that FOTI's private preference for ferry trips would be respected for just a little while longer. But once again, though the Friends of the Island were allowed their day in court, the Confederation Bridge project was not, in the end, derailed.

---

[62] *Prince Edward Island Terms of Union* [R.S.C., 1985, Appendix II, No. 12]

[63] See the summary of the case at http://www.canlii.org/en/ca/fct/doc/1993/1993canlii2942/1993canlii2942.html

[64] Sanford Levinson's pejorative tag for "strict constructionism," "originalism," or "textualism." Sanford Levinson, *Constitutional Faith*. Princeton: Princeton University Press, 1988.

As these cases illustrate, Canadian courts have adopted a liberalized interpretation of the rules of standing, and unlike the case in the United States, there are few judges in Canadian courts who have defended the traditional rules of standing. As in the case with questions of federal jurisdiction over the environment, Canadian courts have adopted a "progressive" position when evaluating these issues. But most interestingly, the revolution in standing has not led to the judicialization of environmental policy. The limits of environmentalism in Canadian law only become apparent through an examination of how Canadian courts deal with disputes over the interpretation of environmental law.

Divergent Paths: Statutory Interpretation and Administrative Discretion in Canadian and American Environmental Law

The "rights revolutions" in Canada and the United States have followed similar trajectories, at least in regards to those novel rights to challenge government that have emerged through the reformation of the law of standing.[65] The expansion of standing, therefore, does not appear dependent upon any factors or motives that emerge from the specific political arrangements in the United States or in Canada. Yet despite these changes, the judicialization of American environmental policy will continue to be more conspicuous than in Canada. This is for two central reasons: the separation of powers, and the greater degree of ideological diversity in the American political system.

In the American system conflicts (actual or anticipated) between the executive and legislative branch creates incentives for legislators to constrain the discretion of the executive branch. The tension and distrust between the executive and the legislature does not exist in modern parliamentary systems—or rather, it does not operate in the same way. Members of the U.S. Congress have an incentive to expand judicial oversight of the executive branch, as well as an incentive to increase the capacity of interest groups to use the courts to challenge executive decision-making.[66] In contrast, there has been an increasing

---

[65] Cass Sunstein, *After the Rights Revolution: Reconceiving the Regulatory State*. Cambridge: Harvard University Press, 1990.

[66] Dodd, Lawrence C. and Richard Schott, *Congress and the Administrative State* (New York: John Wiley and Sons, 1979).

tendency within Parliamentary governments, especially Canadian governments, to vest increasing powers in the cabinet, the federal civil service, and the Prime Minister's office.[67]

Secondly, as the American President does not depend upon the support of the legislature to remain in power, there is less need for party discipline. The policy-making process is affected by this comparative weakness of American parties in a variety of ways.[68] In some circumstances, weak parties produce legislators who are more prone to create ambiguous laws.[69] This is because ambiguous policy proposals are more likely to survive the legislative process in Congress than laws which set clear policy goals. This feature of American law-making is not omnipresent. Particularly after the sub-committee revolution of the 1970s, and perhaps in response to criticisms of Congressional delegation of law-making power, American legislators increased their capacity to insert detailed regulatory provisions into law.[70] But nevertheless, the weakness of American political parties still shapes the legislative process; in the absence of party discipline, legislators use ambiguous statutory language and delegation of power as tools to forge consensus.

Ambiguous laws and delegation of legislative power to executive branch bureaucracies are features of law-making in parliamentary systems of government as well as those in the American separation-of-powers system. Yet the consequences differ in parliamentary systems, where the government is a creature of the legislative branch. When parliamentary governments offer interpretations of ambitious or poorly specified laws, it is difficult for courts to argue that the government is departing from the will of the legislature. This is because the

---

[67] Donald Savoie *Governing From the Center: The Concentration of Power in Canadian Politics.* Toronto: University of Toronto Press, 1999.

[68] Sidney Milkis, *Political Parties and Constitutional Government* (Baltimore: Johns Hopkins University Press, 1999).

[69] R. Shep Melnick, *Between the Lines: Interpreting Welfare Rights.* Washington, D.C.: Brookings Institution, 1994.

[70] R. Shep Melnick, *Regulation and the Courts: The Case of the Clean Air Act.* Washington, D.C.: Brookings Institution, 1983 pp 5-9.

government serves at the will of the legislature. In the United States, the situation is of course very different. While the President has always played a role in the legislative process, whether through the exercise of traditional powers or through the expanded institutions and practices of the modern "legislative" or "plebiscitary" Presidency,[71] the specific enforcement actions of the Presidency and the executive branch cannot with any certainty claim the support of the legislature, at least not in the way that actions of a parliamentary cabinet can claim support from the Commons.

In environmental policy, as in many other fields of government action, the American political system encourages conflict between the legislature and the executive branch. Again, the key difference between the Congressional and Parliamentary system is that the executive in the Parliamentary system exists by virtue of legislative support. A Canadian court that challenges a government decision does not merely challenge an executive branch official, but (in theory) the majority of representatives of the national government. The President's institutional independence from Congress is, in contrast, a source of weakness when confronting the courts. A cabinet minister in Canada, when interpreting ambiguous provisions in law, can claim that their interpretations are implicitly supported by the very people who are responsible for making the laws and maintaining the government. The President, lacking that institutional connection to the legislature, is a more fitting target for judicial suspicion. Given all of these factors, we would expect environmental policy to be more "judicialized" in the United States than in Canada.[72]

Canadian laws, perhaps as often as American, are characterized by ambiguity, utopian aspirations, and the absence of clear standards. But the political context of parliamentary government limits the ability of courts to creatively reconstruct statutory law. Consider the following statement from the preamble to the 1999 *Canadian Environmental Protection Act:*

---

[71] E.g Theodore Lowi, *The "Personal" President: Power Invested, Promise Unfulfilled.* Ithaca: Cornell University Press, 1985.

[72] Martin Shapiro, "Juridicalization of Politics in the United States." *International Political Science Review.* Vol. 15, No. 2 (April, 1994) pp 101-112.

> Whereas the Government of Canada is committed to implementing the precautionary principle that, where there are threats of serious or irreversible damage, lack of full scientific certainty shall not be used as a reason for postponing cost-effective measures to prevent environmental degradation.

In the abstract, we might think that statutory language of this kind has the potential to be a valuable resource for public-interest litigants. Depending upon the seriousness of the commitment, application of the precautionary principle could imply massive restrictions on any number of economic activities. Perhaps this is why the impending ecological damage must be "serious" or "irreversible," and why the preventive measures must be "cost-effective." Yet all of these terms depend upon scientific assessments of environmental impact, as well as economic calculations of the relative benefits of regulation versus development. This clause, like many others that proliferate in Canadian environmental statutes, seems to incorporate both a desire to privilege the post-materialist claims of environmental movements and a desire to not unduly constrain the discretion of federal administrators.[73]

Despite the ambiguities in law that might provide opportunities for the exercise of judicial power, parliamentary governments constrain the opportunities for the "judicialization" of environmental policies in at least two general ways. First, parliamentary governments are usually well-positioned to reverse judicial decisions that hamper executive discretion.[74] Secondly, parliamentary governments are less likely to constrain executive discretion through detailed statutes that impose non-discretionary duties on administrators. Perhaps paradoxically, American courts have the potential to intervene into environmental policy whether Congress writes laws that are broad and vague, or

---

[73] For a discussion of the precautionary principle and its relationship to Canadian environmental policy, see David Boyd, *Unnatural Law: Rethinking Canadian Environmental Law and Policy*. Vancouver: UBC Press, 2003 pp 234-236.

[74] Assuming that, as is usually the case, the government does not allow a "free vote" by its members in relation to the issue; see Thomas Flanagan, "The Staying Power of the Legislative Status Quo: Collective Choice in Canada's Parliament after *Morgentaler*." *Canadian Journal of Political Science*. Vol. 30, No. 1, (March, 1997) pp 31-53.

detailed and wonkish.[75] In Canada, courts are constrained because Lilliputian legislators have fewer incentives to constrain executive Gullivers. If the courts act to restrain executive discretion, legislators have the incentive and the capacity to challenge and reverse those judicial decisions.

In order to assess the ways in which differing institutional environments place limits on judicial policy-making, it is useful to consider one of the major aspects of environmental policy in Canada and the United States: environmental impact assessment. Environmental assessment refers to the process through which governments evaluate the impact that development projects have upon various aspects of the environment, such as the effect of development upon human health, the potential for pollution, the disruption of eco-systems, the threat to endangered species, and so on. By looking at the statutes that govern environmental assessment in the United States and Canada, we can see how American political institutions create a far greater scope for judicial intervention into environmental policy.

The principal environmental assessment law in the United States is the *National Environmental Policy Act*, or NEPA. The key section of NEPA reads as follows:

> The Congress authorizes and directs that, to the fullest extent possible . . . all agencies of the federal government shall include, in every recommendation or report on proposals for legislation and other major Federal actions significantly affecting the quality of the human environment, a detailed statement by the responsible official on the environmental impact of the proposed action.

As other scholars have noted, there are no provisions for enforcement of this law other than through recourse to litigation—no special boards or tribunals were established to oversee the environmental assessment process. Thus, courts have played a key role in implementing NEPA from the very beginning.[76]

---

[75] Melnick, *Between the Lines*, p. 31.

[76] Kenneth Holland, "The Role of the Courts in the Making and Administration of Environmental Policy in the United States." in Holland et al, editors.

In Canada, similarly, environmental assessment involves identifying and reviewing federal projects that are likely to have an environmental impact. "Federal projects" are those projects initiated by federal departments and agencies, using federal funds, or involving federal funds or federal jurisdiction. What is most interesting about the judicial role in environmental assessment policy is the way in which Parliament has circumscribed the role played by judges. Canadian judges have shown some inclination to "judicialize" environmental policy, but here, limits on judicial intervention have been successfully imposed by political actors. Even while Canadian courts were clearly moved by environmental values in their attempt to insert non-discretionary duties into the Canadian environmental assessment process, the capacity of the courts to do this was limited by their institutional environment. All of this is fully consistent with a purely political interpretation of judicial decision-making. What is not consistent is the way in which the generally progressive Canadian judiciary has generally refused to impose "environmental values." In contrast to what we might expect based upon the general trends of Canadian jurisprudence in other areas, Canadian judges have come to accept that, for the most part, courts should not attempt to emulate the role played by American courts in environmental policy.

The Canadian version of environmental assessment began to take shape in the early 1970s, as the desire for development in Canada's resource-dependent economy began to be qualified by concerns with environmental degradation.[77] Environmental assessments of federal projects, as in the U.S.A., were intended to help the national government take into account the "externalities" created by economic development. Yet the concern with environmentalism in Canada took place in the shadow of NEPA, which had already been revealed as heavily dependent upon litigation, with its attendant costs and lack of predictability.[78] As a result, Canadian policy-makers approached

---

Federalism and the Environment: Environmental Policy-Making in Australia, Canada, and the United States. Greenwood Press: Westport, Conn. 1996.

[77] Hessing et al *Canadian Natural Resource and Environmental Policy*, pp 144-145

[78] Ibid., p. 202.

environmental assessment in a cautious, Canadian fashion. In contrast to the USA, where environmental assessment laws were created without an accompanying bureaucratic apparatus, the Trudeau government in Canada created a bureaucracy without an accompanying law to enforce. The Canadian Federal Environmental Assessment Review Office was established by cabinet decision in 1973. From this beginning point, the Canadian analogue to NEPA—the Environmental Assessment and Review Process, or EARP—would evolve over the next several decades. Yet while Canadian and American policies were evolving in similar directions, it is not clear that the role of courts was part of that similar evolutionary trajectory.

In order to compare the role played by Canadian and American courts in the environmental assessment process, I have assembled a sample of fifty American and 50 Canadian environmental assessment cases. The American cases are drawn from Circuit Court cases decided in 2006-2007; the Canadian cases are composed of environmental assessment cases decided by the Canadian Federal Court of Appeals between 1990 and 2009, as well as all environmental assessment cases decided by the provincial and territorial courts of appeal.[76] The decisions of executive branch officials were overturned, in whole or in part, in 20 out of 51 cases in the American federal appellate courts. In the Canadian federal appellate courts and the courts of appeal in Alberta, British Columbia, and Ontario, decisions by government officials were overturned in whole or in part in 10 out of 50 cases. It is interesting to note that in 4 of the 10 cases where Canadian appellate courts overturned government decisions, the courts acted in favor of business or development interests. Judging by these environmental assessment cases, the Canadian appellate courts are no haven for environmentalist interest groups.

Another way to consider the scope of politicization in American and Canadian environmental assessment jurisprudence is to consider the level of unanimity in appellate court decisions. In the fifty NEPA cases decided by American appellate courts which I examined, there were dissenting votes in ten of the cases; there were only 2 dissenting votes in the 50 Canadian environmental assessment cases. This indicates that the moderate,

---

[76] See Appendices C and D for a full list of cases.

deferential approach to government decision-makers in environmental policy is not a particular matter of controversy at the appellate court level. There may well be less of a struggle in Canadian jurisprudence between those who wish to incorporate "green" values into their decision-making, and those who wish to respect the generally pro-development inclinations of government and business. The unwillingness of Canadian appellate courts to intervene into environmental policy, and the low levels of dissent in environmental assessment cases, is a good indicator of the ways in which the parliamentary system places political restraints on even the most progressive judiciaries.

Does this mean that the American environmental law decisions are simply political, not different in kind from the struggles over environmental policy that occur in other forums? The answer, I believe, is that there is less contention and less politicization in American environmental law than we might expect, even if American courts are more interventionist and more divided than their Canadian counterparts. In order to examine the scope of politicization in American environmental law, I conducted a Lexis Nexis search of federal appellate court cases, using the following environmental policy-related statutes as keywords: Clean Water Act (CWA), National Environmental Protection Act (NEPA), National Forest Management Act (NFMA), the Endangered Species Act (ESA), the Clean Air Act (CAA). I selected one hundred cases, based upon whether or not at least one environmental interest group was opposing a position taken by the national government, or by state governments who were participating in a nationally mandated policy.

In analyzing the cases, I divided the cases into the following categories:

1) Cases in which environmentalist petitioners succeeded on at least one of their claims

2) Cases in which environmentalist petitioners were completely rebuffed by the courts

3) Cases in which "anti-environmentalist" (typically, businesses or business associations) petitioners succeeded on at least one of their claims

4) Cases in which "anti-environmentalist" groups lost on all of their claims

Table Seven summarizes the outcomes in these cases.

Table 7: Environmental Law Cases in U.S. Courts of Appeal.

	N = 100	**Cases with Dissenting Votes**	**Court Maj. Dem.**	**Court Maj. GOP**
Environmentalist Petitioner Wins	39	4	19	20
Environmentalist Petitioner Loses	43	3	17	26
Anti-Environmentalist Petitioner Wins	5	2	3	2
Anti-Environmentalist Petitioner Loses	13	0	4	9

What is of most interest in the outcomes of these cases is the absence of any clear partisan divisions on the court. 93 out of 100 of these cases were decided unanimously, despite the fact that most of the cases (86) featured appeals court panels with judges appointed by both parties. Success for environmental interest groups does not seem to depend on facing Democratic appointees on the bench. These decisions show that while the appeals courts are not hesitant to take the side of environmentalist interest groups, they are not fractured by deep partisan divisions. Without detailed knowledge of the specific political preferences of the 126 judges who participated in these cases, it is impossible to reject with certainty that the judges are not simply voting their policy preferences. Still, when one considers the increased attention that both parties have paid to the appointment process in recent decades,[80] the increase of partisan differences amongst political elites,[81] and the intensity of public conflict over environmental issues,[82] it is interesting that the battles over environmental policy that occupy the public, the pundits, and the politicians have not, for the most part, spilled over into the judicial branch. The question of whether judges are "really" judging on the basis of their policy preferences in these cases is in some ways politically irrelevant, if the policy preferences of Democratic and Republican appointees converge (for the most part) when dealing with highly contentious issues such as environmental regulation.

At the Supreme Court level, comparisons are more difficult to make due to the paucity of environmental law decisions in the Canadian Supreme Court, and the even greater paucity of cases dealing with highly significant environmental issues. The Canadian Supreme Court has, in the post-charter era, decided relatively few cases dealing with environmental law and regulation, and those decisions rarely challenge the statutory interpretations or policy determinations of governments. There are some cases in which the courts have forced governments to conduct broader environmental assessments. In the case of *The Friends of the Oldman River Society v. Canada,*[83] for instance, the court ruled that the federal EARPGO process was mandatory, and had to be applied to an Alberta dam that had undergone construction. The federal government underwent the review process, but this had no impact upon the construction of the dam. In addition, the court played a role in halting the James Bay Hydro Electric Project

---

[80] E.g. Thomas Keck, *The Most Activist Supreme Court in History? The Road to Modern Constitutional Conservatism.* Chicago: University of Chicago Press, 2004.

[81] E.g. Marc Hetherington "Resurgent Mass Partisanship: The Role of Elite Polarization." *American Political Science Review.* Vol. 95, No. 3 (Sept. 2001) pp 619-631

[82] E.g Aaron M. McCright and Riley E. Dunlap, "Challenging Global Warming as a Social Problem: An Analysis of the Conservative Movement's Counter-Claims." *Social Problems.* Vol. 47, No. 4 (Nov. 2000).

[83] *The Friends of the Oldman River Society v. Canada* 1992 CanLII 110 (S.C.C.).

by enjoining the federal government to conduct an environmental review. Yet, while the case certainly pitted the court against the Quebec provincial government, it is far from clear whether the federal government was averse to conducting a federal environmental assessment over the project.[84] So, while the court did force the federal to act in this case, judicial intervention did not really supplant the preferred political options of national decision makers. As in the case of *R. v. Crown Zellerbach*, the court has intervened into environmental policy as a supporter of national jurisdiction and national policymaking. This is judicial activism of a sort, but it difficult to construe it as anti-democratic or counter-majoritarian judicial activism.[85]

The American Supreme Court has been more willing, in general, to rule against national, state, and local governments based upon statutory interpretation. This can be seen by looking at decisions addressing one of the central national environmental regulatory statutes, the Clean Air Act. The Clean Air Act and its various amendments has been one of the most highly litigated aspects of American Environmental policy, and courts have played a major role in shaping the implementation of the act since its inception.[86] The court's decisions in Clean Air Act cases do not always reveal the clear political divisions apparent in other controversial areas of law.87 This is not to say that political divisions

---

[84] The federal government had attempted to initiate jurisdiction over the process, but backed down in response to the intransigence of decision-makers in Quebec. The court's decision to make the federal review process mandatory in some ways provided "cover" for a government, a way for it to avoid the political fallout of hampering a multi-billion dollar project that was central to the economic interests of Quebec. See Oliver A. Houck, "O Canada! The Story of Rafferty, Oldman, and the Great Whale." *Boston College International and Comparative Law Review*. Vol. 29 (Spring, 2006).

[85] See the discussion in Barry Friedman, "The Birth of An Academic Obsession: The History of the Counter-Majoritarian Difficulty, Part V." *The Yale Law Journal*. Vol. 112, No. 2 (Nov. 2002) pp 153-259.

[86] R. Shep Melnick, *Regulation and the Courts*. Washington, D.C.: Brookings Institution, 1983. pp 343-394.

87 *Pennsylvania v. Delaware Valley Citizens Council for Clean Air et al,* 1986 *Pennsylvania v. Delaware Valley Citizens Council for Clean Air et al*, 1987 *General Motors Corporation v. United States,* 1990

are entirely absent. The case of *Massachusetts v. EPA*, discussed earlier in regards to the question of standing, is one example of a clear "liberal vs. conservative" split over the scope of the EPA's duties under the Clean Air Act. A similar division is apparent in *Alaska Department of Environmental Conservation v. EPA*, in which a majority on the court endorsed the EPA's determination to enforce a more rigorous air protection policy on the government of Alaska.[88] But liberal justices have not maintained anything like a general endorsement of environmentalist claims in regards to this law.

Between 1985 and 2007, the U.S. The Court decided eight cases dealing with the Clean Air Act. It directly overturned the statutory interpretations of national policy-makers in only two of those cases. The key thing to note is that the political divisions on display in *Massachusetts v. EPA* are not necessarily reflected in all of the cases dealing with the Clean Air Act; if the judges are voting on the basis of policy preferences in these cases, then their preferences cannot be determined by their general ideological orientations. For instance, in the six CAA cases where the court ruled in favor of the national government, there is little indication that judicial deference to the government shifted depending upon whether an individual judge favored a more or less active approach to government regulation. In one instance, liberal judges argued in dissent that the power of the national government to enforce environmental policy had to be restrained by the criminal law provisions of the Bill of Rights—a clear case of legal commitments trumping policy preferences.[89] One unanimous decision upheld government regulatory power over the legalistic objections of General Motors,[90] another more recent case (with Souter in lone dissent) held that federal law pre-empted some of

---

[88] *Alaska Department of Environmental Conservation v. EPA*, 540 U.S. 461 (2004)

[89] *Dow Chemical v. USA*, 476 U.S. 227 (1986.)

[90] *General Motors Corporation v. United States*, 496 U.S. 530 (1990)

California's more rigorous clean air regulations.[91] Similarly, in 2004, the Court ruled unanimously against the claim that the EPA must be required to exercise its authority over cross-border transportation operations between Mexico and the United States.[92] These unanimous (or near unanimous) decisions indicate that, while the American political system provides considerable opportunity for judicial intervention into environmental policy, the ways in which judges choose to challenge (or not challenge) government decisions is not determined by their individual assessment of environmental regulation alone. A closer look at several examples of American appeals court decisions that address the Clean Air Act will help to illustrate how the division of powers in American politics and the nature of statutory law-making affect the role of courts in the environmental policy process.

Whitman v. American Trucking Association[93] reveals how distinctly legal factors shape the response of American courts to questions in environmental policy. The case originated in disputes over the Clean Air Act's "national ambient air quality standards," or NAAQS.[94] These standards establish the maximum amount of pollutants allowable in the air, standards that are developed and enforced by the EPA. The interpretation and implementation of NAAQS has been a central problem in environmental law, because a great deal of uncertainty has been built into the relevant statutory framework.[95] As a consequence, this aspect of American environmental policy has been subjected to considerable judicial scrutiny. In this case, however, the Supreme Court was presented with a challenge not merely to the implementation NAAQS, but a challenge to the validity of the

---

[91] *Engine Manufacturers Association/ Western States Petroleum Association v. South Coast Air Quality Management District*, 541 U.S. 246 (2004)

[92] *Department of Transportation v. Public Citizen et al.*, 541 U.S. 752 (2004)

[93] *Whitman v. American Trucking Association*, 531 U.S. 457 (2001)

[94] For a discussion of the development of the Clean Air Act, see Marc Allen Eisner, *Governing the Environment: The Transformation of Environmental Regulation.* Boulder: Lynne Rienner Publishers, 2007. pp 18-23.

[95] Daniel J. Fiorino, *The New Environmental Regulation.* MIT Press: Cambridge, 2006. pp 208-209.

underlying law. Specifically, the American Trucking Association and the other parties to the case claimed that the Clean Air Act unconstitutionally delegated legislative power to the EPA administrator.

To challenge the delegation of legislative power to the executive is in many ways to challenge the basis of the post-New Deal administrative state.[96] According to some liberal commentators, the attempt to limit delegation of legislative power to bureaucracies is part of a larger project that aims to return the "Constitution in Exile," the jurisprudential regime that once placed significant limits not only on the ability of Congress to blur the lines between creating law and enforcing it, but also limited the scope and ambitions of the national government as a whole.[97] Thus, the various industries involved in this case were not merely challenging the EPA, but were raising some basic constitutional challenges to the modern administrative state.[98]

The non-delegation doctrine was based on the premise that the powers given to branches of government could not be given to other individuals, groups, organizations, or (most relevant here) other branches of government The rule made a good deal of sense—after all, legislators are elected to create laws, not to create new legislatures, however much this might help them focus on more pleasing tasks such as campaign fund raising. In times when the responsibilities of government were rather limited, as in the 19th century United States, the non-delegation doctrine was rarely employed by courts because legislators rarely attempted to delegate power.[99] When the problem of delegation of power was raised, (for instance, in relation to tariff setting

---

[96] For a succinct summary of the issue, see David H. Rosenbloom, "Retrofitting the Administrative State to the Constitution: Congress and the Judiciary's Twentieth Century Progress." *Public Administration Review*. Vol. 60, No. 1 (Jan. 2000) pp 39-46.

[97] For an overview of the debate over the New Deal's relationship to the Constitutional order, see William Forbath, "The New Deal Constitution in Exile." *Duke Law Journal*. Vol. 51, No.1 (Oct., 2001) pp 165-222.

[98] David Schoenbrod, *Power without Responsibility: How Congress abuses the people through delegation*. New Haven: Yale University Press, 1993.

99 See Rabkin, *Judicial Compulsions*, pp 11-12.

decisions that could not be easily made on a case-by-case basis by Congress as a whole), courts usually required that Congress had only to determine a practical principle that could guide executive decision making.

In the early 20th century, the increased significance of bureaucratic rule-making in the modern administrative state raised questions about whether the means employed by progressive reformers were compatible with traditional standards of legality and American constitutionalism. By the end of the 1930s, the court had shown that it was willing to be more deferential when reviewing Congressional delegations of power to the executive branch.[100] But the non-delegation doctrine has re-emerged in recent years, after an almost century-long hiatus.

In the case of *Whitman v. American Trucking Association*, the circuit court for the District of Columbia had used the non-delegation doctrine, or at least a version of it, to challenge the ways in which the EPA had interpreted its responsibility to establish air quality standards. Under the Clean Air Act, Congress gave the EPA the responsibility to set standards for ozone and particulate matter "requisite to protect the public health" and with an "adequate margin of safety." In is 1997 revisions of the "national ambient air quality standards" (NAAQS) for ozone, the EPA decided to reduce the allowable "parts per million" (ppm) from 0.08 to 0.07. In American law, litigation has sprung from things even smaller than one-one hundredth of a part per million of ozone. The question was whether Congress could allow an executive branch bureaucracy to change "the law" in this way.

In an opinion by Judge Williams, joined by Judge Ginsburg and in part by Judge David Tatel, the D.C. Circuit Court of Appeals ruled that the EPA had not provided an intelligible principle for reducing the allowable ppm's.[101] Section 109 of the Clean Air Act states that the standards must be set at a level "requisite to protect the public health" with and "adequate margin of safety." The EPA had determined that ozone was definitely a "non-threshold" pollutant—that is, a pollutant that has adverse health impacts at any level. Given this fact, it was

---

[100] See David Schoenbrod, "The Delegation Doctrine: Could the Court Give it Substance?" *Michigan Law Review*. Vol. 98, No. 2 (April, 1985) pp 1223-1290.

[101] *American Trucking Association v. EPA*, 175 F.3d 1027 (1999).

necessary for the EPA to provide an explanation of their decision to reduce the ppm level. As Judge Williams put it, "here it is as though Congress commanded the EPA to select 'big guys,' and the EPA announced that it would evaluate candidates based on height and weight, but revealed no cut-off point. The reasonable person responds 'how tall? how heavy?'" Yet a reasonable person might also question how Williams' critique relates to non-delegation doctrine.

Williams used the "non-delegation doctrine" in this case to question an administrative agency's interpretation of a statute, not to challenge the way Congress had delimited the responsibilities of the agency. Under this new guise, the non-delegation doctrine was used not to constrain or prevent delegations of power by Congress, but rather to prevent "unprincipled" or arbitrary decisions made by administrative agencies. In effect, the court was telling the agency that the violation of the non-delegation doctrine could be avoided if the agency adopted the principles that Congress had failed to provide it. In order to be "principled," however, the agency would have to explain to the court why it had adopted the 0.07ppm standard as opposed to 0.08, or 0.09, or "0," or "killer fog" levels of pollution.

The decision of the D.C. Circuit court was in many ways typical of a certain strain of modern judicial conservatism that aims to restrict the modern state without returning to the standards of pre-New Deal jurisprudence. The non-delegation doctrine was not resurrected in its pre-New Deal form in this case. Instead, the courts adopted a somewhat curious approach: the law was not an unconstitutional delegation of legislative power in itself, but was only un-Constitutional as interpreted by the EPA. Of course, had the court adopted a more strict approach[102] to the non-delegation doctrine, the implications would have been far more severe. If courts were to require Congress to do all of the rule-making currently undertaken by federal agencies, then the entire

---

[102] Admittedly, it is not entirely clear that there was a consensus approach to the non-delegation doctrine even prior to the new deal. Nevertheless, some of the earliest decisions by the Supreme Court that struck down aspects of the New Deal (such as ALA *Schecter Poultry Corp. v. United States,* 295 U.S. 495 (1935) were unanimous, and not merely a consequence of Four Horsemen of Laissėz-Faire standing in the path of progress. The *Schecter* case involved the delegation of legislative power to private groups, however, not the executive branch, which might have explained the outcome in this case.

structure of the modern administrative state would (potentially) be thrown into disarray.[103] By interpreting the non-delegation doctrine as simply a demand for "principles" in the rule-making process, the circuit court must have hoped to place restrictions on the scope of administrative discretion and arbitrariness without initiating a Constitutional counter-revolution.[104]

The appeals court concluded that the EPA had to assume the responsibilities of a legislature; that is, the court required that the executive establish its own principles for action that Congress had neglected to provide. Some would conclude that this decision can easily be explained under "attitudinalist" model of judicial making. This may be the case, but the most relevant attitude or preference in this case is not the judge's views of environmental policy, but rather his view on the form that law and policy should take: the law should be principled, and if the legislature will not make laws that reveal principles, then executive agencies must take this burden upon themselves.

The U.S. Supreme Court's decision in *Whitman* was shaped more by considerations of the relationship between Congress and the executive branch, as opposed to policy outcomes. The Court upheld Congress' delegation of legislative power to the EPA, while at the same time it questioned whether the EPA could consider the costs of environmental regulation. Essentially, the Court held that Congress can absolve itself from the responsibility of considering the costs of environmental legislation, and in doing so it can also prevent the executive branch from assuming that responsibility. The opinion upholding this peculiar policy arrangement, which made certain that neither the legislature nor the executive should consider the costs of a national policy, was penned by Justice Antonin Scalia. Scalia's opinion (joined by Rehnquist and Thomas, in addition to Ginsburg, Kennedy, O'Connor, and Breyer) is best interpreted not as a consequence of his

---

[103] See John F. Manning, "The Non-Delegation Doctrine as a Canon of Avoidance." *The Supreme Court Review*, Vol. 2000, (2000) pp 223-277.

[104] The decision is therefore similar to the Supreme Court's recent federalism decisions, which place some restraints on national power (particularly in regards to Congressional power over state government) without returning to the pre-New Deal understanding of the commerce clause. *United States v. Lopez* 514 U.S. 549 (1995), *United States v. Morrison* 529 U.S. 598 (2000)

support for the particular policy, but rather as a result of his attempt to determine congressional intent.[105] Whether or not the policy arrangement is constitutional is a question that perhaps should have detained Justice Scalia longer. Whether the arrangement was politically wise is an easier to question to answer, at least for a conservative.

Can Congress prevent the executive from making decisions based on the costs of policy, while at the same time declining to make that calculation itself? The Court's opinion in *Whitman* suggests that this somewhat irrational outcome is constitutionally legitimate. In order to meet the Constitutional requirements of Article I, which vests the legislative power in Congress, Scalia suggested that Congress must carefully circumscribe executive discretion—in this case, by eliminating the discretion of the EPA to consider the costs of national regulation. The decision is based upon Scalia's conception of the proper function of Congress as a law-making body, and his conception of the proper relationship between Congress and the executive. That conception might be conservative in some ways, but it is a conservative interpretation of constitutional law, not environmental policy, that determines the outcome in this case.

Scalia's opinion is based on the fiction that Congress has not delegated legislative power in establishing the National Ambient Air Quality Standards policy. It is not surprising that the court was unwilling in this case to apply an expansive understanding of the non-delegation doctrine—though it is a sign that the prophecies about the return of the Constitution in Exile are surely exaggerated.[106] Yet it might be surprising to some that the "conservative wing" of the 2001 court showed no inclination to resurrect the pre-New Deal version of the non-delegation doctrine. Or rather, the conservative wing of the court signed onto the fiction that the non-delegation doctrine had never been abandoned, that there was no delegation of legislative power in

---

[105] Scalia's best argument against the administration's "spirited" attempt to rationalize environmental decision-making was that Congress, in other pieces of environmental regulation, had left no doubt when it wanted to grant executive agencies the power to take costs into account.

[106] Thomas Keck, *The Most Activist Supreme Court in History? The Road to Modern Constitutional Conservatism*. Chicago: University of Chicago Press, 2004.

this case, because the Court had rubber-stamped much vaguer laws in other circumstances.

Justices Stevens and Souter, in a concurring opinion, argued that the Court should simply stop pretending that agencies like the EPA have not been delegated "legislative power":

> The Court has two choices. We could choose to articulate our ultimate disposition of this issue by frankly acknowledging that the power delegated to the EPA is "legislative" but nevertheless conclude that the delegation is constitutional because adequately limited by the terms of the authorizing statute. Alternatively, we could pretend, as the Court does, that the authority delegated to the EPA is somehow not "legislative power." Despite the fact that there is language in our opinions that supports the Court's articulation of our holding, I am persuaded that it would be both wiser and more faithful to what we have actually done in delegation cases to admit that agency rulemaking authority is "legislative power.[107]

It is true that theoretical differences lie beneath the surface of the concurring opinions in this case. Stevens and Souter, for instance, argue that even though the Constitution lodges the "legislative power" in Congress, there is no explicit prohibition on the delegation of that power. Therefore, Congress can delegate that power to the executive branch (or, presumably, to private business associations, management consulting firms, etc.) as long as it provides "intelligible principles." Justice Thomas, while apparently accepting the fiction that no delegation of power has occurred in the case, was clearly uncomfortable with the courts broad deference to congressional delegations of power. But despite their clear theoretical differences, Stevens, Souter and Thomas ultimately agreed to support a policy whose "rationale" is that policy is best made with only minimal attention to cost and context. It is not even clear that non-conservatives could support such a policy. Yet in the context of legal decision-making—or rather, within the context of a legal tradition that combines

---

[107] Justice Stevens, concurring opinion, *Whitman v. United States Trucking Association*, 531 U.S. 457.

deference to Congressional regulatory decisions, suspicion of executive discretion, and general indifference to the logic of the non-delegation doctrine—the decision was entirely predictable.

Ultimately, this kind of decision reflects a distrust of executive power that is produced by the structure of American institutions—the decision cannot be understood if looked at simply as a dispute over "preferences" in environmental policy. Distrust of executive discretion is much less evident in Canadian courts, because the government is based upon the direct support of the legislature. Paradoxically, the American President, directly elected by the people, is subjected to more scrutiny because he is not directly dependent upon legislators. The form of judicial politics revealed in this case is a product not simply of the politics of the judges involved, but is instead a consequence of the institutional setting in which they operate. The preferences of the court are best characterized as a desire for "lawfulness" combined with deference to Congress' determination not to provide the principles necessary for the rule of law.

The complicated case of *New York et al v. EPA,*[108] decided by the D.C. circuit in 2005, provides a further example of how legal factors structure judicial decisions in complex and controversial cases. In this case, the EPA's 2002 interpretation of "new source review" (NSR) provisions in the Clean Air Act and its amendments was challenged by a variety of state governments, environmental interest groups, and industry representatives.[109] The NSR provisions in the Clean Air Act are meant to address problems that emerge from attempts to balance environmental improvements and economic efficiency. Under the Clean Air Act, the EPA can impose environmental standards on the construction of new plants, but it does not necessarily require existing plants to be retrofitted or scrapped if they fail to meet those standards. However, in order to limit the capacity of older sources of pollution to be maintained for extensive periods of time, the NSR provisions require that modifications to existing plants be subjected to review by the

[108] *New York et al v. EPA*, 367 U.S. App. D.C. 3; 413 F.3d (2005)

[109] For a discussion of the NSR provisions of the Clean Air Act, see Todd B. Adams, "New Source Review Under the Clean Air Act: Time for More Market-Based Incentives?" *Buffalo Environmental Law Review*. Vol. 8, No. 1, (Fall, 2000).

EPA, at least if those modifications lead to an increase in pollution. Interpreting these provisions is complicated, as Congress never defined "modification" or "increase in pollution." As a consequence, the EPA has been forced to defend its interpretation of NSR against challenges from industries, states, and environmental groups.[110]

In *New York v. EPA*, there were several sources of controversy over the EPA's 2002 interpretations of NSR. First, the EPA introduced new standards for interpreting the "baseline" of emissions from a source. In order to determine whether or not modifications of existing plants leads to increased pollution, the EPA must evaluate the amount of pollution that the source or plant currently emits. The Clean Air Act assumes that this is a relatively straightforward process, but in practice it is extremely complicated to find a useful standard for evaluating the pollution emitted during the production process.

On the one hand, it is possible to determine how much pollution is emitted during the production of any given unit of widget X. But the production of an individual unit cannot be the starting point for measuring increases in pollution, as differing plants will have differing levels of overall production—some will operate around the clock, some will sit dormant for long periods of time, etc. A temporal element has to be introduced to accurately measure the amount of overall pollution produced by the source. It isn't clear, however, what temporal frame should be used to evaluate the amount of pollution released by a production process, as patterns of production will vary from day to day, week to week, and year to year. In order to establish baseline standards for evaluating increases in pollution, in 2002 the EPA promulgated a rule which allowed firms to select any continuous 24 month period from the previous ten year period.

The EPA also changed the ways in which it measured increases in emissions. Once a baseline of emissions has been established, it is necessary to determine the amount by which proposed changes will increase emissions (if at all) in the production process. Based upon 1980 rule, the EPA had come to the conclusion that increases should be measured by the potential annual emission rate of the source, compared against the "baseline" period discussed above. In response, industry petitioners argued that this "actual to potential" test was invalid, as the

---

[110] For a further discussion of new source review, see Christopher McGrory-Klyza and David Sousa, *American Environmental Policy, 1990-2006: Beyond Gridlock*. Cambridge: MIT Press, 2008 pp 135-147.

1980 regulation provided that an "increase" in emissions occurs only if the maximum hourly emissions rate goes up as a result of the physical or operational change. The practical difference between the two interpretations was that, if the industry position was adopted, a plant might adopt technology that could produce the same amount of widgets while reducing emissions, but the overall emission rate might nevertheless increase due to increased overall production.

The EPA rule was upheld in court. But by 1992, the EPA wanted to introduce more flexibility into the regulatory process by abandoning the "actual to potential" rule. Instead, increases would be measured on the basis of projected emissions. More importantly, changes in emissions that resulted from demand-related increases in production would not be counted as "increases" in terms of NSR requirements. At first, the actual to projected test and the "demand growth exclusion" were applied only to utilities. By 2002, the "actual to projected test" and "demand growth exclusion" were adopted for all sources. Obviously, the expansion of these rules was very much in line with long-term commitment of the GOP to regulatory flexibility. From the perspective of many states and environmental groups it represented yet another example of the Bush Administration's indifference to the "rule of law."[111]

In addition to changing the standards for measuring past emissions and universalizing the actual to projected test and demand growth exclusion, the EPA also adopted several new exemptions to the NSR policy. In situations where changes were not anticipated to have any real possibility of increasing emissions, firms were exempted from certain onerous record keeping requirements. In addition, the EPA adopted several programs that, if followed, would exempt firms from NSR: the Plantwide Applicability Limitations ("PAL") program, the Clean Unit option, and the Pollution Control Project ("PCP") exemption.

As is usual in American politics, the new rules provoked lamentations and gnashing of teeth from all sides of the political spectrum. The outcome in the case does not reveal any obvious partisan or political influence, however. What the case does reveal is that the

[111] E.g Patrick Parenteau, "Anything Industry Wants: Environmental Policy Under Bush II." *Vermont Journal of Environmental Law*. Vol. 6, No. 1 (2004/2005).

structure of American law-making creates a situation in which judges are more likely to challenge executive discretion, not on the basis of their own policy preferences, but on the basis of their understanding of congressional law. This is, in its own way, just as troubling as an overtly "politicized" court. The court denied all of the petitions made by the industry, state government, and environmentalist petitioners, vacating only those provisions adopted by EPA in relation to the "Clean Unit Rule," "Pollution Control Projects," and record-keeping requirements. A closer look at the judges' reasoning in relation to these specific provisions reveal how legalism, not politicization, becomes a problem once judges have adopted a flexible conception of standing to sue.

The Clean Unit Rule was adopted by the EPA in order to prevent NSR from creating disincentives against the adoption of the "best available control technology" or "BACT." The rule stated that, if a firm has adopted BACT as part of plant modifications, then additional collateral emissions will not necessarily trigger NSR. Pollution Control Projects would be treated in a similar manner. The problem with these policies was that exemptions of this kind were not authorized by the Clean Air Act itself. As a consequence, the court ruled that even if it seemed irrational to conclude that the Clean Air Act mandated perverse incentives with anti-environmental consequences, the precise words of the statute were controlling. If those words mandated a policy approach that was manifestly irrational in the context of the broader goal of environmental protection, then the EPA was forced to accept an irrational policy.

In regards to other aspects of the law where the political stakes were much more apparent, such as the EPA's new interpretation of baseline emissions or the expansion of the "demand growth exclusion," the court found statutory justification for deference to the EPA's policy judgments. But the statute could not be stretched so far as to endorse the new exemptions proposed by the EPA, for the very simple reason that there were no discussions of exemptions in the Clean Air Act and its amendments. The court even seemed to endorse the policy-judgments made by the EPA regarding the perverse incentives of the Clean Air Act, in the very act of striking down those policies. While this is very much an example of "judicial activism," in the sense that the court invalidated the decisions of another branch of government, it is very difficult to say that this decision was motivated by the policy preferences of the judges. The most pressing policy issues were left untouched by the court. The outcome of the decision is better explained as an attempt by the court to enforce a strict conception of legality, and therein lies the problem. What we see here is not a politicized court, but a court that is committed to an abstract conception of the "rule of law," a strictness that does not take into account the limits of legality.

The kind of legality defended by the court is curiously one-sided. Judges approach the terms of congressional law with an almost Talmudic reverence, and are eager to constrain executive discretion within the terms of statutory language. When evaluating environmental statutes, judges (regardless of their political affiliations) overwhelming appear to be committed textualists; there is little evidence of either environmentalist ideology or libertarian economics leading judges to ignore the explicit language of law. But just as judges have, for the most part, been unwilling to adhere to the formal limits on judicial power contained in the Article III "case and controversy" requirements, courts have been unwilling to place formal limits on the scope of congressional power. Thus while environmental law decisions show that judges have not been co-opted by either environmentalism or free-market anti-environmentalism, they have been swept into the legislative vortex.

The cases I have discussed in this section—*Whitman v. American Truckers Association* and *New York v EPA*—reveal federal courts caught in a struggle not over policy, but a struggle over the role of the courts in the modern political state. While clearly political in some sense, it is also distinctively judicial politics, not simply partisan politics in robes. The key problem for the courts is determining the scope of judicial power. In cases such as *New York v. EPA*, Democratic and Republican appointees reached agreement over a broad range of complicated statutory issues. A similar dynamic is apparent in the unanimous Supreme Court decision in *Whitman*. What these cases illustrate is that the greater judicialization of American environmental law is more than a product of the greater ideological tensions in the American political system. The American political system itself—rooted in the separation of powers—has come to be a major source of judicialization.

The Judicialization of Environmental Policy in Canada: A Delayed Revolution?

There are many reasons to think that the role played by American courts in overseeing the details of environmental policy will not be replicated in Canada. Yet as we have also seen, Canadian courts have altered the law of standing in relation to environmental issues. With little or no help from parliamentary enabling legislation, Canadian courts have created a broad potential for citizens groups to challenge the details of environmental policy. But the opportunity to challenge policy should not be equated with success in the courtroom.

Michael Howlett has argued that even if the rules of standing were to be liberalized in Canada, it would not necessarily lead to the complete "judicialization" of environmental policy; that is, he suggested that environmentalists might not get the desired results from judges, even if they were granted their day in court. His reasoning was based primarily on the institutional differences between the Canadian and American regimes. In the United States, a combination of fragmented parties and separation of the legislative and executive branches creates a number of conditions which can promote judicial power. Legislators often have an incentive to enlist courts in their struggles with the executive branch, and it is often extremely difficult for legislators to respond to judicial statutory interpretations which they find uncongenial.[112] In Canada, there is no institutional separation between the executive and legislative branches; furthermore, the disciplined nature of the Canadian party system often makes it easier for legislators to respond to the statutory interpretations of judges. These institutional differences could probably be supplemented by cultural and historical factors, such as the United States' longer experience with judicial activism, the prevalence of "rights consciousness" and anti-statist libertarianism in America, etc. Yet if the rules of standing have proven so malleable, it is worthwhile to question whether institutional and cultural differences will be able to support the traditional deference of Canadian courts.

Judging by the cases which I have examined for this chapter, it seems clear that Canadian judges are still far less active challengers of administrative discretion that are their American counterparts. There

---

[112] Melnick, *Between the Lines*, pp. 8-13.

are perhaps some reasons to suspect that judicialization in Canada is beginning to follow the American model, albeit at a slower pace, and despite the remaining institutional and cultural differences between the two countries. Ted Morton, who has studied the development of judicial activism in Canada across a broad range of issues, argued that judicial activism is likely to extend into environmental policy. Judicial "values," not constitutional structure or constitutional language, will determine the role played by Canadian courts in governing the environment.[113] But, as we have seen by looking at the Supreme Court decisions dealing with environmental issues and lower appeals court cases dealing with environmental assessment, there are few signs that Canadian courts are playing, or are likely to play, a key role in the development of environmental policy. The courts have pursued a revolution in the ability of groups to participate in Canadian environmental policy, but judicialization has not led to many substantive challenges to the discretionary power of government in environmental policy.[114]

If we consider the actual successes of environmental interest groups, it is clear that the judicialization of Canadian environmental policy is proceeding at a glacial pace, if at all. We should not be surprised by the slow progression. In the United States, the judicialization of public policy through administrative law did not emerge all at once, fully formed like Athena from the head of Zeus. The starting point was the advent of the New Deal, which from a Constitutional perspective introduced the following changes: courts

---

[113] E.g. "While the Charter has had little direct impact on environmental policy, there is a consensus that Charter-inspired activism in other policy fields has spilled over into the Court's environmental docket, making the court more 'receptive' to legal challenges to government decisions...The new constitutional culture that has taken root around the Charter not only has legitimized judicial intervention in policy matters but also has devalued the principle of respect for provincial autonomy, heretofore the two most important restraints on judicial activism in the area of environmental jurisdiction." F.L. Morton, "The Constitutional Division of Powers with Respect to the Environment in Canada." in Kenneth Holland, et al., editors *Federalism and the Environment: Environmental Policymaking in Australia, Canada, and the United States*. Greenwood Press: Westport, Conn., 1996. pp 37-55 (p. 50).

[114] Boyd, *Unnatural Law*, pp 237-248.

appeared to abandon their traditional solicitude for "economic rights,"[115] they endorsed a "looser" understanding of the scope of national regulatory power under the commerce clause,[116] and they endorsed a broader role for the executive branch in policy-making, based upon the delegation of Congress' legislative powers.[117]

Courts did not simply wash their hands of administrative law and regulatory policy, however. Starting sometime in the 1960s—perhaps in response to the influence of well-organized interest groups on federal policy making[118]—judges began to open up access to the courts (i.e. they liberalized the rules of standing.) Shapiro refers to this as a shift from a "deferential" to a "pluralist" or "polyarchical" model of judicial decision-making.[119] Gaining access to the courts meant little if the applicants were unable to raise meaningful challenges to administrative decisions. For the process of administrative rule-making to be truly polyarchical, all power and information could not reside with the administrators. So judges started to spread power and information around.

In order to facilitate the polyarchical litigation process, courts began to expand upon the simple procedural rules found in the Administrative Procedure Act of 1946. Federal agencies were forced to not only notify the public of their intention to promulgate a new rule of regulation, but also to provide increased information regarding the need for the rule, and the grounds upon which they based their decision regarding the rule's content. Similarly, courts gradually became more willing to demand that agencies not merely receive comments from

---

[115] Hadley Arkes, *The Return of George Sutherland: Restoring a Jurisprudence of Natural Rights*. Princeton: Princeton University Press, 1994.

[116] Randy Barnett, "The Original Meaning of the Commerce Clause." *The University of Chicago Law Review*, Volume 68, Number 1, pp 101-147.

[117] David Schoenbrod, *Power Without Responsibility: How Congress Abuses the People Through Delegation* New Haven: Yale University Press, 1993.

[118] Theodore Lowi, *The End of Liberalism: The Second Republic of the United States*. New York: W.W. Norton Press, 1979.

[119] Shapiro, *Who Guards the Guardians? Judicial Control of Administration*. Athens, Ga.: University of Georgia Press, 1988.

interested parties, but also provide responses to those comments. These judge-made rules—what Shapiro refers to as "dialogue requirements"—still fit within a polyarchical model. The next stage of judicial decision-making emerged when courts required agencies to not simply provide responses, but to provide fully adequate, rationally justified responses. The next two steps moved beyond polyarchalism. First, courts began to demand that agencies respond not to all significant issues that were raised, but to all significant issues. Secondly, courts began to demand that the agencies prove that they reached the correct or most rational regulatory decision. Shapiro refers to this final stage as "synoptic rationalism."

There are few indications that Canadian federal courts will march down the path towards "synoptic rationalism" in environmental policy. But there are some indications. First, some Canadian judges have challenged the statutory interpretations of administrative decision makers. Secondly, there are indications that some Canadian judges are willing to challenge the scientific bases of administrative decision makers as well, in emulation of the "hard look" doctrine propagated by American courts. Examples of these two modes of judicialization are relatively sparse. The groundwork has been laid for Canadian courts to move from a "polyarchical" to a "synoptic-rationalist" model of decision-making. It is true that the Canadian Parliament will usually have more capacity to respond to judicial statutory constructions that finds uncongenial, especially in comparison with its American counterparts. It is unlikely that Canadian environmental policy will experience the same levels of judicialization as American environmental policy. But changes in the law of justiciability make it possible that, in the future, Canadian courts will not be as deferential to governments in environmental policy.

Some Canadian judges are developing the legal tools necessary to expand the power of courts to intervene into environmental policy. One crucial theme in the federal court's environmental law cases over the past two decades is the absence of any clear distinction between "judicial review based upon statutory interpretation" and "judicial review based upon 'hard looks' at facts/scientific evidence." Canadian judges almost never directly challenge the scientific bases of administrative decisions. Though courts immerse themselves in the minutiae of environmental assessments, such open exercises in policy analysis are usually resolved in favor of the government. However, it is often quite easy for judges to re-interpret factual disputes as disagreements over the meaning of statutes. While judges seem to doubt their capacity to examine scientific findings, they are more confident in their ability to interpret the law.

A good example of how factual disputes are transformed into statutory disputes can be seen in the Federal Trial Court decision in *Friends of the Oldman River Society v. Canada.*[120] This case illustrates that judicialization does not occur simply when judges challenge scientific evidence. The collapse of the rules of standing permit judges to exercise control over the discretion of administrative officials, despite the fact that judges need not go far beyond the letter of the law to do this.

Friends of the Oldman River Society v. Canada dealt with final federal authorization of a dam construction project in Alberta, the planning for which had begun in the 1950s. By May of 1987, the federal government had reached an agreement with the province not to make any claims of jurisdiction over the dam project, thereby avoiding federal duplication of the already extensive environmental review process. By March of 1989, the dam was 40% complete. In April of that year, the Friends of the Oldman River Society filed a motion for certiorari to quash the Minister of Transportation's approval of the project, on the grounds that the minister had failed to comply with the environmental assessment and review process guidelines order (EARPGO.) The Friends of the Oldman River were basically claiming that the federal decision to abstain from conducting further environmental assessments was illegal.

This case illustrates that the problem of judicialization is often not the result of judges moving beyond the letter of the law, but is instead the result of strict adherence to statutory constraints in regards to policy decisions that do not affect private rights. In other words, judicialization emerges from a kind of misguided legalism, that is, the belief government decisions must be constrained by courts even when those decisions do not affect individual rights . Before judges can use legalism to hamper executive discretion, they need to allow the rules of standing to erode so that they no longer pose a significant barrier to access. Once this has occurred, judges are well-positioned to impose

[120] *Friends of the Oldman River Society v. Canada* 2 F.C. 18 • (1990), 68 D.L.R. (4th) 375.

strict legality upon government actions. In enforcing legalism, judges are supported several crucial myths. The first is the myth that all executive action must be in strict accordance with the letter of "the law," regardless of whether or not the departure from law affects individual rights. The second myth is that "the law" provides clear indications of the scope of executive discretion. The third myth is that public-interest groups are entitled to enjoin enforcement of the law, even when there are no private rights at stake.

In *Friends of the Oldman River Society v. Canada*, the trial judge could have dismissed the application on the grounds that the applicant was simply moving a policy dispute into a legal arena. No individual or property rights were at stake; the Friends of the Oldman River were simply perturbed that the government of Canada was not exercising the full scope of its own powers. Instead, the trial judge simply assumed that the applicants had standing; there is literally no discussion of the issue at all in the decision. In the end, the judge dismissed the application of Friends of the Oldman River society, yet his reasoning was far from water-tight. Indeed, if one accepts that public-interest groups have the right to enforce strict legalism upon government decision-makers, one would probably have to accept that the trial judge erred in this case.

Simplifying for the sake of brevity, the trial judge concluded that the EARPGO was not applicable to the decision to approve the dam. Alberta's application for approval was made under section 5(1) of the Navigable Waters Protection Act, an act which made no reference to environmental assessments. The judge concluded that the Minister of Transportation was only required to take navigation issues into account when assessing the dam project. A further legal issue was whether or not the Department of Fisheries and Oceans had to undertake an environmental assessment in relation to this project, given that it was not an "initiating department" faced with a "project" (i.e. the project was being undertaken by the Alberta government, not the government of Canada.) Essentially, the trial judge gave an extremely narrow reading of the EARPGO, a reading which caused this statute to be subordinated to other statutes such as the Navigable Waters Protection Act, a reading which implied that only a fairly narrow range of ministerial decisions should be subject to the environmental assessment process.

This narrow reading of the EARPGO was frankly implausible. The statute is meant to be of broad application: all decisions and authorizations made by federal ministers should be able to trigger the environmental assessment process, not merely a decision to directly engage in the construction of dams. Secondly, the EARPGO would have been meaningless if it could only come into effect when directly incorporated in other statutes. The appeals court—which upheld the application of the Friends of the Oldman River Society—gave a much more plausible reading of the scope and intention of the EARPGO. Their reasoning was fairly straightforward. EARPGO is triggered whenever a federal minister makes a decision which is likely to have a significant impact upon an area of federal jurisdiction; the dam is likely to affect fisheries, Indians, and Indian lands; thus, the Ministry of Fisheries and Oceans and the Minister of Transportation must conduct a federal environmental assessment.

This plausible statutory reading hides the fact that the court's decision still rested on contestable interpretations of the facts. The appeals court had many opportunities to defer to the federal authorities. The simplest way would have been to accept the federal government's contention that the dam posed no significant threat to an area of federal jurisdiction. This decision of the federal ministers to accept the validity of the provincial environmental assessment process, a process that had been going on for years if not decades, was certainly not beyond the bounds of rationality. Once the court had asserted its own version of the facts—i.e. the potential impact upon fisheries, Indians, and Indian lands—it was quite easy for the appeals court to maintain that they were simply enforcing the letter of the law when they demanded the federal government to conduct another environmental assessment.

There were several other opportunities that the court could have taken in order to rule in the government's favor. The application of the 1984 EARPGO legislation to a dam project initiated decades earlier was a retroactive application of the law. The extremely late filing date of the motion (recall that the dam was almost half completed) would under most circumstances have been regarded as a reasonable grounds for dismissal. What cases of this kind illustrate is that the image of a deferential Canadian federal court is incomplete, as judges can judicialize public policy without appearing to move beyond their traditional focus upon statutory interpretation into the realm of "hard looks" at scientific evidence. The appeals court did not have to engage in a wild deconstructive reading of federal statutes in order to rule in favor of the Friends of the Oldman River. In this case, the judges had in some ways a plausible legal basis for intervening into a highly complex area of federal-provincial negotiations. But such intervention is only legitimate if we assume that old rules of standing are no longer legitimate, an assumption that is dubious despite being widely accepted.

The rules of standing were meant to prevent abstract legal claims from trumping political prudence, and they were based on the insight that the rule of law does not require us to ignore the theoretical and practical difficulties of legalism. Though it may seem that the courts are simply following the law in this case, we should consider whether attention to legalism is of any value when it is divorced from any concern with concrete private rights. The rules of standing were meant to insure (amongst other things) that the discretion of government officials would be restrained only when government actions actually affect individuals, their rights, and their property. The reason that the ultimate responsibility for the execution of laws is entrusted to elected officials is that the execution of public policy cannot and should not be a mechanical process. General laws can never anticipate the multiplicity of particular situations in which they must be applied, and cabinet officials are entrusted to adjust the laws to those circumstances, provided that they do not infringe upon individual rights. The practical judgment of elected officials is needlessly hampered, however, once groups are able to dispute those judgments, not because their rights have been violated, but because they hold a different (and often idiosyncratic) vision of the public good. Thus Michael Howlett was wrong when he asserted that liberalized rules of standing would be unlikely to judicialize Canadian environmental policy. Liberalized rules of standing allow judges to wrest control of public policy from responsible officials, despite the fact that judges claim they are only following the law when doing so. Judicialization can occur even when judges refrain from imposing "new rights," even when judges refrain from conducting "hard looks" at scientific evidence that they are typically not qualified to evaluate. Once the rules of standing have been liberalized, judges can judicialize public policy simply by applying the black letter of the law. This will seem desirable only to those who regard legalism as the supreme political value.

In addition to using statutory interpretation as a vehicle for asserting control over public policy, Canadian federal courts have shown that they are prepared to adopt some version of the American "hard look" doctrine. As mentioned in the previously discussed case, disputes over facts can sometimes be disguised as disputes over the meaning of statutes. Federal judges have indulged in direct, ad-hoc analyses of scientific evidence on some occasions. Such analyses do not often lead judges to overturn administrative decisions, but we can presume that a familiarity with factual analysis will eventually yield more confident judicial edicts on the meaning of those facts. At any rate, it is no longer true that Canadian judges restrict themselves to questions of law in cases that deal with environmental policy.

A few examples will suffice to illustrate how Canadian courts are moving beyond legal interpretation into the realm of factual analysis. *The Friends of the West Country Association v. Canada*[121] dealt with an authorization, granted by the Minister of Transportation, for the Sunpine Logging Company to construct bridges over two waterways in rural Alberta. After an initial screening process, ministry officials concluded that there was no risk of environmental harm from the project. The Friends of the West Country Association, disagreed. In their application, they contended that the initial screening process was conducted in an unlawful manner. The government argued, as we might expect, that the group was simply contesting the factual evidence and professional judgments of the Ministry of Transportation officials, and really had no legal right to contest the authorization.

The trial court judge, in ruling for the Friends of the West Country Association, argued that the Ministry of Transportation had failed to take into account the full range of possible environmental effects that might result from bridge construction. The idea that the effects of this proposal should be assessed in a broad manner was extracted by the trial judge from something called the "independent utility principle." According to this principle, if a given project (e.g. a bridge) has no worth ("independent utility") in itself, except as a means for accomplishing another project (e.g. logging) then the effects of the latter project should be considered in the assessment process. Of course, this principle was never actually enshrined in any parliamentary

---

[121] *The Friends of the West Country Association v. Canada;* 1997 CanLII 5107 (F.C.).

legislation. Guided by an esoteric reading of a single paragraph from a Supreme Court decision, as well as a pamphlet from the Canadian Environmental Assessment Administration, Judge Gibson felt confident in imposing the independent utility principle in this case. It would be difficult to imagine a more explicit example of judicial law-making, or a more worrying sign of the decline of deference amongst Canadian judges.

It is important to remember examples of the decline of judicial deference in Canadian environmental law are very rare. "Post-materialist" environmentalism has not supplanted the Canadian judiciary's traditional patterns of deference towards the federal government. Michael Howlett's thesis—that environmental policy is unlikely to be judicialized in Canada due to institutional constraints—and the Shapiro-Bzdera thesis—that federal courts tend to partisans of centralized government—find considerable support environmental law decisions in Canadian courts. The activism that the Court has shown in other areas of law has not been apparent in environmental policy.

Yet those same cases also show that there is a certain amount of flux in the Canadian court. Rules of standing have collapsed, which has allowed courts to exercise control over the execution of environmental policy without having to move beyond statutory interpretation. These cases also reveal that the primary battle lines in environmental policy are not between federal and provincial governments, but are instead between governments and interest groups. Courts are rarely given the opportunity to favor the federal government over the provincial government, and when such conflicts arise, the federal government is not the invariable winner. The willingness of federal courts to respect federal-provincial bargaining in regards to environmental policy may be wavering, however. The collapse of the rules of standing, and the combination of ambiguous legislative standards and utopian legislative aspirations, provides fertile ground for the further cultivation of judicial power.

The transformation of the laws of standing in relation to Canadian environmental policy reveals that institutions do not fully determine the nature of judicial power. It is also interesting to consider why the Canadian Government itself continues to accept the judicially-created policy of private attorneys general. Perhaps Canadian governments accept a mild level of judicialization in order to create a façade of participation in governmental decision making. No elected official would echo my argument against the legitimacy of "public interest" litigation; it would seem authoritarian, despite the fact that it is implicit in the very structure of responsible government. Yet in the long run it is dangerous for governments to rely on the public's firm belief in the mystique of law and courts. If Canadian courts increase their interference with the details of environmental policy, the federal government will find it very difficult to challenge the legitimacy of judicial decision making, even if those decisions have moved beyond the law. But thus far, the influence of the Supreme Court, so prominent in Canadian Indian policy, has not been extended to environmental policy. Canadian judges have given environmentalists their day in court, but in terms of ultimate outcomes in environmental policy, Canadian courts have not directly challenged the authority of elected governments.

In contrast with the United States, the Canadian judiciary has had little influence over the development of environmental policy. The absence of environmentalism activism in Canada—in particular, the absence of detailed judicial oversight over the interpretation of environmental laws—illustrates how institutions constrain judicial power. In the United States, the tensions between Congress and the Presidency have produced a system of environmental policy that, due to a combination of statutory inflexibility and distrust of executive power, remains a paradigmatic case of "judicialization." Despite the recognition of the problems of "judicialized" environmental policy, it has proven very difficult for American political leaders to craft an alternative. While the Canadian political system is unlikely to create a judicialized form of environmental policy, the American political system often seems unable to escape it.[122] This has little to do with the political proclivities of judges. The opportunities available to judges to influence environmental policy are shaped much more decisively by the institutional arrangements of the two nations.

---

[122] Daniel J. Fiorino, *The New Environmental Regulation*. Cambridge, Mass.: MIT Press, 2006. pp 27-59.

CHAPTER FIVE: CONCLUSION

This study has attempted to assess the constraints imposed on judicial power institutional differences--what I have called "constitutional architecture." The central conclusion is that differences in constitutional language and executive-legislative organization between Canada and the United States, not merely the political differences between the Canadian and American judiciary, impose different constraints on judicial power. This is not to revert to a purely legalistic interpretation of judicial decision-making. Rather, my argument is that institutional differences create differing opportunities for political jurisprudence.

In Canada, the adoption of the Constitution Act of 1982 paved the way for a court-led revolution in Indian policy, as the document included new and expansive protections for Indian rights without clarifying the content of those rights. The specific intentions of the framers were unclear, but the desire to "judicialize" this area of public policy was not. The United States has not experienced any similar constitutional modifications in the area of Indian rights, and as a consequence, judicial decisions in American Indian law operate in a framework that accords fewer possibilities for aboriginal rights activists. Within this framework, there are some clear differences between conservative and liberal justices on the American Supreme Court. But on the whole, both liberal and conservative justices on the American Supreme Court have adopted a more constrained conception on the scope of aboriginal rights and aboriginal sovereignty.

This is not to say that the development of Canadian Indian law over the past two decades was *determined* by the Constitution Act or by the specific intentions of its framers. It is difficult to determine if the framers of the Constitution Act even had a clear conception of exactly how Section 35 of the Constitution Act would affect the relationship between First Nations and the provincial and federal governments of Canada. The intentions of constitutional framers can be obscure, even when the framing has occurred in living memory. It is undeniable, however, that the language of Section 35 limits the power of the national and provincial governments to alter and abridge aboriginal rights and the treaty rights of Indian tribes. The justices of the Supreme Court of Canada can make a good case that the Constitution Act calls for judicial activism in the field of Indian affairs. This is not to say that the decisions of the court have always been wise. But the Court's activism in this area is a product of constitutional, not judicial, supremacy. At the very least, the judicial activism in Indian policy could not have occurred without the decisions of other political actors

The activism of the Canadian court in Indian law does not necessarily support the "Court party" thesis, advanced by Canadian critics of judicial power which suggests that the jurisprudence of the court has been shaped largely by interest-group pressure and the influence of the left-leaning Canadian legal academy. The court has used Section 35 to advance the interests of aboriginal litigants in many important cases, but it has not endorsed the visions of aboriginal sovereignty that command near unanimous support amongst academics, aboriginal leaders, and even government experts who deal most closely with aboriginal affairs.[1] This suggests that the connection between the courts and the national government—the "centralization thesis"—plays a considerable role in limiting judicial activism. Or, alternatively, it may provide further evidence in support of Ran Hirschl's "juristocracy thesis": courts are willing to transform policy in regards to many social issues, but they are unlikely promote those aspects of the progressive agenda that threaten the interest of economic and political elites.[2] It is important not to miss the forest for the trees, however. The Canadian Supreme Court has not re-defined the relationship between Indian tribes and the Canadian polity as a relationship between separate sovereigns. But it *has* transformed the meaning and scope of aboriginal and treaty rights, by adopting both an evolutionary understanding of treaty agreements and through novel approaches to the use of evidence. This judicially managed transformation of Indian law was not dictated by the Constitution Act of 1982, but for, better or worse, Section 35 of the Constitution Act authorized this transformation by judicializing this area of public policy. The more limited success of Indian litigants in the American Supreme Court is a consequence of the more limited

---

[1] For discussion of the near unanimity of the aboriginal rights establishment, manifested most prominently in the Canadian government's 1996 *Royal Commission on Aboriginal Peoples*, see Thomas Flanagan *First Nations? Second Thoughts*. pp 5-10.

[2] Hirschl, *Towards Juristocracy* pp 213-214.

protections for aboriginal rights in the Constitution of 1787—not simply a result of the more conservative character of American justices.

In contrast, the differences between parliamentary and Presidential-Congressional government help to explain the contrasting approach to environmental law adopted by Canadian and American courts. Canadian courts have transformed many of the *procedural* aspects of environmental decision-making, particularly in regards to the law of standing. But Canadian courts have typically refrained from challenging the statutory interpretations and scientific conclusions of environmental policy makers. Thus, while the values of what might be called legal pluralism or even participatory democracy have opened Canadian courts to environmentalist claimants, Canadian courts have rejected substantive environmentalist claims. In the United States, the transformation of procedure in environmental law has more often lead to a transformation in the substance of environmental policy. This is because American political institutions, particularly the separation of powers, create greater space for judicial intervention into environmental policy. When American courts adjudicate environmental policy, they typically encounter not "the government" but rather a conflict within government, conflicts between the often vaguely-expressed intentions of Congress and the decisions of the executive branch. Despite the impact of the *Chevron* decision, American courts are still more likely than Canadian courts to justify intervention into environmental policy-making based upon the tension between legislative intent and executive decision-making.

The absence of environmental activism by the Canadian court is an anomaly for those scholars who view judicial decision-making through a political or ideological lens. Judged by its decisions in Indian law but also in areas related to gay right, women's rights, and criminal rights, the Canadian court has been liberal or left-leaning in the post-Charter era.[3] Why has this liberal trend not been extended to environmental law decisions? It is difficult to believe that this is simply because of the idiosyncratic policy preferences of the judges—particularly when a broad number of Canadian trial and appellate courts judges have all rejected the substantive claims of environmentalist litigants. The

---

[3] Though, of course, never leftist enough for those still waiting for the revolution. E.g. Joel Bakan *Just Words: Constitutional Rights and Social Wrongs*. Toronto: University of Toronto Press, 1997.

simplest explanation is that the legal and institutional conditions for judicial activism in environmental law do not exist in the Canadian political system. In particular, the institutional dependence of the government on the legislature in a parliamentary system makes it difficult for courts to claim that executive branch decisions have departed from legislative intent. Canada's constitutional transformations have increased the power of the courts to protect certain spheres of individual rights, but judging by the case of environmental policy, the capacity and willingness of courts to make policy through statutory activism remains largely unchanged. I have also suggested that a purely political perspective cannot fully account for the pattern of environmental law decisions in American appellate courts, though this claim is not central to my overall argument. What is central is the fact that American judges, in contrast with their Canadian counter-parts, are more likely to intervene into the details and substance of environmental policy-making.

The conclusions of this study have important implications for those scholars who are interested in what courts do and how they make their decisions, and for those citizens and scholars who are interested in what courts should (or should not) be doing. The contrasting roles of Canadian and American courts in Indian and environmental law challenges the views of those who regard the court decisions as being largely a consequence of the ideological preferences of justices. Environmentalist litigation has limited success in Canada, and Indian rights litigation has had considerable success, not simply because of the values and preferences of Canadian judges, but because of the constitutional and institutional features of the Canadian regime. The contrasting experience of environmentalist and Indian litigants in the United States provides support for this claim. For the remainder of this conclusion, I will assess how these findings relate to other comparisons of judicial power in Canada and the United, and consider some possible implications and areas for future research. I will also explain how attention to the constitutional and institutional limits on judicial power might help to shape political debate over the legitimacy of political jurisprudence and judicial activism.

The case of gay and lesbian rights, for instance, appears to provide support for those who regard judicial ideology and cultural differences as the primary causes of disparate outcomes in Canadian and American jurisprudence. Over the last decade, Canada has experienced a judicial transformation in gay rights related to matters such as employment and marriage. Gay rights decisions in American courts have not gone as far in endorsing gay rights, and they have elicited far more political and legal opposition. James Pierceson explains the contrasting development of gay rights in Canada and the United States as a consequence of cultural differences between the two nations, emphasizing in particular the richer liberalism that has come to dominate Canadian political culture, a liberalism that endorses a broader notion of equality than the negative liberalism that predominates in the United States.[4] Despite these differences, Pierceson suggests that the case of gay rights illustrates a new dynamic in North American constitutional law. While influence in constitutional doctrine has usually flown south to north, Pierceson argues that American courts and American legal culture is likely to follow Canadian developments areas such as same-sex marriage, spousal benefits, adoption rights, and so forth.

Pierceson's analysis contrasts with the analysis of environmental and Indian law presented here because it explains different legal outcomes as a consequence of cultural differences. Furthermore, he argues that those legal differences are likely to decline as a consequence of cultural convergence. According to his argument, the "Canadianization" of gay rights litigation in the United States is driven by broader cultural changes, and depends primarily on the changing ideology of judges. Pierceson does not extend his analysis beyond the issue of gay rights, and does not consider whether or in what way the convergence of Canadian and American jurisprudence in gay rights is a sign of a broader trend. If, as I have argued, Canadian and American jurisprudence is not converging in environmental and Indian law, and if this is not likely to be affected by the general ideological predispositions of judges, what accounts for the case of gay rights jurisprudence?

One hypothesis is that the convergence of Canadian and American jurisprudence is most likely to occur in areas of law and policy that are most readily cognizable under the rubric of individual rights. In many instances, the kinds of questions that must be addressed by Canadian and American courts when dealing with individual rights (e.g. whether a given act is speech, whether a classification is a violation of equality

---

[4] Jason Pierceson, *Courts, Liberalism, and Rights: Gay Law and Politics in the United States and Canada*. Philadelphia: Temple University Press, 2006.

rights, etc.) are identical.[5] Environmental law cases in Canada differ from those in the United States because of tensions between executive action and legislative intent that emerge in the American context. Section 25 of the Charter and Section 35 of the Constitution Act cast a shadow over aboriginal law in Canada, one that is not present in American law. In the case of issues related to gay rights, the institutional or legal environment is essentially the same—both nations have provisions that guarantee equal protection of the law, and courts in both countries must consider in what instances legislatively-drawn categories violate equal protection. In regards to some equal protection issues, the debate in Canadian courts has been less contentious, not only because of the greater ideological unity of Canadian judges but also because the framers of the Constitution insulated affirmative action programs from equal protection challenges. But in both Canada and the United States, the meaning of equal protection of the law raises identical issues; the uncertainty over the meaning of equal protection creates the space for ideological divisions amongst judges.[6] The ultimate outcome of these judicial conflicts depends very much on the political forces which influence the court, whether in terms of public opinion, the ideological development of individual justices, or—most importantly—the appointment process. Indian law in the United States is not susceptible to political forces and ideology in the same way or to the same degree, and this is also true regarding environmental law in Canada.

The Supreme Court of Canada's gay rights jurisprudence raises questions about the legitimacy of judicial power, and this contrasts with the role of Canadian courts in Indian and environmental law. The Constitution Act empowers the Courts to intervene into Indian policy, and the court has done so; the Constitution Act changes nothing in regards to Canadian environmental policy, and Canadian courts have

---

[5] Ronald J. Krotozynski, Jr. *The First Amendment in Cross-Cultural Perspective*. New York: New York University Press, 2006 p. 4.

[6] The uncertainty over the meaning of equal protection of the law may arise as much from the limitations of the judges, as from the complexity of the questions they address. For a critique of the premises of gay marriage litigation, see Robert P. George, *In Defense of Natural Law*. Oxford: Oxford University Press, 1999 pp 276-287.

for the most part remained deferential to the environmental policy decisions of governments (especially the national government). Environmentalist litigants have achieved some successes regarding the procedures involved in environmental policy, but courts in Canada have not gone as far as American courts in challenging the substance and details of environmental policy. In endorsing the idea that gays and lesbians form a suspect class, the Court cannot rely on the specific intentions of the framers or the specific words of the Constitution Act and the Charter of Rights and Freedoms. Instead, they act as Philosopher-Kings, constitutional prophets, and comparative anthropologists, assaying the development of the world-spirit in order to push the Canadian polity along the path to enlightenment and true freedom; or at least, that is how conservative critics of the court would view it. And here the critics would be correct—to some extent. The court has certainly acted as the vanguard of the intelligentsia in endorsing gay rights, as have their liberal counterparts in certain American states. The intelligentsia, however, may well be leading the Canadian people. The gay rights decisions of the Court have not sparked public outcry, and the Court remains the political institution with the highest degree of public approval. The gay rights decisions of the Canadian Supreme Court rest on thin legal justifications, but it is difficult to say that the cases raise a counter-majoritarian problem.

Canadian gay rights jurisprudence nevertheless illustrates the "court party" thesis of Morton and Knopf, the idea that the judicial power is directed by judges and interest groups, not by the text of the Charter or the intentions of its framers. In the case of gay rights, the similarities between Canadian judges and their liberal counterparts in the American judiciary also suggests that a political interpretation, rooted in individual policy preferences of judges, is more useful in explaining this aspect of law than in the case of Indian and environmental law. Is this a sign that there is an emerging liberal, North American jurisprudence of *individual* rights? This is a possibility. Though gay rights decisions, and even to some extent decisions dealing with women's rights, raise acute cultural and religious controversies, they are in some ways *less* controversial from a legal perspective than many Indian and environmental rights claims, in which private groups attempt to direct public policy, place limits on the sovereignty of the state, assign access to natural resources based upon ethnicity, etc. Gay rights decisions deal with momentous moral questions, but from a legal perspective the claims are not so strange: they deal with *individuals* and their relationship to the state, in particular, the claims of individuals to have been denied a benefit, due to an arbitrary classification by the state. In dealing with controversies of this kind, differing judicial decisions are based upon differing assessments of what classifications are arbitrary. Those differences will not be affected by the institutional differences between Canada and the United States, but will instead be shaped by judicial ideology.

However, the evidence for the convergence of Canadian and (liberal) American jurisprudence in other aspects of individual rights is incomplete. Part of the problem is that the rights provisions of the Canadian and American constitutions do differ in some significant ways. Ronald Krotoszynski, in his comparative study of free speech jurisprudence, argues that the Canadian Supreme Court has occupied a middle ground between the libertarian "market place of ideas" model that dominates in American law, and post-war German jurisprudence in which freedom of speech has been subordinated to other values such as human dignity.[7] In his attempt to explain the Canadian Court's willingness to accept government limitation on free speech, Krotoszynski emphasizes the limits that have been built into the Charter of Rights and Freedoms itself—not so much the dead letter Section 33 "notwithstanding clause", but rather the Section 1 "reasonable limitations" clause, which allows the court to uphold limits on the rights of free speech, as long as those limits are justified according to the requirements of a free and democratic society.[8] Through Section 1, the Canadian Constitution endorses Felix Frankfurter's approach to freedom of speech, not the First Amendment absolutism of Hugo Black. As a consequence, the Canadian Court has given government considerable leeway to enact restrictions on speech in relation to hate crime, obscenity, and the content of commercial advertising.

The issue which Krotoszynski does not fully address is whether the "reasonable limits" clause leads to outcomes in Canadian jurisprudence

---

[7] Krotoszynski, *The First Amendment in Cross-Cultural Perspective.* New York: New York University Press, 2006.

[8] Janet Hiebert, *Limiting Rights: The Dilemma of Judicial Review.* Montreal-Buffalo: McGill-Queen's University Press, 1996.

that cannot be explained on the basis of ideology alone. Is the Canadian Supreme Court's perception of what constitutes a reasonable limit on free speech determined by party affiliation and ideological predispositions? Based on the limited range of cases addressed in *The First Amendment in Cross-Cultural Perspective*, the answer would seem to be no. However, one problem with evaluating the ideological aspects of free speech cases is that they raise issues that are not easily mapped onto a liberal-conservative continuum. For instance, in endorsing government prosecution of a prominent Native Canadian leader for anti-semitic ravings that violated hate crime laws, was the Court adopting a progressive or conservative agenda? What about the willingness of Canadian Courts to uphold anti-obscenity laws? Krotoszynski makes the case that the court's free speech jurisprudence tends to have conservative consequences. In accepting hate crime laws, the Court has also accepted the government's highly selective approach to hate crime enforcement: expressions of racial hatred made by marginal groups leads to prosecution, while equally inflammatory statements from government officials (particularly in Quebec) are left un-prosecuted. In accepting anti-obscenity laws, the Court has also accepted the disparate treatment that gay and lesbian publications receive from Canadian customs officials. We might be inclined to interpret the Canadian Supreme Court's willingness to uphold hate-crime and anti-pornography laws as part of a general progressive project, one that is fully consistent with the Court's gay rights jurisprudence. But the ideological issues are blurred. As is well known, conservative legal scholars have long argued against the expansive interpretations of First Amendment rights—perhaps less well known is the fact that conservative legal scholars are not only concerned with the ways in which First Amendment jurisprudence has been used as a shield for pornography and obscenity. Hadley Arkes, for instance, has argued that freedom of speech should not be extended to include group defamation, including the defamation of racial groups.[9] Krotosyznski has raised some interesting hypotheses about the consequences of Canadian free-speech cases, but further investigation—and a broader range of cases—is necessary to evaluate the ideological and political dimensions of free speech jurisprudence in Canada.

---

[9] Hadley Arkes, *The Philosopher in the City: The Moral Dimensions of Urban Politics* (Princeton: Princeton University Press, 1980) pp 23-56.

Such an investigation would have to focus on whether the judicial balancing promoted by Section One of the Canadian Charter has led Canadian courts to defer to government in a consistent way, or whether the deference shown by the court varies depending upon the political goals of speech regulations, or the characteristics of those whose speech is being regulated. Further comparative analysis of Canadian and American free speech jurisprudence is still necessary as well, as Krotozynski is too quick to accept the claim that American courts have accepted the Holmesian ``marketplace of ideas`` metaphor as their guide to free speech. American judges—at least, many of them—accept restrictions on freedom of speech in relation to political expression that are every bit as draconian as those imposed by the Canadian state. Furthermore, it may be the case that the attitudinal model may be particularly apt in explaining the hypocrisy of American free speech jurisprudence, in which liberal judges have endorsed restrictions on peaceful abortion protesters and conservatives endorse restrictions on political pamphleteering in supposedly private spaces such as shopping malls and housing developments.[10] It is still an open question whether Section One of the Charter, in allowing for reasonable limits on free speech rights, encourages a consistently deferential approach by Canadian Courts or whether it allows them to favor some groups over others.

Other studies have attempted to show how, much like in the case of freedom of speech, the specific features of the Canadian Charter of Rights and Freedoms have shaped post-Charter jurisprudence, thereby undermining the claims of those who argue that Canadian Courts have imposed judicial supremacy in the post-Charter era. James Kelly has argued that the Canadian Supreme Court, in supervising police conduct and the criminal process, has not simply aped the due process model of American jurisprudence developed during the Warren Era, but has instead maintained many aspects of the ``crime control`` model of criminal rights.[11] So, for instance, the court has adopted a version of the exclusionary rule that, in contrast with the general approach of

---

[10] Margaret Kohn, *Brave New Neighborhoods: The Privatization of Public Space*. New York: Routledge, 2004.

[11] James B. Kelly, *Governing with the Charter: Legislative and Judicial Activism and Framers' Intent*. (Vancouver: UBC Press, 2005) pp 107-110.

American courts, is less likely to lead to the exclusion of evidence as a remedy for procedural errors committed by police officers.

Canadian jurisprudence in the area of criminal rights is best characterized, according to Kelly, as being moderately activist, in that it recognizes, perhaps more adequately than American criminal rights jurisprudence, the need to balance the imperatives of crime control and due process when overseeing the actions of police and prosecutors. The liberalism on display in the Canadian Supreme Court's gay rights jurisprudence has been more qualified in the area of criminal rights. Similarly, and perhaps most surprisingly, the Canadian court has engaged in what might be called conservative or even libertarian activism in cases dealing with Canadian health policy. The differences between Canada's state-monopolized health care regime and the USA's mixed government-private system are great enough that a comparison of health care litigation is very difficult. The significance of the Court's activism in health care policy is worth considering, however, because it seems to contrast with the findings of this study in the area of environmental policy. The health care decisions of the court are an anomaly, because health care law seems to be more similar to environmental law than issues in gay law, aboriginal law, and criminal law, in that the Constitution Act and Charter did not create any specific rights related to health care. More specifically, and unlike the case of criminal rights discussed by Kelly, there are no indications that the framers of the Charter and Constitution Act thought that their constitutional innovations would affect the health care policy status quo. Why have Canadian courts challenged the statism of Canadian health care, in a way that promotes greater individual freedom and even threatens to undermine the state monopoly on health care, when it has refrained from endorsing the substantive goals of environmental litigants?

The answer may lie in the fact that, while the framers of the Constitution Act and Charter did not specifically consider the question of how these documents would affect health care policy, courts found it reasonable to extend enumerated rights to cover health policy related claims. That Canadian courts have not, for the most part, found the Constitution Act and Charter sufficiently flexible so as to encompass environmental rights is a good sign that the judiciary has not been captured by liberal litigants. In the case of *Waldman v. Medical*

Services of British Columbia[12] the Supreme Court of British Columbia found that the province's attempt to control the geographic dispersion of physicians in the province violated the equality and mobility rights protected by the Charter.[13] Similarly, in the case of *Chaolli v. Quebec*[14] the Supreme Court of Canada struck down two provincial statutes in Quebec that limited access to private health care, on the grounds that long waiting lists for medical treatment violated Quebec's Charter of Human Rights and Freedoms. The latter case is particularly interesting, in terms of the ideological dimensions of the case, because it is one of the few examples of judicial elaboration of the Charter in a way that protects economic rights from arbitrary government action. According to one of the Quebec appeals court judges who rejected Chaolli's claims, the Charter was not intended to protect economic rights of any kind—an interpretation that is probably correct, though one that also reveals the severe limits of the Charter as a statement of human rights. *Chaolli*'s challenge to the government health care monopoly may indicate an unexpected potential of Canadian jurisprudence to serve as a limit on Canadian statism. That this decision was reached by many of the same justices who endorsed expansive readings of aboriginal, criminal, and gay rights is yet another indication that, even if the court is driven by policy preferences, those preferences are not narrowly partisan or merely post-materialist.

A closer reading of the *Chaolli* decision reveals that libertarians should not hold their breath in anticipation of a Canadian economic rights revolution, however. The Court did not provide a principled justification for overturning the state health care monopoly—the kind of consideration that, in reflecting on the problem of state monopolies and restrictions on economic freedom in general, would have had implications for many other areas of public policy. Instead of reasoning

---

[12] *Waldman v. Medical Services of British Columbia*, 1997 CanLII 3113 (BC S.C.).

[13] Christopher Manfredi and Antonia Maioni, "Courts and Health Policy: Judicial Policy-Making and Publicly Funded Health Care in Canada." *Journal of Health Politics, Policy and Law.* Volume 27, Number 2 (April, 2002) pp 223-240.

[14] *Chaolli v. Quebec* (Attorney General) 1 S.C.R. 791 (2005)

on the basis of principles and rights, the Court engaged in a sort of ad hoc comparative policy analysis: because most other countries with public health care do not forbid private insurance and private provision of health care, and because this does not appear to have a deleterious effect on public health systems, the Quebec government is not justified in maintaining a health care monopoly which imposes long waiting times on patients. The arbitrariness of law is measured by the state of international public opinion and international public policy, not by the logic of individual rights. The three dissenting justices argued, hysterically, that the Chaolli decision was a northern version of the discredited, even demonic *Lochner v. New York,* a decision that would threaten Canadian values (presumably, envy, resentment, and lousy health care for the very ill.) But the decision was hermetically sealed off from principled reasoning, and thus its effects are likely to be felt only in the area of health care access. Those effects have already started to be felt, however: regardless of the decision's philosophical merits, it shows that the court is willing to challenge and even re-structure the most significant area of public policy in Canadian politics.

The pattern of Canadian jurisprudence in gay rights, criminal law, and health care litigation does not reveal a consistent ideological pattern—just as the court's activist Indian rights jurisprudence contrasts with its reticence in environmental law. The recent health care decisions undermine the centralization thesis, the idea that courts tend to reflect the political interests of the established regime. In addition, those decisions challenge the idea that Canadian jurisprudence is shaped solely by the supposedly collectivist and statist values of Canadian society. It is possible, of course, that the patterns of judicial decision making—bracketed by the liberal activism of the gay rights decisions, and the conservative activism of the health care decisions—reflect the idiosyncratic policy preferences of the Supreme Court, even if they do not reflect (at least not entirely) a partisan agenda. Is there any unifying theme to the activism of Canadian courts, if partisan ideology and "capture" by the "court party" fail to account for the various forms of activism and deference in Canadian jurisprudence? This is a possible area for future exploration, and one possible answer may lie in the way the views of judges are shaped, not by partisanship, but by their professional experiences as lawyers, and as member of international legal elites.

My central claim, however, is that whatever the role or sources of ideology and political preferences, the policy-making of courts is limited by constitutional language and political structure. Institutional differences explain why Canada has not had the experience of the judicialization of public policy through statutory activism. The convergence of judicial power in Canada and the United States has occurred in areas of law that deal with constitutionally protected individual rights, and this convergence requires both similarity between legal elites, and similarities in constitutional language. The differences that remain are most likely explained as consequence of the array of political forces in Canadian and American society that shape the ideological predispositions of Canadian and American Courts.

The debate over the legitimacy of judicial activism is enhanced by paying attention to the limits placed upon judicial power by legal and political institutions. Proponents of judicial power have come perilously close to suggesting that judges should not hesitate to impose their own conceptions of public policy, notwithstanding the evidence of the limits of judicial effectiveness in shaping significant social change. Critics of judicial power, particularly in Canada, have emphasized that the courts are already politicized, and are dominated by ideologies that are systematically biased in a liberal or left-leaning direction. The response of judges, for the most part, is that their decisions are guided by the law, not by their personal politics, and that those who object to judicial-policymaking actually object to constitutionalism. This is only a half-truth, but it is still a *half*-truth. The deference of Canadian courts in environmental policy illustrates that the courts do not simply march lock-step with the post-materialist intelligentsia. Environmental law decisions in the United States are more political in character (though, as I suggest, they are less political or at least less partisan than one might expect.) But the more activist character of American environmental law jurisprudence is a consequence of the institutional features of the American regime, most prominently, the endless tension between executive discretion and congressional intent. In Indian law, the claim that Canadian judges are guided by constitutional imperatives is not simply boilerplate. The Framers of the Constitution Act did not specify what policies they wanted to inaugurate in the area of Indian rights, but they clearly wanted—or at least agreed—to judicialize this area of public policy. In the absence of a similar constitutional imperative, American courts—and to a great extent, liberal American judges—have adopted a deferential approach to government decisions regarding aboriginal policy. Political jurisprudence will always exist, and the dream of a completely impartial judiciary will always be a dream. But political jurisprudence exists within legal and institutional limits, limits that are created by constitutional architecture, limits that have not been erased by judicial ideology.

APPENDIX A

INDIAN LAW CASES IN THE SUPREME COURT OF CANADA, 1985-2008 (OUTCOME= OUTCOME FOR INDIAN LITIGANT/INTERVENERS)

Case/Year	Subject	Outcome
Simon v. The Queen , 2 S.C.R. 387 (1985)	Are Indian hunting rights in Nova Scotia protected by 1752 treaty?	Win
.*Dick v. the Queen*, 2 S.C.R. 309 (1985)	Are hunting regulations applicable to Indians?	Loss
R. v. Horse, 1 S.C.R. 187 (1988)	Do Indians have hunting rights on private lands, whether under the i)Wildlife Act, or by virtue of ii) treaty ii)or aboriginal rights? (Custom/usage)	Loss
R v Sparrow, 1 S.C.R. 1075 (1990)	Did the Fisheries Act extinguish aboriginal rights prior to the adoption of Section 35 of the Constitution Act?	Win
.*R. v Sioui,* 1 S.C.R. 1025 (1990)	Do provincial logging regulations- violate treaty rights protected by Section 35?	Win

Case/Year	Subject	Outcome
.*Mitchell v. Peguis Indian Band*, 2 S.C.R. 85 (1990)	Is personal property of Indians on reservation subject to garnishment?	Win
R v Horseman, 1 S.C.R. 901 (1990)	Are Indians subject to Alberta Wildlife Act regulations re. Sale of animal skins?	Loss
Ontario v. Bear Island Foundation, 2 S.C.R. 570 (1991)	Do the Temagami Indians have aboriginal title to various tracts of land in Ontario?	Loss
Williams v. Canada, 1 S.C.R. 877 (1992)	Are unemployment benefits exempt from taxation?	Win (partial)
R v Howard , 2 S.C.R. 299 (1994)	Were fishing rights extinguished by 1923 treaty?	Loss
Native Women's Association v.Canada, 3 S.C.R.627 1994	Is the government under any obligation to provide equal funding for aboriginal women's groups?	Loss

Case/Year	Subject	Outcome
Blueberry River Indian Band v. Canada, 4 S.C.R. 344 (1995)	Did the government owe fiduciary duty to the Blueberry River Indian Band regarding the transfer of reserves and mineral rights?	Win
Canadian Pacific Ltd. v. Matsqui Indian Band 1 S.C.R 3 (1995)	Do Indian tribunals have jurisdiction to determine if rail lines are on reserves, for purposes of tax assessment?	Loss
R v. Vanderpeet, 2 S.C.R. 507 (1996)	Do fisheries regulations infringe upon aboriginal right to sell fish?	Loss
*R v Cote,*3 S.C.R. 139, (1996)	Are Indian fishing rights dependent upon aboriginal title, or can they be free standing rights	Win
R v Pamajewon, 2 S.C.R. 821 (1996)	Can an Indian tribe refuse to submit to casino licensing regulation, based upon right to self-government	Loss
R v Gladstone, 2 S.C.R. 723 (1996)	Challenge to BC fishing regulations; have commercial fishing rights been extinguished?	Win

Case/Year	Subject	Outcome
R v NTC Smokehouse, 2 S.C.R. 672 (1996)	Is there an aboriginal right to commercial fishing?	Loss
R v Lewis, 1 S.C.R. 921 (1996)	Can fishing regulations be extended to reserves?	Loss
Nikal v the Queen, 1 S.C.R. 1013 (1996)	Can an Indian fish on a reserve without a license?	Loss
R. v. Badger, 1 S.C.R. 771 (1996)	Can Indians hunt on privately owned property within land that was ceded by treaty?	Loss
Delgamuukw v. British Columbia, 3 S.C.R. 1010 (1997) .	Do the Indian bands have aboriginal title over thousands of square miles of British Columbia?	Win (on evidentiary issues)
St. Mary's Indian Band v. Cranbrook, 2 S.C.R. 678 (1997)	Does the inclusion of rider mean that surrender of land (for airport) not absolute, therefore designated land, therefore subject to tribal taxation?	Loss
Opetchesaht Indian Band v. Canada 2 S.C.R. 119 (1997)	Can BC maintain an easement on tribal land that does not appear to have any termination date?	Loss

Case/Year	Subject	Outcome
Union of New Brunswick Indians v. New Brunswick, 1 S.C.R. 1161 (1998)	Can a provincial government tax consumption items purchased off reserve?	Loss
R v Sundown, 1 S.C.R. 393 (1999)	Can Indian cut down trees, in violation of provincal regulations, when the trees are used for shelter during hunting (a protected aboriginal right in this instance) ?	Win
R v Marshall, 3 S.C.R. 456 (1999)	Do treaty rights (1770s) confer exemptions from fishing regulations for Indians, based on "oral terms" of the treaty?	Win
. *R v. Marshall II* 3 S.C.R. 533 (1999)	Scope of government power to regulate treaty right -- Whether judgment should be stayed pending disposition of rehearing if so ordered?	Win
R. v. Gladue, 1 S.C.R. 688 (1999)	In a trial for manslaughter, did the sentencing judge take proper account of the aboriginal background of the defendant, in regards to sentencing	Loss

Case/Year	Subject	Outcome
R. v. Wells, 1 S.C.R. 207 (2000)	Criminal rights case; did sentencing judge fail to consider aboriginal background when applying custodial sentence?	Loss
Osoyoos Indian Band v Oliver 3 S.C.R. 746 (2001)	Are land taken by province still Awithin the reserve@ for purposes of taxation by the Indian tribe?	Win
Mitchell v. M.N.R., 1 S.C.R. 911 (2001)	Do the Mohawks of Akwesane have the right to trade cross-border without paying customs duties?	Loss
Wewaykum Indian Band v. Canada, 4 S.C.R. 245 [2002]	Two bands claim each other's reserves as their own; has this been precluded by the statute of limitations	Loss
Ross River Dena Council Band v. Canada, 2 S.C.R. 816 (2002)	Do lands which had been Aset aside in the 1950s have reserve status?	Loss

Case/Year	Subject	Outcome
. *Kitkatla Band v. British Columbia* 2 S.C.R. 146*)* (2002)	Is the power to make exceptions to heritage preservation laws intra vires, in regards to the alteration and destruction of native cultural objects?	Loss
Paul v. British Columbia (Forest Appeals Commission) 2 S.C.R. 585, [2003]	Can Province constitutionally confer on an administrative tribunal the power to determine questions of aboriginal rights and title as they arise in course of tribunal=s duties	Loss
R. v. Powley, 2 S.C.R. 2007 (2003)	i)Do Metis have aboriginal right to hunt in Sault Ste. Marie environs? ii) If so, are licensing limitations justified?	I)Win i) Win
Haida Nation v. BC Minister of Forests 3 S.C.R. 511 (2004)	i) Does the Crown have a duty to consult and accommodate Aboriginal peoples prior to making decisions that might adversely affect their as yet unproven Aboriginal rights and title claims ii) Does this duty extend to third parties?	i)Win ii) Loss

Case/Year	Subject	Outcome
R. v. Marshall; R. v. Bernard, 2 S.C.R. 220 (2005)	Can Indians harvest logs for commercial purposes, without provincial licenses, as a result of treaty rights or aboriginal title?	Loss
Mikisew Cree First Nation v. Canada (Minister of Canadian Heritage),3 S.C.R 388 (2005)	Does the Crown have a duty to consult Indian tribes regarding the construction of road on crown land, in which Indians retain aboriginal hunting rights	Win
R. v. Sappier; R. v. Gray, 2 S.C.R 686 (2006)	Do two Indian tribes have the right to harvest wood on traditional territory? Application of Van der Peet Test : is wood harvesting part of the distinctive culture of the Indian tribes?	Win
R. v Morris 2 S.C.R. 915 (2006)	Does treaty right to hunt include right to hunt at night with illuminating device?	Win
God's Lake Band v McDiarmid Lumber 2 S.C.R. 846 (2006)	Are band funds exempt from seizure in commercial dispute?	Loss

Case/Year	Subject	Outcome
R v. Kapp 2 S.C.R. 483 (2008)	Do communal fishing licenses for aboriginal Canadians discriminate on the basis of race?	Win
R. v. Lameman 1 S.C.R. 372 (2008)	Are tribal land claims barred by *Limitations of Actions Act*?	Loss

APPENDIX B

INDIAN LAW CASES IN THE SUPREME COURT OF THE UNITED STATES, 1985-2008 (OUTCOME= OUTCOME FOR INDIAN LITIGANT)

Case/ Year	Issue	Outcome
United States v. Dann, 470 U.S. 39 (1985)	Has the tribe's aboriginal title to the land been extinguished by an earlier monetary award by the Indian Claims Commission?	Yes/ Loss
County of Oneida v. Oneida Indian Nation, 470 U.S. 226 (1985)	Can the Oneida sue for damages over 18th century transfer of land that occurred in violation of Non-Intercourse Act of 1793?	Yes/Win
Kerr-McGee Corp. v. Navajo Tribe of Indians, 471 U.S. 195 (1985)	Are two tribal ordinances imposing taxes on business activities conducted on the tribe's land invalid because they had not been approved by the Secretary of the Interior?	No/Loss

Case/ Year	Issue	Outcome
National Farmers Union Insurance Co. v. Crown Tribe of Indians, 471 U.S. 845 (1985)	Does the a tribal court have jurisdiction over a personal injury suit between tribe memeber and school district, when school land located on reservation but owned by the state?	Yes / Win
Montana v Blackfeet Tribe of Indians, 471 U.S. 759 (1985)	Are state taxes applied to tribal royalty interest in oil and gas production authorized by Indian Mineral Leasing Act?	No/Win
Mountain States Telephone and Telegraph Co. v. Pueblo of Santa Ana, 472 U.S. 237 (1985)	Was an easement granted by the Pueblo to a telephone company invalid under the Non-Intercourse Act and the Pueblo land Act?	No /Loss
Oregon Department of Fish and Wildlife v. Klamath Indian Tribe 474 U.S. 753 (1985)	Did later agreements ceding land extinguish hunting and fishing rights of Klamath Indian tribe, thus subjecting them to state regulation?	No /Loss

Case/ Year	Issue	Outcome
South Carolina et al v. Catawba Indian Tribe, Inc., 476 U.S. 498 (1986)	Was a tribal claim that 1840 transfer of land to South Carolina invalid under the Non Intercourse itself invalid, due the termination of the tribe's existence in the 1950's?	No/Loss
United States v. Mottaz, .476 U.S. 834 (1986)	Was a claim for damages regarding an invalid sale of Indian land time barred?	No/Loss
U.S. v. Dion, 476 U.S. 734 (1986)	Do tribal members have a treaty right to exemptions from the Endangered Species Act?	Yes /Loss
Bowen v. Roy, 476 U.S. (1986)	Is an American Indian entitled to receive AFDC despite refusal to obtain social security number, due to religious beliefs?	Yes/Loss
Three Affiliated Tribes of the Fort Berthold Reservation v. Wold Engineering, 476 U.S. 877 (1986)	Is a state statute that requires Indian tribes to consent to suit in all civil actions unduly intrusive on the Indian's common law sovereign immunity?	Yes/Win

Case/ Year	Issue	Outcome
Iowa Mutual Insurance Co. v. Laplante 480 U.S. 9 (1987)	Is a federal court required to exercise diversity jurisdiction, where case with same parties is pending in trial court?	Yes /.Win
California v. Cabazon Band of Mission Indians, 480 U.S. 202. (1987)	Must federally approved Indian bingo games comply with state regulations?	No/Win
Amoco Production Co. v. Village of Gambell 480 U.S. 531(1987)	Did sale of leases for oil and gas exploration adversely affect aboriginal hunting and fishing rights? Did the Secretary of the Interior fail to comply with the Alaska National Interest Lands Conservation Act?	I)Yes /Loss II) Yes /Loss
United States v. Cherokee Nation of Oklahoma 480 U.S. 700 (1987)	Did a federal navigation project that affected the riverbed interests of Indian require just compensation to be paid by the federal government, under the fifth amendment?	Yes /Loss

Case/ Year	Issue	Outcome
Hodel v. Irving, 481 U.S. 704 (1987)	Does Indian Land Consolidation Act, which allows individual land allotments to escheat to tribe rather than descend by intestacy or devise, violate the Fifth Amendment by taking private property for public use without just compensation?	No/Loss
Lyng v. Northwest Indian Cemetery Protective Association, 485 U.S. 439 (1988)	Can federal government authorize timber harvest near areas used by Indians for religious ceremonies?	No/Loss
Oregon v. Smith, 494 U.S. 872 (1988)	Does dismissal for drug use (drugs part of Indian religious ritual) constitute unjustified infringement on free exercise of religion?	Yes/Loss
Oklahoma Tax Commission v. Graham, 489 U.S. 838 (1989)	Has a federal question been properly pleaded in dispute over application of state taxes to Indian gaming venture?	Yes/Loss
Mississippi Band of Choctaw Indians v. Holyfield, 490 U.S. 30 (1989)	Are Indian children born outside reservation "domiciled" within the reservation for purposes of adoption proceedings?	Yes/Win

Case/ Year	Issue	Outcome
Cotton Petroleum Corp. v. New Mexico, 490 U.S. 163 (1989)	Can New Mexico impose a severance tax on non-Indian gas/oil facilities on Indian reservation?	No/Loss
Brendale v. Yakima Indian Nation, 492 U.S. 408 (1989)	Do the Yakima have zoning authority over fee lands owned by non-members in i) the reservation's "closed area" and ii) the reservation's "open" area	i)Yes/ win ii)Yes/ win
Employment Division v. Smith, 494 U.S. 872 (1990)	Can Oregon prohibit the use of Peyote in Native American religious ceremonies?	No/Loss
Duro v. Reina, 495 U.S. 676 *(*1990*)*	Can a non-member Indian be subject to tribal criminal jurisdiction, when a non-Indian would not be subject to tribal jurisdiction?	Yes/Loss
Blatchford v .Native Village of Noatak and Circle Village, 501 U.S. 775 (1991)	Does the 11th Amendment bar suits by Indian Tribes against states without their consent?	No/Loss

Case/ Year	Issue	Outcome
Oklahoma Tax Commission v. Potawatomi Indian Tribe, 498 U.S. 505 (1991)	i. May a state that has not asserted jurisdiction over Indian Land under Public Law 280 collect taxes for on-reservation sales of cigarettes to non-members? ii. Did the tribe waive its sovereign immunity by filing an action for injunctive relief?	i) No/Loss ii) No/loss
County of Yakima v. Yakima Indian Nation, 502 U.S. 251 *(*1992*)* .	Can the county impose i) excise tax and ii) ad valorem tax on land, sale of land that had been alloted under the 1887 Dawes Act?	i)No/win ii)No/loss
Lincoln v. Vigil, 508 U.S. 182 (1993*)*	Did the Indian Health Service violate the Administrative Procedure Act when it discontinued a program for handicapped children?	Yes/Loss
South Dakota v. Bourland, 508 U.S. 679 (1993)	Can tribes regulate hunting and fishing rights over non-members in disputed territory?	Yes/Loss

Case/ Year	Issue	Outcome
Negonsott v.Samuels, 507 U.S. 99 (1993)	Does the Federal government have jurisdiction regarding Indian on Indian, on reservation crime?	Yes/Loss
Oklahoma Tax Commission v. Sac and Fox Nation, 508 U.S. 114 (1993)	Must an Indian live on reservation for presumption against state tax jurisdiction to be applied, in the context of a challenge to state taxation?	No/Win
Department of Taxation and Finance of New York v. Milhelm Attea & Bros Inc, 512 U.S. 61 (1994)	Is a New York regulatory scheme enacted to prevent non-Indians from purchasing untaxed cigarettes an invalid exercise of a federal regulatory power?	Yes/Loss
Hagen v. Utah 510 U.S. 399 (1994)	Does crime fall under state jurisdiction, when the crime has taken place in Indian lands that have been opened to settlement by non-Indians? .	No/Loss
Oklahoma Tax Comm'n v. Chickasaw Nation 515 U.S. 450 (1995)	Can the state I) tax fuel sold on reservation and ii) wages paid to Indians who live off of the reservation (claim rooted in 1837 Treaty)?	i)No/win ii)No/loss

Case/ Year	Issue	Outcome
Seminole Tribe of Florida v. Florida, et al. 517 U.S. 44 (1996)	Can Seminole Tribe sue the state of Florida for violation of duty to negotiate in good faith regarding gaming industry?	Yes/Loss
Babbit v. Youpee 519 U.S. 234 (1997)	Does Indian land consolidation act violate property rights?	No/loss
Strate v. A-1 Contractors, 520 U.S. 438 (1997)	Can tribe member (widow of tribe member) sue company that she had an accident with on federal highway on Indian reservation in tribal court?	Yes/Loss
Idaho et al. v. Cour d'Alene Tribe of Idaho, 521 U.S. 261 1997	Does a tribe have title to banks/beds of a navigable water course, and thus rights to exclusive use and exemption from state regulation, based on 1873 executive order?	Yes/Loss
Montana v. Crow Tribe of Indians, 523 U.S. 696 (1998)	Can Crow Tribe get restitution for state taxes imposed upon mining company that had leased land from the tribe?	Yes/Loss

Case/ Year	Issue	Outcome
Cass County v. Leech Lake Band of Chippewa Indians, 524 U.S. 103 (1998)	Is the tribe exempt from county taxation on reservation land that had been sold to individuals but was re-purchased by the tribe?	Yes/Loss
Alaska v. Native Village of Venetie Tribal Government,. 522 U.S. 520 (1998)	Are the tribe's ANCSA land "Indian country," therefore entitling the tribe to tax business conducted on the land?	Yes/Loss
Kiowa Tribe of Oklahoma v. Manufacturing Technologies, 523 U.S. 751 (1998)	Is the Kiowa tribe subject to a breach of contract suit in Oklahoma courts?	No/Win
South Dakota v. Yankton Sioux Tribe, 522 U.S. 329 (1998)	Did the Yankton Sioux cede governing authority over land it sold in the 19th century?	No/Loss
Arizona Depatment of Revenue v. Blaze Construction, 526 U.S. 32, 1999	Does federal law pre-empt application of state tax to Indian-owned company?	Yes/Loss
El Paso Natural Gas v. Neztsosie, 526 U.S. 473 (1999)	Does Price-Anderson Act establish federal court jurisdiction for torts for regarding nuclear waste?	No /Loss

Case/ Year	Issue	Outcome
Minnesota v. Milles Lacs Band of Chippewa Indians, 526 U.S. 172 (1999)	Did 1850 executive order extinguish tribes usufructuary rights established in1837 Treaty?	No /Win
Amoco Production Co. v. Southern Ute Indian Tribe, 526 U.S. 865 (1999)	Does a tribe that has been given rights to coal deposits also have rights to coalbed methane gas (alternative energy source)?	Yes/Loss
Rice v. Cayetano, 528 U.S. 495 (2000)	Does a Hawaii statute permitting only descendants of aboriginal peoples inhabiting Hawaiian Islands in 1778 to vote for trustees of state agency violate the Federal Constitution's Fifteenth Amendment?	Yes/Loss
C & L Enterprises v. Citizen Band Potawatomi Indian Tribe of Oklahoma, 532 U.S. 411 (2001)	Has tribe waived soverign immunity regarding contract dispute?	No/Loss

Case/ Year	Issue	Outcome
Atkinson Trading Company v. Joe Shirley, 532 U.S. 645 (2001)	Can Indian Tribe impose a hotel tax on nonmember guests in hotel rooms that were located on non-Indian fee land within exterior boundaries of tribe's reservation?	Yes/Loss
Chickasaw Nation v. United States, 534 U.S. 84 (2001)	Tax question regarding exemptions; do Indian tribes receive identical exemptions as do state governments?	Yes/Loss
Nevada v. Hicks, 533 U.S. 353 (2001)	Does a tribal court have jurisdiction over civil claims against state official	Yes/Loss
Arizonav.California, 530 U.S. 392 (2001)	Are water rights claims of Indian tribe precluded by claims commission decision?	No/Win
United States v. Navajo Nation 537 U.S. 488 (2003)	Did payment rate for private company which has licensed to mine coal on federal Indian land violate the federal government's fiduciary duty to the Navajo?	Yes/Loss

Case/ Year	Issue	Outcome
Inyo County v. Paiute-Shoshone Indians of the Bishop Community, 538 U.S. 701 (2003)	Can a state search an Indian casino as part of an investigation of welfare fraud?	No /Loss
United States v. White Mountain Apache Tribe, 537 U.S. 465 (2003)	Does the US gov't have a fiduciary duty regarding military base on Native American land? Must the government pay monetary compensation for decay of fort?	Yes/Win
United States. v. Lara, 541 U.S. 193 (2004)	Does trial by Indian court and subsequent trial by federal court violate double jeopardy clause?	No/Win
City of Sherrill v. Oneida Indian Nation, 544 U.S. 197 2005	Does open market purchases of land that was previously part of Indian territory restore tax immunity privileges?	Yes/Loss
Wagnon v. Prairie Band Potatwatomi Nation, 546 U.S. 95 2005	Can Kansas impose a gas tax on suppliers for Indian reservation?	No/Loss

Case/ Year	Issue	Outcome
Cherokee Nation of Oklahoma v. Leavitt, 534 U.S. 631 (2005)	Under the Indian Self-Determination and Education Assistance Act (ISDEAA) (25 USCS §§ 450 et seq.) which authorized the Federal Government and Indian tribes to enter into contracts in which the tribes promised to supply some federally funded services that a government agency would otherwise provide, there is a provision which) specified that the government had to pay a tribe's "contract support costs," which included some indirect administrative costs; is this a legally enforceable contract?	Yes/Win

APPENDIX C

CANADIAN ENVIRONMENTAL ASSESSMENT CASES

Case[1]	Description	Outcome
Eastmain Band v. Canada, 1 F.C. 501 (1992) (FCA)	Government : Attorney General, Hydro Quebec Project: James Bay Hydro Electric Dam Law: EARPGO Issue: Federal duty to conduct environmental assessments Judicial Actions: In regards to EARPGO claims, a "project" is no longer in the "project" stage once irrevocable steps have been taken to complete the project.	pro-gov anti-env

[1] FCA= Federal Court of Appeal; BCCA= British Columbia Court of Appeals; NSCA= Nova Scotia Court of Appeal; ONCA= Ontario Court of Appeal; SKCA= Saskatchewan Court of Appeal; NLCA= Newfoundland Court of Appeal; MCA= Manitoba Court of Appeal; ABCA= Alberta court of appeal; NBCA= New Brunswick Court of Appeal ; NWTCA= North West Territories Court of Appeal; QCA= Quebec Court of Appeal

Case[1]	Description	Outcome
Curragh Resources Inc. v. Canada, 3 F.C. 729 (1993) (FCA)	Government : Minister of Indian and Northern Affairs, Minister of Fisheries and Oceans Project: water license for mining company Law: EARPGO Issue:Do the ministers have the authority under EARPGO to impose additional conditions for water license? Judicial Actions: Minister of Indian and Northern Affairs had the authority to impose conditions	partial pro-gov pro-env
Metropolitan Authority v. Coalition of Citizens for a Charter Challenge, 125 N.S.R. (2d) 241 (1993) (NSCA)	Government : Metropolitan Authority (regional government) Project: solid waste management system Law: N.S. Environmental Protection Act Issue: Does incineration of waste violate Section 7 Charter right to security of the person? Was the decision to authorize the project ultra vires the Metropolitian Authority? Judicial Decision: The appellants lack standing to pursue the challenge.	Pro-gov Anti-env

Case[1]	Description	Outcome
Kynock v. Bennet, 131 N.S.R. (2d) 334 (1994) (NSCA)	Government : Nova Scotia Utility and Review Board Project: gravel pit quarry Law: Nova Scotia Planning Act, Environmental Assessment Act Issue: Does the Board have the ability to conduct environmental assessments? Judicial Decision: The board does not have the power to conduct environmental assessments	Anti-gov Anti-env
Banks v. Northumberland (County), 114 D.L.R. (4th) 360 (1994) (ONCA)	Government : Ministry of the Environment Project: resource recovery facility Law: Ontario Environmental Assessment Act Issue: Is the project a waste disposal site, thus requiring a public hearing required for approval? Judicial Decision: The project is not a waste disposal site, and a public hearing is not required.	Pro-gov Anti-env

Case[1]	Description	Outcome
Sea to Sea Greenbelt Society v. Greater Victoria Water District, CanLII 2752 1996) (BCCA)(	Government : Ministry of the Environment/ GVWD Project: expansion of reservoir capacity Law: BC environmental assessment act Issue:does the BC EAA apply to this project? Judicial Action: appeal dismissed, lower court upheld	pro-gov anti-env.
Canadian Parks and Wilderness Society v. Superintendent of Banff National Park, 1 F.C. 832 1996) (FCA)	Government : Parks Canada Project: ski resort Law: EARPGO, CEAA Issue: do developments fall under the EARPGO and CEAA? Had project received valid final approval, or was it subject to ongoing environmental review? Judicial Action: project subject to ongoing environmental review	Pro-gov pro-env

Case[1]	Description	Outcome
Kelvington Super Swine v. Irving, et al, 163 Sask. R. 87 (1997) (SKCA)	Government : Ministry of the Environment, Ministry of Agriculture Project: intensive livestock operation Law: Environmental Assessment Act Issue: Is the project a "development" under the terms of the Environmental Assessment Act? Judicial Decision: The project is not a development.	Pro-gov Anti-env
Labrador Inuit Assn. v. Newfoundland (Minister of Environment and Labour) 155 Nfld. & P.E.I.R. 93 (1997) (NLCA)	Government : Ministry of Environment and Labour Project: mining development Law: Nfld. Environmental Assessment Act Issue: Can infrastructure development be treated separately from the main project, for purposes of environmental assessment? Judicial Decision:The development cannot be treated separately from the main project.	Anti-gov Pro-env
Vuntut Gwitchin First Nation v. Canada (Attorney General) CanLII 7819 (1998) (FCA)	Government : DIAND Project: well-testing Law: CEAA Issue: challenge to permit decision Judicial action: application denied; lower court affirmed	pro gov anti env

Case[1]	Description	Outcome
Alberta Wilderness Association v. Canada, 1. F.C. 483 (1998) (FCA)	Government : Department of Fisheries and Oceans Project: open pit coal mine in Jasper national park Law: CEAA Issue: failure to complete EA prior to issuing authorizations Judicial Action: application allowed ; environmental assessment must be conducted ; lower court overturned	anti- gov pro-env
Algonquin Wildlands League v. Ontario (Minister of Natural Resources), 117 O.A.C. 174 (1998) (ON CA.)	Government:Minister of Natural Resources Project: Forest management plans Law: Crown Forest Sustainability Act Issue: Did the plans comply with the act? Judicial Action: Statutory requirements are mandatory, not directory	anti-gov pro-env
Caddy Lake Cottagers Association v. Nora Road Access, Inc. 8 W.W.R. 514 (1998) (MCA)	Government: Project: Road construction in a provincial park Law: The Environment Act Issue: Was the public notice regarding the development sufficient? Judicial Decision: The notice was sufficient	Pro-gov Anti-env

Case[1]	Description	Outcome
Friends of the West Country Association v. Canada (Minister of Fisheries and Oceans) 1999 2 F.C. 263 (1999) (FCA)	Government : Coast Guard Project: bridge Law: CEAA Issue: Scoping, application of independent utility principle (projects cannot be separated for purpose of EA if they have no independent utility) Judicial Action: appeal dismissed; Coast Guard decision re. scoping of project invalid	pro env anti gov
Sharp v. Canada (Transportation Agency) 4 F.C. 363 (1999) (FCA)	Government : Canada Transportation Agency Project: railway line construction Law: CEAA, Canadian Transportation Act Issue: Does law require that new the need for new rail line constructions be demonstrated? Judicial Action: application dismissed	pro gov anti-env

Case[1]	Description	Outcome
Alberta Cement Corporation v. Alberta Environmental Protection, 212 CanLII (1999 (ABCA)	Government : Alberta Environmental Protection Project: quarry Law: Land Surface Conservation and Reclamation Act Issue: Validity of request for environmental impact assessment Judicial Action: appeal dismissed	pro-gov pro-env
Canada (Minister of Environment) v. Hamilton Wentworth (Municipality), 213 F.T.R. 57 (2001) (FCA)	Government: Environment Canada vs. municipal government Project: highway construction Law: CEAA Issue: Does the CEAA apply to a project that had been initially approved in the early 1980s? Judicial Actions: CEAA not applicable to 45 year old highway project now nearing completion; lower court decision favoring federal position overturned	Anti fed gov anti-env

Case[1]	Description	Outcome
Bow Valley Naturalists Society v. Canada (Minister of Canadian Heritage) 2 F.C. 461 (2001) (FCA)(	Government : Parks Canada Project: construction of meeting facility in Banff National Park Law: CEAA Issue: scoping of project, cumulative environmental effects assessment, Court Action: application dismissed	Pro gov anti env
Inverhuron & District Ratepayers Ass. v. Canada (Minister of The Environment), 206 F.T.R. 318 (2001) (FCA)	Government : Environment Canada Project: Nuclear Waste Storage Facility Law: CEAA Issue: adequacy of review Judicial Actions: application denied; lower court decision upheld	pro gov anti env
Tsawwassen Indian Band v. Canada (Minister of Enviornment), 213 F.T.R. 316 (2001) (FCA)	Government : Ministry of the Environment Project: ocean dumping Law: CEAA, Ocean Dumping Control Act Issue: do the actions constitute a "project" under CEAA? Judicial Actions: application denied; CEAA only applies to proposed projects	pro gov anti env

Case[1]	Description	Outcome
Cook v. Alberta (Environmental Protection), 293 A.R. 237 2 (2001)(ABCA)	Government : Minister of Environmental Protection Project: wilderness camping facility Law: Public Lands Act Issue: Could the Minister reject lease application Judicial Actions: Minister must reconsider application, provide reason for decisions	anti-gov anti-env
Athabasca Chipewyan First Nation v. British Columbia Hydro and Power Authority 3 F.C. 412 (2001) (FCA)	Government : National Energy Board Project: export of hydro-electric energy Law: National Energy Board Act Issue: adequacy of review process Judicial Actions: appeal allowed, Board's decision quashed	anti-gov pro-env
Lavoie v. Canada (Minister of the Environment), 228 F.T.R. 318) (2002) (FCA)	Government : Minister of the Environment, Department of Fisheries and Oceans Project: hydroelectric project Law: CEAA Issue: Did project approval comply with environmental assessment process? Judicial Actions: application dismissed; ministerial decision upheld	Pro gov anti-env

Case[1]	Description	Outcome
Fenske v. Alberta (Minister of Environment), 2002 ABCA 135 (2002) (ABCA)	Government : Minister of the Envir onment Project: landfill expansion Law: Environmental Protection and Enhancement Act Issue: Ministerial decision to approve expansion of the project, against recommendations of environmental review board Judicial Actions: lower court decision overturned	pro-gov anti-env
Taku River Tlingit First Nation v. Ringstad, 211 D.L.R. (4th) 89 (2002)(BCCA)	Government : Environmental Assessment Office et al Project: mining project Law: BC EAA Issue: adequacy of environmental review process Judicial Action: as a matter of administrative law (BC EAA) the certificates authorizing the project were valid	pro gov anti env (dissent)

Case[1]	Description	Outcome
Canadian Parks and Wilderness Society v. Minister of Canadian Heritage,4 F.C. 672 (2003) (FCA)	Government : Minister of Canadian Heritage Project: wilderness road Law: Canadian National Parks Act Issue: Can the Minister approve road construction for non-park related purposes? Did the minister breach her duty to uphold the ecological integrity of the park? Were road permits issued for t he purpose of park management ? Judicial Action: application dismissed	Pro gov anti env
Society Promoting Environmental Conservation v. Canada (Attorney General) (C.A.),4 F.C. 959 (2003) (FCA)	Government :A.G., Ministry of Defense Project: Expropriation of seabed and foreshore for torpedo testing Law: Expropriation Act Issue: Did the hearings officer properly notify the public, properly inform the minister of the nature of the objections Judicial Action: application rejected, lower court overturned	Pro gov anti env

Case[1]	Description	Outcome
Western Canada Wilderness Committee v. British Columbia (Ministry of Forests, South Island Forest District) 1 Admin. L.R. (4th) 167,(2003) (BCCA)	Government : Ministry of Forests Project: four logging cutblocks Law: Forest Practices Code of B.C. Issue: Did the decision to approve a logging project adequately take into account dangers to the spotted owl? Judicial Action: application dismissed; lower court decision upheld	Pro gov anti env
North American Tungsten Corporation Ltd. v. Mackenzie Valley Land and Water Board, 1 Admin. L.R. (4th) 293 (2003) (NWTCA)	Government : Mackenzie Valley Land and Water Board Project: water license Law: Mackenzie Valley Resource Management Act, CEAA Issue: Is the license a new or continuing license? Decision: The continuing licenses are not subject to new environmental assessments	Pro-federal gov Anti-env

Case[1]	Description	Outcome
2016596 Ontario Inc. v. Ontario, 2003 CanLII 30021 (ON C.A.)	Government : Minister of Natural Resources Project: Use of forest access road. Law: Ontario Environmental assessment act Issue Motion by environmental groups for leave to intervene as "friend of the court." Judicial Decision: Leave is granted	Pro-gov Pro-env
Inter-Church Uranium Committee Educational Co-operative v. Canada (Atomic Energy Control Board) 1 F.C.R. 372 (2004) (FCA)	Government : Atomic Energy Control Board Project: licensing for component of uranium mine Law: CEAA Issue: retroactive applicability of CEAA Judicial Action: lower court decision overturned, appliation of ICUCEC rejected	pro-gov anti-env
Lone Pine (Committee) v. Alberta (Natural Resources Conservation Board), 361 A.R. 209 (2004) (ABCA)	Government : Natural Resources Conservation Board Project: expansion of cattle feedlot Law: Agricultural Operations Practices Act Issue: Did the Board err in application of the transitional provisions of the act? Judicial Action: decision of the board quashed	anti-gov pro-env

Case[1]	Description	Outcome
Sutcliffe v. Ontario (Minister of the Environment), 72 O.R. (3d) (2004) (ONCA)	Government : Ministry of the Environment Project: landfill site Law: Environmental Assessment Act Issue: Can the minister approve an assessment that is tailored for a specific project? Judicial Action: appeal allowed; ministerial decision re-instated	pro-gov anti-env
1359629 Ontario Inc. v. New Brunswick (Minister of the Environment) 17 Admin. L.R. (4th) 149 (2004) (NBCA)	Government : Ministry of the Environment Project: ground water extraction/bottling plant Law: N.B. Clean Environment Act Issue: Can minister attach a condition to an exemption granted under the Clean Environment Act? Judicial Action: The conditions can be imposed	Pro-gov Pro-env

Case[1]	Description	Outcome
Canada (Minister of the Environment) v. Bennett Environmental Inc. 29 Admin. L.R. (4th) 256, 2005 (FCA)	Government : Environment Canada Project: High Temperature Thermal Oxidizer Law: CEAA Issue: challenge to federal decision to refer facility to a review panel; facility was largely complete at the point when the federal review process began ; was the facility still a "project" subject to review? Judicial Action: lower court decision that the facility was not a "project" at this stage was correct	anti-env anti-gov

Case[1]	Description	Outcome
Sumas Energy 2 Inc. v. Canada (National Energy Board), FCA 377 (CanLII) 2005 (FCA)	Government : National Energy Board Project: international power line Law: National Energy Board Act, Canadian environmental assessment act Issue: can the board consider the environmental impact of an international project? Judicial Action: application for review of Board's decision rejected	pro gov pro env
Castle-Crown Wilderness Coalition v. Alberta (Director of Regulatory Assurance Division, Alberta Environnment), 371 A.R. 370 (2005) (ABCA)	Government : Director of Regulatory Assurance, Ministry of the Environment Project: ski facility Law: Alberta Environmental Protection and Enhancement Act Issue: Was an EIA (environmental impact assessment) necessary for all aspects of the development? Judicial Action: appeal allowed, lower court overturned	pro gov ant env

Case[1]	Description	Outcome
South Etobicoke Residents & Ratepayers Association Inc. v. Ontario Realty Corp. 75 O.R. (3d) 641, (2005) (ONCA)	Government : Ontario Realty Corp, Ministry of the Environment Project: crematorium Law: Ontario Environmental Protection Act Issue: challenge to adequacy of environmental assessment Judicial Action: application denied; lower court upheld	pro gov anti env
R. v. Terroco Industries Limited, 367 A.R. 1 (ABCA) (2005)	Government : Alberta A.G. Law: Environmental Protection and Enhancement Act, S.A. 1992, c. E-13.3 ("EPEA") Project/Issue: conviction for release of dangerous chemicals; fine Judicial Action: mixed decision; summary convictions appeal court upheld in part; one fine maintained at a higher level; one fine reduced	pro-gov pro-env
Québec (Procureur général) c. Germain Blanchard ltée 52 Admin. L.R. (4e) (2005) (QCA)	Government : Ministry of the Environment Law: Environmental Quality Act Project/Issue: conversion of gravel pit into dry materials disposal site Judicial Action: government refusal of application allowed	Pro-gov Pro-env

Case[1]	Description	Outcome
Eagleridge Bluffs & Wetlands Preservation Society v. H.M.T.Q., 65 B.C.L.R. (4th) 53 (2006) (BCCA)	Government : Project: highway construction Law: B.C. environmental assessment act Issue: have those responsible for the construction project complied with environmental assessment certificate? Judicial Action: application dismissed; lower court decision upheld	Pro gov anti env
Do Rav Right Coalition v. Hagen, 61 B.C.L.R. (4th) 25 (2006) (BCCA)	Government : Project: RAV rapid transit line Law: BC environmental assessment act Issue: consultation on project was inadequate due to recent changes in construction method Judicial Action: application dismissed, lower court decision upheld	pro gov anti env

Case[1]	Description	Outcome
Prairie Acid Rain Coalition v. Canada (Minister of Fisheries and Oceans) 265 D.L.R. (4th) 2006 (FCA)	Government : Department of Fisheries and Oceans Project: Oil sands project Law: CEAA Issue: scoping of oil sands project , delegation of aspects of environmental assessment to Alberta Court Action: application for review dismissed, lower court upheld	Pro gov anti env
Labrador Métis Nation v. Canada (Attorney General) 277 D.L.R. (4th) 60 (2006) (FCA)	Government : Attorney Project: Provincial bridges/causeways Law: Fisheries Act Issue:Aboriginal right to consultation re. Termination of federal prosecution against provinces, based upon Section 35 of the Constitution Act. Ruling: Appeal dismissed; Attorney General only accountable to Parliament	pro-gov anti-env
R.K. Heli-Ski Panorama Inc. v. Glassman, 61 B.C.L.R. (4th) 316 (2007) (BCCA)	Government : Environmental Assessment Office, Minister of Sustainable Resource Management, etc Project: ski resort Law: BC environmental assessment act Issue: procedural unfairness and bias in assessment process Judicial Action: appeal dismissed	pro gov anti env

Case[1]	Description	Outcome
Tsawwassen Residents Against Higher Voltage Overhead Lines Society v. British Columbia (Utilities Commission) 67 B.C.L.R. (4th) 376, (2007) (BCCA)	Government : BC Utilities Commission Project: construction of overhead electrical power lines Law: Utilities Commission Act Issue: Must the government rely on the "precautionary principle" when undertaking environmental assessment Judicial Action: appeal dismissed	pro gov anti env
MiningWatch Canada v. Canada (Minister of Fisheries and Oceans), 2 F.C.R. 21 (2008) (FCA)	Government : Natural Resources Canada, Ministry of Fisheries and Oceans Project: mine Law: CEAA Issue: Did the project require a public consultation under the CEAA? Judicial Decision: A public consultation was not required.	Pro-gov Anti-env

Case[1]	Description	Outcome
Moses c. Canada (Procureur général) 1 C.N.L.R. 169 (2008) (QCA)	Government : Attorneys General of Quebec and Canada Project: vanadium mining operation Law: CEAA, James Bay and Northern Quebec Agreement Issue: Is the project subject to a federal environmental assessment? Judicial Decision: The project is subject to federal environmental assessment.	Pro-federal gov. Pro-env
Sincennes v. Alberta (Energy and Utilities Board), 454 A.R. 121 (2009) (ABCA)	Government : National Energy Board, Alb. Energy and Utilities Board Project: international power line Law: CEAA, National Energy Board Act Issue: Jurisdiction of National Energy Board and Energy and Utilities Board Judicial Decision: The EUB interpretation of its jurisdiction was correct.	Pro-gov Anti-env

Case[1]	Description	Outcome
1162209036 QUEBEC INC (Les Amis de la Rivière Kipawa) v. Canada (Attorney General), 2008 FCA 267 (CanLII) (FCA)	Government:A.G. of Canada et al Project: river dam Law: CEAA Issue: Does the project require mitigating measures in order to preserve navigation on the river? Judicial Decision: Mitigating measures are not required.	Pro-gov Anti-env

APPENDIX D

50 NATIONAL ENVIRONMENTAL POLICY (NEPA) CASES, AMERICAN CIRCUIT COURTS, 2006-2007

Case /Year/Circuit	Issue	Outcome
Lands Council v. McNair, 494 F.3d 771, 2007 (9th)	Government :USFS Project: logging in National Forest Law: NFMA, NEPA Issue: Is project approval invalid because USFS failed to include a full discussion of scientific uncertainty surrounding its strategy for improving wildlife habitat? Judicial Action: Appeal allowed; EIS is insufficient	Pro env anti-gov
City of Dania Beach v. FAA, 485. F.3d 1181, 2007 (DC)	Government : Federal Aviation Administration Project: Change to runway procedures at Florida airport Law:NEPA Issue: Has the FAA followed the proper NEPA review process? Judicial Action: petition for review granted	Pro-env anti-gov
Environmental Protection Info Center v. United States Forest Service, 2007 (9th)	Government :USFS Project: forest thinning project Law: NEPA Issue: Has USFS met NEPA requirements in its EIS Judicial Action: petition for review granted	anti-gov pro-env (dissent)

Case /Year/Circuit	Issue	Outcome
Citizens for Alternatives v. United States DOE, 485 F.3d 1091 2007 (10th)	Government : Department of Energy Project: Nuclear Waster Repository Law: NEPA Issue: Did DOE rely on faulty data in its environmental review? Judicial Action: request for injunction denied	pro-gov anti env
Utah Environmental Congress v. Richmond, 483 F.3d 1127, 2007, 10th	Government : USFS Project: timber sale Law: NEPA, NFMA Issue: review of license Judicial Action: petition for review granted	pro env anti gov
Consejo De Desarrollo Economico De Mexicali, A.C. v. United States 482 F.3d 1157, 2007 (9th)	Government : Bureau of Reclamation Project: Concrete-lined canal Law: NEPA and APA Issue: Failure to prepare supplementary environmental impact statement Judicial Action: environmental and statutory claims are moot	pro gov anti env
Utah Environmental Congress v. Troyer, 479 F.3d 1269 (10th, 2007)	Government : United States Forest Service Project: six separate logging projects Law: NEPA Issue: Adequacy of approval process Judicial Decision: 3 project approvals affirmed, 3 reversed	partial pro-env anti-gov

Case /Year/Circuit	Issue	Outcome
Navajo Nation v. United States Forest Service, 479 F. 3d 1024, (9th,2007)	Government : USFS Project: expansion of ski resort Law: Religious Freedom Restoration Act, NEPA Issue: Did FEIS comply with NEPA? Judicial Decision: challenge to USFS allowed	pro env anti-gov
Lands Council v. Martin, 479 F3d 643 (9th ,2007)	Government : US Forest Service Project: post-fire logging sales Law: NEPA, NFMA Issue: authorization of logging operation Judicial Decision: Preliminary injunction halting logging operations to allow for consideration on merits	pro env anti-gov
Forest Guardians v. Forsgren, 478 F.3d 1149 (10th, 2007)	Government : US Forest Service Project: Forest Management Plan Laws: ESA Iaaue: Does the plan threaten an endangered species? Judicial Decision: action dismissed, lower court affirmed	anti-env pro-gov
Hale v. Norton, 476 F.3d 694 (9th, 2007)	Government : National Park Service Project: moving large vehicles through park for home construction Laws: NEPA Issue: challenge to NPS decision to submit decision to NEPA analysis Judicial Decision: appeal rejected	pro env pro gov

Case /Year/Circuit	Issue	Outcome
Karst Environmental Education and Protection v. EPA, 475 F.3d 1291(DC, 2007)	Government : EPA, TVA, HUD Project: Transit Park development Laws: NEPA Issue: challenge to environmental assessment Judicial Decision: appeal rejected	anti-env. Pro-gov
O'Reilly v. U.S. Army Corps of Engineers, 477 F.3d 225 (5th, 2007)	Government : US Army Corps of Engineers Project: dredging of wetlands for housing project Laws: NEPA Issue: challenge to environmental assessment Judicial Decision: environmental assessment inadequate, but the analysis does not need to include two possible future phases of the project.	partial anti-gov pro-env
Siskiyou Reg'l Educ. Project v. Goodman, 2006 (9th)	Government : United States Forest Service Project: salvage of dead wood from fire Laws: NEPA Issue: adequacy of environmental assessment Judicial Decision: lower court upheld, injunction denied	anti env pro gov (dissent)

Case /Year/Circuit	Issue	Outcome
Mayo Foundation vs. Surface Transportation Board, 472 F.3d 545 (8th, 2006)	Government : surface transportation board Project: railway construction Laws: NEPA Issue: adequacy of environmental assessment Judicial Decision : petition denied	anti-env pro gov
Enivironmental Law and Policy Center v. NRC, 470 F.3d 676(7th, 2006)	Government : Nuclear Regulatory Commission Project: permit for nuclear power facility Laws: NEPA Issue: adequacy of environmental assessment Judicial Decision: injunction denied	anti-env pro-gov
Or. Natural Res. Council v. United States Bureau of Land Management, 470 F.3d 818 (9th, 2006)	Government : Bureau of Land Management Project: logging project Laws: NEPA Issue: adequacy of environmental assessment Judicial Decision: injunction granted,	Anti gov pro env (dissent)

Case /Year/Circuit	Issue	Outcome
Wildwest Institute v. Bull, 472 F.3d 587 (9th, 2006)	Government : United States Forest Service Project: Forest fuel reduction project Laws: NEPA (service committed resources prior to full EIS) Judicial Decision: lower court affirmed, preliminary injunction denied	anti-env pro-gov
Pit River Tribe v. United States Forest Service, 469 F.3d 768 (9th Cir. 2006)	Government : US Forest Service Project: geothermal plant Laws: NEPA Issue: adequacy of environmental assessment Judicial Decision: permit overturned	pro-env anti-gov
Klamath Siskiyou Wildlands Ctr. v. Boody, 468 F.3d 549, 554 (9th Cir.2006)	Government : Bureau of Land Management Project: timber sales Law: Federal Land Policy & Management Act ("FLPMA") and NEPA Issue: adequacy of environmental assessment/ adherence to FLPMA procedures Judicial Decision: lower court overturned, injunction against timber sales entered	Anti-gov Pro-env

Case /Year/Circuit	Issue	Outcome
Tri Valley Cares v. DOE, No. 04-17232 (9th 2006)	Government : Department of Energy Project: proposed construction of biological weapons research lab Law: NEPA Issue: must environmental assessments take into account potential terrorist attacks? Judicial Decision: DOE must consider the effects of a terrorist attack on the project vis a vis the environment, and conduct EIS accordingly	pro env anti-gov
Islander East Pipeline Co. V. Conn. Dept. Of Environmental Protection, 482 F3d 79 (2nd, 2006)	Government : FERC, Conn. Dept of Environmental Protection Project: natural gas pipeline between Conn. and NY; Conn. denied approval permits Law: Natural Gas Act, NEPA Issue: adequacy of environmental assessment Judicial Decision: Conn. Dept. must reverse decision	anti-env anti- state gov (dissent)
Forest Conservation Council v. United States Forest Service, 2006 (9th)	Government : US Forest Service Project: four timber sales from four national forests; Law: NEPA Issue: does the failure to "monetize" non-timber resources violate NEPA? Judicial Decision: lower court's summary judgment in favor of US affirmed	pro gov anti env

Case /Year/Circuit	Issue	Outcome
Ilio'Ulaokalani Coalition v. Rumsfeld, 464 F3d 1083 (9th, 2006)	Government : US Army Project: Expansion of army base in Hawaii Law: NEPA Issue: adequacy of environmental assessment Judicial Decision: Army has not fully considered alternatives	anti gov pro env (dissent)
Utah Shared Access Alliance v. Carpenter, 463 F.3d 1125 (10th, 2006)	Government : Bureau of Land Management Project: limitation of off road vehicle use in Utah Law: NEPA, FLPMA Issue: adequacy of environmental assessment Judicial Decision: lower court affirmed BLM's decision upheld	pro gov pro env
Coliseum Square Ass'n v. Jackson, 465 F.3d 215 (5th, 2006)	Government : HUD Project:Federal funding for housing redevelopment project Law: NEPA Issue: Must HUD funding for project cease prior to completion of environmental assessment? Judicial Decision:HUD actions upheld	pro gov anti env

Case /Year/Circuit	Issue	Outcome
Ouachita Watch League v. Jacobs, 463 F.3d 1163 (11th, 2006)	Government : US Forest Service Project: change to forest management plans in the southern region of USA; standing Law: NEPA Issue: standing Judicial Decision: lower court ruling overturend; standing of environmental groups upheld	pro env anti gov (standing)
La. Crawfish Producers Ass'n v. Rowan, 463 F.3d 352 (5th, 2006)	Government : U.S. Army Corps of Engineers Project: restoration of swampland Law: NEPA Issue: adequacy of environmental assessment Judicial Decision: lower court affirmed; government action upheld	pro gov anti-env
Northwest Envtl. Advocates v. Nat'l Marine Fisheries Serv., 460 F.3d 1125 (9th, 2006)	Government : Fisheries Service, Army Corp of Engineers Project: Deepening of Columbia River navigation channel Law: NEPA Issue: adequacy of environmental assessment Judicial Decision: lower court affirmed; Corp did take hard look at the evidence	pro gov anti env (dissent)

Case /Year/Circuit	Issue	Outcome
The Fund for Animals, Inc. v. U.S. Bureau of Land Management , 460 F.3d 13 (DC, 2006)	Government : Bureau of Land Management Project: regulations re. Wild Horse and Burros Law: NEPA , Wild Horses and Burros Act Issue: challenge to general BLM strategy Judicial Decision: The Fund does not challenge any justiciable agency actions	pro gov anti env (dissent)
Highway J Citizens Group v. DOT, 456 F.3d 734 (7th, 2006)	Government : DOT Project: Highway expansion Law: NEPA , APA, CWA Issue: variety of claims related to NEPA, APA, CWA Judicial Decision: lower court affirmed, claims barred	pro gov anti-env
Great Basin Mine Watch v. Hankins, 456 F.3d 955 (9th, 2006)	Government : Department of Interior, Bureau of Land Management Project: gold mining project Law: NEPA, APA, CWA– Issue: scoping of the project Judicial Decision: some aspects of EIS insufficient	partial pro-env. Anti-gov (dissent)
Nuclear Information and Resource Service v. NRC, 457 F.3d 941 (9th, 2006)	Government : Nuclear Regulatory Commission Project: exemption standards for transportation of nuclear material Law: NEPA Issue: adequacy of environmental assessment Judicial Decision: petition for review dismissed	pro gov anti env

Case /Year/Circuit	Issue	Outcome
California Sportfishing Protection Alliance v. FERC, 472 F.3d 593 (9th, 2006)	Government : FERC Project: hydroelectric project Law: NEPA, ESA Issue: Does authorized project violate ESA? Judicial Decision: petition for review dismissed	pro gov anti env
Idaho Rivers United v. FERC, No. 05-72513 (9th, 2006)	Government : FERC Project: 5 hydro-electric projects Law: NEPA Issue: adequacy of environmental assessment Judicial Decision: petition for review denied	pro gov anti env
Ecology Center v. United States Forest Service, 451 F.3d 1183 (10th, 2006))	Government : US Forest Service Project: Logging Law: NFMA, NEPA Issue: procedural violation of NEPA; failure to comply with forest plan under NFMA Judicial Decision: affirmed in part, reversed in part NEPA claim rejected claim sustained under national forest management act	partial pro-env anti-gov
Environmental Protection Info Center v. U.S. Forest Service, 451 F.3d 1005 (9th, 2006)	Government : US Forest Service Project: timber sale Law: NEPA, NFMA Issue: adequacy of environmental assessment/ violation of forest management plan Judicial Decision: petition denied, lower court affirmed	pro gov anti env

Case /Year/Circuit	Issue	Outcome
Gulf Restoration Network v. DOT, 452 F.3d 362 (5th,2006)	Government : DOT Project: license for liquefied natural gas facility Law: NEPA Issue: adequacy of environmental assessment Judicial Decision: Petition for review denied	pro gov anti env
San Luis Obispo Mothers for Peace v. NRC, 449 F.3d 1016 (9th, 2006)	Government : Nuclear Regulatory Commission Project: nuclear facility Law: NEPA; Issue: must the environmental assessment take into account the possibility of terrorist attack ? Judicial Decision: petition of SanLuis Obispo granted in part ;NEPA claim upheld	partial pro env. Anti gov
Cherokee Forest Voices v. United States Forest Service, 2006 (6th)	Government : United States Forest Service Project: logging projects Law:NFMA, NEPA Issue: adequacy of environmental assessment Judicial Decision : Cherokee Forest Voices wins on NFMA claim, but lower court upheld on NEPA claim	Partial pro-env; Anti-gov

Case /Year/Circuit	Issue	Outcome
Utah Environmental Congress v. Bosworth, 443 F.3d 732 (10th, 2006)	Government : United States Forest Service Project: Forest thinning Law: NEPA, APA, NFMA Issue: failure to consider cumulative impact, failure to apply proper rules, inadequate data collection Judicial Decision: USFS plan upheld	pro gov anti env
Sierra Club v. US Army Corps of Engineers, 446 F.3d 808 (8th, 2006)	Government : US Army Corps of Engineers Project: levee Law: NEPA, FEMA Issue: failure to prepare environmental assessment Judicial Decision: lower court reversed; NEPA claims of Sierra Club upheld ; environmental assessment insufficient	pro env anti-gov
Wyoming v. United States DOI 442 F.3d 1262 (10th, 2006)	Government : Department of the Interior Project: failure to de-list gray wolves from endangered species list Law: ESA, NEPA Issue: Has statutorily required action been withheld? Judicial Decision: standing denied	pro env pro gov

Case /Year/Circuit	Issue	Outcome
Earth Island Institute v. United States Forest Service, 442 F.3d 1147 (9th, 2006)	Government : US Forest Service Project: post-fire restoration projects Law: NEPA, NFMA Issue: use of evidence Judicial Decision: Preliminary injunctions against Forest Service granted	Pro env anti gov
Ripplin Shoals Land Co. v. US Army, Corps of Engineers, 440 F.3d 1038 (8th, 2006)	Government : US Army Corps of Engineers Project: bridge construction as part of development project Law: NEPA Issue: can US Army Corpus refuse to consider new application for approval, based upon previous judicial decision which overturned a separate approval? Judicial Decision: US Army Corps of Engineers ordered to reconsider application	anti-gov anti-env (dissent)
Utah Environmental Congress v. Bosworth, 439 F.3d 1184 (10th, 2006)	Government : USFS Project: timber harvesting project Law: National Environmental Policy Act, NFMA Issue: Did the USFS properly monitor Management Indicator Species? Did it properly analyze alternatives? Judicial Decision: USFS did not properly monitor Management Indicator Species, but it did properly consider NEPA alternatives; USFS project approval vacated	anti-gov anti-env

Case /Year/Circuit	Issue	Outcome
Turtle Island Restoration Network v. United States DOC, 438 F.3d 937 (9th, 2006))	Government : Department of Commerce, National Marine Fisheries Service Project: re-opening swordfish fisheries Law:NEPA, Migratory Bird Treaty Act, Endangered Species Act, APA, Magnuson-Stevens Fishery Conservation and Management Act Issue: compliance with multiple statutory requirements Judicial Decision: action is time-barred	Pro-gov anti-env
Sierra Nev. Forest Prot. Campaign v. United States Forest Service, 2006 (9th)	Government : United States Forest Service Project: Meadow Valley Defensible Fuel Profile Zone Law: NEPA Issue: Was an EA/ FONSI appropriate, or was an EIS required to approve this project? Judicial Decision: EA was appropriate; USFS decision upheld	pro gov anti env
Colorado Wild v. United States Forest Service, 435 F.3d 1204 (10th, 2006)	Government : United States Forest Service Project: salvage of dead trees Law: NEPA Issue: Can dead trees be salvaged without EA? Judicial Decision: All claims by conservation groups rejected	pro gov anti env

Case /Year/Circuit	Issue	Outcome
Silverton Snowmobile Club v. United States Forest Serv., 433 F.3d 772 (10th, 2006)	Government : United States Forest Service Project: Changes in access to Molas Pass recreational area Law: NEPA, NFMA Issue: failure to take "hard look" at proposed actions Judicial Decision: USFS decision upheld	pro gov pro env

Bibliography

Abell, Charles S. "Ignoring the Trees for the Forests: How the Citizen Suit Provision of the Clean Water Act violates the Constitution's Separation of Powers Principle." *Virginia Law Review*, Vol. 81, No. 7 (Oct., 1995) pp 1957-1987.

Ackerman, Bruce. *We The People, Volume Two: Transformations*. Cambridge: Harvard University Press, 1998.

Ackerman, Bruce A. and William T. Hassler, *Clean Coal/Dirty Air*. New Haven: Yale University Press, 1981.

Adams, Michael. *Fire and Ice: The United States, Canada, and the Myth of Converging Values* Toronto: Penguin, 2003.

Adams, Todd B. "New Source Review Under the Clean Air Act: Time for More Market-Based Incentives?" *Buffalo Environmental Law Review*. Vol. 8, No. 1, (Fall, 2000).

Adler, Johnathan H. "Wetlands, Waterfowl, and the Menace of Mr. Wilson: Commerce Clause Jurisprudence and the Limits of Federal Wetland Regulation. " *Environmental Law*, Vol. 29, No. 1 (Spring, 1999).

Agresto, John. *The Supreme Court and Constitutional Democracy*. Ithaca: Cornell University Press, 1984.

Alston, J.P., T.M. Morris, and A Vedlitz, "Comparing Canadian and American Values: New Evidence from National Surveys." *American Review of Canadian Studies* Vol. 26, No. 3, (1996) pp 301-314.

Arkes, Hadley. *The Return of George Sutherland: Restoring a Jurisprudence of Natural Rights*. Princeton: Princeton University Press, 1994.

--- *Beyond the Constitution*. Princeton: Princeton University Press, 1990.

--- *The Philosopher in the City: The Moral Dimensions of Urban Politics* (Princeton: Princeton University Press, 1980.

Arthurs, H.W. "The Political Economy of Canadian Legal Education." *Journal of Law and Society*. Vol. 25, No. 1, (March, 1998).

Atiyah, Patrick and Robert S. Summers. *Form and Substance in Anglo-American Law: A Comparative Study in Legal Reasoning, Legal Theory, and Legal Institutions.* London:Clarendon Press, 1987.

Baer, D., E. Grabb, and W. Johnston. "Reassessing Differences in Canadian and American Values." in *Images of Canada: The Sociological Tradition*. ed. J. Curtis and I Tepperman Scarborough, ON: Prentice-Hall Canada, 1999.

Baier, Gerald. *Courts and Federalism: Judicial Doctrine in the United States, Australia, and Canada.* Vancouver and Toronto: UBC Press, 2006.

Bakan, Joel. *Just Words: Constitutional Rights and Social Wrongs*. Toronto: University of Toronto Press, 1997.

Balfour, Lawrie. "Reparations after Identity Politics." *Political Theory*, Vol. 33, No. 6 (Dec., 2005), pp. 786-811

Barnett, Randy. "The Original Meaning of the Commerce Clause." *The University of Chicago Law Review*, Volume 68, Number 1, pp 101-147.

Bateman, Thomas M.J. "Rights Application Doctrine and the Clash of Constitutionalisms in Canada." *Canadian Journal of Political Science*. Vol. 31, No. 1, (March, 1998) pp 3-29.

Beatty, David. *Talking Heads and the Supremes: The Canadian Production of Constitutional Review*. Toronto: Carswell, 1990.

Bogart, W.A. *Good Government? Good Citizens? Courts, Politics, and Markets in a Changing Canada*. Vancouver: UBC Press, 2005.

Bogart, W.A. "Understanding Standing, Chapter IV: *Minister of Finance v. Finlay*," *Supreme Court Law Review*, Volume 10, 1988. pp 377-97.

Borrows, John. *Recovering Canada: The Resurgence of Indigenous Law* Toronto, University of Toronto Press, 2002.

----- "Let Obligations be Done." In Hamar Foster, Heather Raven, and Jeremy Webber, ed. *Let Right Be Done: Aboriginal Title, the Calder Case, and the Future of Indigenous Rights*. Vancouver: UBC Press, 2007. Pp 201-216

Boucher, Christian. 'Canada-U.S. Values: Distinct, Inevitably Carbon Copy, or Narcissism of Small Differences? *Horizons* Vol. 7, No. 1(2004).

Brisbin, Richard A., Jr. "The Reconstitution of American Federalism? The Rehnquist Court and Federal-State Relations." *Publius*, Vol.28, No. 1 (Winter, 1998) pp 189-215.

Brodie, Ian *Friends of the Court: The privileging of interest group litigants in Canada*. Albany, N.Y.: State University of New York Press, 2002

Bzdera, Andre. "Comparative Analysis of Federal High Courts: A Political Theory of Judicial Review." *Canadian Journal of Political Science*. Volume 26, Number 3 (January, 1993) pp 3-29.

Cairns, Alan. *First Nations and the Canadian State*. Kingston: Queen's University, The Institute of Inter-Governmental Relations, 2005.

--- *Citizens Plus: Aboriginal Peoples and the Canadian State*. Vancouver: UBC Press, 2000.

--- "The Judicial Committee and its Critics." *Canadian Journal of Political Science*. Vol. 4, No. 3 (Sept., 1971) pp 301-345.

Cairns, Robert D. "Natural Resources and Canadian Federalism: Decentralization, Recurring Conflict, and Resolution." *Publius*, Vol. 22, No. 1 (Winter, 1992) pp 55-70.

Canada. *Report of the Royal Commission on Aboriginal Peoples* 5 Volume. Ottawa: Canada Communication Group Publishing, 1996.

Carlson, Kirsten Matoy. "Towards Tribal Sovereignty and Judicial Efficiency: Ordering the Defenses of Tribal Sovereign Immunity and Exhaustion of Tribal Remedies." *Michigan Law Review*. Vol. 101, No. 2 (Nov., 2002) pp 569-601.

Castile, George Pierre. *Taking Charge: Native American Self-Determination and Federal Indian Policy, 1975-1993*. Tucson: University of Arizona Press, 2006.

Chandler, Marsha A. "Constitutional Change and Public Policy: The Impact of the Resource Amendment (Section 92a)" *The Canadian Journal of Political Science*. Vol. 19, No. 1, pp 103-126.

Clark, Bruce. *Native Liberty, Crown Sovereignty: The Existing Aboriginal Right of Self Government in Canada*. Montreal and Kingston: McGill-Queen's University Press, 1990.

Cohen, F. *Handbook of Federal Indian Law*. Washington, D.C.: US Government Printing, 1982.

Cooper, Phillip J. *Hard Judicial Choices: federal district court judges and state and local officials*. New York and Oxford: Oxford University Press, 1988.

Dacks, Gurston. "British Columbia after the *Delgamuukw* Decision: Land Claims and Other Processes." *Canadian Public Policy*. Volume 28, No. 2, (June, 2002) pp 239-255.

Dahl, Robert. "Decision-Making in a Democracy: The Supreme Court as a National Policy-Maker." *Journal of Public Law*, Vol. 6, (1957).

Dalton, Jennifer E. "Aboriginal Title and Self-Government In Canada: What is the true scope of comprehensive land claim agreements?" *Windsor Review of Legal and Social Issues*. Vol. 29 (Dec. 2006).

Derthick, Martha. *Up in Smoke*: *From Legislation to Litigation in Tobacco Policy*. Washington, D.C.: CQ Press, 2005.

Dietz T., et al. "Social structural and social psychological bases of environmental concern." *Environment and Behavior*, Vol.3, No. 4 (1998).

Dodd, Lawrence C. and Richard Schott, *Congress and the Administrative State* New York: John Wiley and Sons, 1979.

Dufriamont, L. "From Regulation to Recolonization: Justifiable Infringement of Aboriginal Rights at the Supreme Court of

Canada." *University of Toronto Faculty Law Review*, Volume 58, Number 3, 2000.

Dunlap, R.E. and R.E. Jones, "Environmental attitudes and values." in R. Fernandez-Ballesteros, editor, *Encyclopedia of Psychological Assessment* Volume One. London: Sage Publishers, 2003.

Eisner, Marc. *Governing the Environment: The Transformation of Environmental Regulation*. Bolder, CO.: Lynne Rienner Publishers, 2007.

Elgie, S. "Environmental Groups and the Courts: 1970-1992." in G. Thompson, M. McConnell, and L. Huestis, editors. *Environmental Law and Business in Canada*. Toronto: Canada Law Books, 1993.

Ellis, Richard. "Romancing the Oppressed: The New Left and the Left Out." *Review of Politics*. Volume 58, Number 1, (Winter, 1996) pp 109-154.

Epp, Charles. *The Rights Revolution*. Chicago: University of Chicago Press, 1998.

Epstein, David and Sharyn O'Halloran. *Delegating Powers*. New York: Cambridge University Press, 1999.

Epstein, Lee and Jack Knight, "Toward A Strategic Revolution in Judicial Politics: A Look Back, a Look Ahead." *Political Research Quarterly*. Vol. 53, No. 3, (September, 2000) pp 625-661.

Fallon, Richard H., Jr. "The 'Conservative' Paths of the Rehnquist Court's Federalism Decisions." *University of Chicago Law Review*. Vol. 69, No. 2 (Spring, 2002) pp 429-494.

Farber, Daniel A. "Stretching the Margins: The Geographic Nexus in Environmental Law." *Stanford Law Review*. Vol. 48, No. 5 (May, 1996) pp 1247-1278.

Feeley, Malcolm M. and Edward L. Rubin. *Judicial Policy-Making and the Modern State*. Cambridge: Cambridge University Press, 2000.

Fiorino, Daniel J. *The New Environmental Regulation*. MIT Press: Cambridge, 2006.

Flanagan, Thomas. *First Nations? Second Thoughts*. Ithaca and Kingston: McGill-Queen's University Press, 2000.

Flanagan, Thomas. "The Staying Power of the Legislative Status Quo: Collective Choice in Canada's Parliament after *Morgentaler*." *Canadian Journal of Political Science*. Vol. 30, No. 1, (March, 1997) pp 31-53.

Forbath, William. "The New Deal Constitution in Exile." *Duke Law Journal*. Vol. 51, No.1 (Oct., 2001) pp 165-222.

Franck, Matthew. *Against the Imperial Judiciary: The Supreme Court vs. The Sovereignty of the People* Lawrence: University Press of Kansas, 1996.

Franks, C.E.S "Indian Policy: Canada and the United States Compared." in Cook and Lindau, editors, *Aboriginal Rights and Self-Government*. McGill University Press: Montreal, 2000.

Friedman, Barry "The Birth of An Academic Obsession: The History of the Counter-Majoritarian Difficulty, Part V." *The Yale Law Journal*. Vol. 112, No. 2 (Nov. 2002) pp 153-259.

George, Robert P. *In Defense of Natural Law*. Oxford: Oxford University Press, 1999.

Gibson, Gordon. *A New Look at Canadian Indian Policy*. Vancouver: Fraser Institute, 2009.

Gillman, Howard."More on the Origins of the Fuller Court's Jurisprudence: Reexamining the Scope of Federal Power over Commerce and Manufacturing in Nineteenth-Century Constitutional Law." *Political Research Quarterly*, Vol. 49, No. 2 (Jun., 1996), pp. 415-437

--- *The Constitution Besieged: The Rise and Decline of Lochner Era Police Powers Jurisprudence*. (Durham: Duke University Press, 1993).

Grafton, R. Quentin and Daniel E. Lane. "Canadian Fisheries Policy: Challenges and Choices" *Canadian Public Policy*. Vol. 24, No. 2 (June, 1998) pp 133-147.

Greve, Michael. *The Demise of Environmentalism in American Law*. Washington: AEI Press, 1996.

Guillemin, Jeanne. "The Politics of National Integration: A Comparison of United States and Canadian Indian Administrations." *Social Problems*, Volume 25, Number 3, (February, 1978).

Heard, Andrew. *Canadian Constitutional Conventions: The Marriage of Law and Politics*. Toronto: Oxford University Press, 1991.

Heineke, Peter S. "Chevron and the Canon Favoring Indians." *University of Chicago Law Review*. Vol. 60, No. 3/4 (Summer, 1993) pp 1015-1042.

Hessing, Melody and Michael Howlett. *Canadian Natural Resource and Environmental Policy: Political Economy and Public Policy*. Vancouver: UBC Press, 1997.

Hetherington, Marc. "Resurgent Mass Partisanship: The Role of Elite Polarization." *American Political Science Review*. Vol. 95, No. 3 (Sept. 2001) pp.

Hiebert, Janet L. *Charter Conflicts: What Is Parliament's Role?* Montreal: McGill-Queen's University Press, 2002.

Hiebert, Janet L. *Limiting Rights: The Dilemma of Judicial Review.* Montreal-Buffalo: McGill-Queen's University Press, 1996.

Hirschl, Ran. *Towards Juristocracy: The Origins and Consequences of the New Constitutionalism*. Cambridge: Harvard University Press, 2004.

Horowitz, Donald. *The Courts and Social Policy* Washington, D.C.: The Brookings Institution, 1977.

Houck, Oliver A. "O Canada! The Story of Rafferty, Oldman, and the Great Whale." *Boston College International and Comparative Law Review*. Vol. 29 (Spring, 2006).

Howe, Daniel Walker. *What Hath God Wrought? The Transformation of America, 1815-1848.* New York: Oxford University Press, 2007

Howlett, Michael. "The Judicialization of Canadian Environmental Policy, 1980-1990: A Test of the Canada-United States Convergence Thesis." *Canadian Journal of Political Science*. Vol. 27, No. 1, (March, 1994). pp 99-127.

Hoxie, Frederick E. *A Final Promise: The Campaign to Assimilate the Indians, 1890-1920*. Lincoln: University of Nebraska Press, 1984.

Huntington, Samuel. *American Politics: The Promise of Disharmony*, New York: Belnap Press, 1981.

Hutchinson , Celeste. "Case Comment on *R. v. Kapp*: An Analytical Framework for Section 25 of the Charter."52 *McGill L.J.* 173 (2007)

Kanji, Mebs and Neil Nevitte. "Who are the most deferential: Canadians or Americans?" in *Canada and the United States: Differences that Count*. ed. David M. Thomas Peterborough, ON: Broadview Press, 2000.

Katzmann, Robert. *Institutional Disability: The Saga of Transportation Policy for the Disabled.* Washington, D.C.: The Brookings Institution, 1986.

Keck, Thomas. *The Most Activist Supreme Court in History*. Chicago: University of Chicago Press, 2004.

Kelly, James B. *Governing with the Charter.* Vancouver: UBC Press, 2005.

Kelly, James B."Reconciling Rights and Federalism during Review of the Charter of Rights and Freedoms: The Supreme Court of Canada and the Centralization Thesis, 1982-1999." *The Canadian Journal of Political Science*, Volume 34, Number 2, 2001. pp 321-355.

Kelly, James B. "The Charter of Rights and Freedoms and the Re-balancing of Liberal Constitutionalism in Canada, 1982-1997." *Osgood Hall Law Journal*, Number 37, 1999.

Kelly, Lawrence C. *The Assault on Assimilation: John Collier and the Origins of Indian Policy Reform.* Albuquerque: University of New Mexico Press, 1983.

Kessler, David. *A Question of Intent: A Great American Battle with a Deadly Industry*. New York: Public Affairs, 2001.

Knopff, Rainer and J.E. Glen. "Courts, Tribunals, and the Environment in Canada." In Kenneth Holland et al, editors, *Federalism and the Environment: Environmental Policymaking in Australia, Canada, and the United States*. Greenwood Press: Westport, Conn., 1996.

Kohn, Margaret. *Brave New Neighborhoods: The Privatization of Public Space*. New York: Routledge, 2004.

Kritzer, Herbert M. "Federal Judges and their Political Environment: The Influence of Public Opinion," *American Journal of Political Science*, Vol. 23, No. 1, (1979).

Krotozynski, Ronald J., Jr. *The First Amendment in Cross-Cultural Perspective*. New York: New York University Press, 2006.

Levinson, Sanford. *Constitutional Faith*. Princeton: Princeton University Press, 1988.

Lippert, Owen Paul. *Beyond the Naas Valley: national implications of the Supreme Court's* Delgamuukw *decision*. Vancouver: Fraser Institute, 2000.

Lomborg, Bjorn. *The Skeptical Environmentalist: Measuring the Real State of the World*. Cambridge: Cambridge University Press, 2001.

Lowi, Theodore. *The "Personal" President: Power Invested, Promise Unfulfilled*. Ithaca: Cornell University Press, 1985.

Lowi, Theodore. *The End of Liberalism: The Second Republic of the United States*. New York: W.W. Norton Press, 1979.

Macklem, Patrick. "First Nations Self-Government and the Borders of the Canadian Legal Imagination." *McGill Law Journal*, Volume 36, No. 1 (1992).

Macklem, Patrick. *Indigenous Difference and the Constitution of Canada*. Toronto: University of Toronto Press, 2001.

Mandel, Michael. *The Charter of Rights and the Legalization of Politics in Canada*. Toronto: Thompson Press, 1994.

Manfredi, Christopher. *Feminist Activism in the Supreme Court: legal mobilization and the Women's Legal Education Action Fund.* Vancouver: UBC Press, *2004*.

Manfredi, Christopher and Antonia Maioni. "Courts and Health Policy: Judicial Policy-Making and Publicly Funded Health Care in Canada." *Journal of Health Politics, Policy and Law*. Volume 27, Number 2 (April, 2002) pp 223-240.

Manfredi, Christopher. "Judicial Review and Criminal Disenfranchisement in Canada and the United States." *The Review of Politics*, Volume 60, Number 2, 1998 pp277-305.

--- *Judicial Power and the Charter* Toronto: McLelland and Stewart, 1993.

--- "The Use of United States Decisions by the Supreme Court of Canada under the Charter of Rights and Freedoms." *Canadian Journal of Political Science*. Vol. 23, No. 3. 1990 pp 499-518.

Manning, John M. "The Non-Delegation Doctrine as a Canon of Avoidance." *The Supreme Court Review*, Vol. 2000, (2000) pp 223-277.

McCright, Aaron M. and Riley E. Dunlap. "Challenging Global Warming as a Social Problem: An Analysis of the Conservative Movement's Counter-Claims." *Social Problems*. Vol. 47, No. 4 (Nov. 2000).

McGrory-Klyza, Christopher and David Sousa, *American Environmental Policy, 1990-2006: Beyond Gridlock.* Cambridge: MIT Press, 2008.

McKenzie, Judith I. *Environmental Politics in Canada: Managing the Commons into The 21st Century*. Oxford University Press: London, 2002.

McNeil, Kent. "Aboriginal Rights in Canada: From Title to Land to Territorial Sovereignty." *Tulsa Journal of Comparative and International Law*. Vol. 5, No. 1, 1998. pp 278-98.

McSloy, Steven Paul. "The Miner's Canary: A Bird's Eye View of American Indian Law and Its Future." *New England Law Review*, Volume 37, (Spring, 2003).

Melnick, R. Shep. *Between the Lines: Interpreting Welfare Rights*. Washington, D.C.: Brookings Institution, 1994.

Melnick, R. Shep. *Regulation and the Courts: The Case of the Clean Air Act*. Washington,D.C.: Brookings Institution, 1984.

Melnick, R. Shep. "Environmental Litigation and Institutional Analysis: Wenner and Ackerman & Hassler." *American Bar Foundation Research Journal*. Vol. 8, No. 3 (Summer, 1983) pp 740-751.

Milkis, Sidney. *Political Parties and Constitutional Government* Baltimore: Johns Hopkins University Press, 1999.

Mishler, William and Reginald S. Sheehan. "Public Opinion, the Attitudinal Model, and Supreme Court Decision Making: A Micro-Analytic Perspective," The *Journal of Politics* Vol. 58, No. 1 (Feb., 1996).

Morgan, Edmund. "Hearsay and Non-Hearsay." *Harvard Law Review*, Vol. 48, No. 7 (May, 1935)

Morrison, Trevor W. " Private Attorneys General and the First Amendment." *Michigan Law Review*, Vol. 103, No. 4, (Feb., 2005), pp. 589-675.

Morton, F.L. and Avril Allen. "Feminists and the Courts: Measuring Success in Interest Group Litigation in Canada." *Canadian Journal of Political Science*. Vol. 34, No. 1, (March, 2001).

Morton, F.L. and Rainer Knopff. *The Charter Revolution and the Court Party*. Peterborough, Ontario: Broadview Press, 2000.

Morton, F.L. and Troy Riddell. "Reasonable Limitations, Distinct Society, and the Canada Clause: Interpretive Clauses and the Competition for Constitutional Advantage." *Canadian Journal of Political Science*. Volume 31, Number 3, (April, 1998) pp 467-493.

Morton, F.L. "The Constitutional Divisions of Powers with Respect to the Environment in Canada." Ed. *K. Holland, Federalism and the Environment: Environmental Policymaking in Australia, Canada, and the United States*. Wesport, Conn.: Greenwood Press, 1996.

---. *Pro-Choice vs. Pro-Life: Abortion and the Courts in Canada* Norman, Ok: University of Oklahoma Press, 1992.

--- "The Supreme Court's Promotion of Sexual Education: A Case Study of Institutional Capacity." *Polity*. Vol. 16, No. 3 (Spring, 1984) pp 467-483.

Murphy, Michael. "Culture and Courts: A New Direction in Canadian Jurisprudence on Aboriginal Rights?" *Canadian Journal of Political Science*. Vol. 34, Number 1 (Mar. 2001) pp 109-129.

Newman, Dwight G. "Prior Occupation and Schismatic Principles: Toward a Normative Theorization of Aboriginal Title; Newman, Dwight G. *Alberta Law Review*, Volume 44, Issue 4, pp 779-802

Norgren, Jill. *The Cherokee Cases: two landmark decisions in the fight for sovereignty*. Norman, OK: Oklahoma University Press, 2004.

Note, "International Law as an Interpretive Force in Federal Indian Law." *Harvard Law Review*, Vol. 116, No. 8, (June, 2003) pp 1751-1773.

Olson,Walter. *The Litigation Explosion*. Truman Talley Books: New York, 1991.

Ostberg, Cynthia and Matthew Wetstein. *Attitudinal Decision-Making in the Supreme Court of Canada*. Vancouver: UBC Press, 2007.

P., J.Y. Jr., "Toward a Constitutionally Protected Environment." *Virginia Law Review*. Vol. 56, No. 3, (April, 1970.) pp 458-486.

Pagden, Anthony "Human Rights, Natural Rights, and Europe's Imperial Legacy." *Political Theory*. Vol. 31, No. 2, pp 171-199.

Panagos, Dimitrios. "The Plurality of Meanings Shouldered by the Term "Aboriginality." *Canadian Journal of Political Science*. Volume 40, Issue 3, September 2007 pp591-613

Parenteau, Patrick. "Anything Industry Wants: Environmental Policy Under Bush II." *Vermont Journal of Environmental Law*. Vol. 6, No. 1 (2004/2005).

Pearson , Mary. " Hunting Rights: Retention of Treaty Rights after Termination." *American Indian Law Review* , Vol. 4, No. 1 (1976), pp. 121-133

Peretti, Terri Jennings. *In Defense of a Political Court*. Princeton: Princeton University Press, 1999.

Pierceson, Jason. *Courts, Liberalism, and Rights: Gay Law and Politics in Canada and the United States*. Philadelphia, Pa.: Temple University Press, 2005.

Powe, Lucas. *The Warren Court and American Politics*. Cambridge: Harvard University Press, 2001.

Prims, Harold E. L. *The Mi'Kmaq: Resistance, Accommodation, and Cultural Survival*. Harcourt Publishers: Fort Worth, 1996.

Prucha, Francis. *American Indian Treaties: The History of a Political Anomaly*. Berkeley: University of California Press, 1994.

Redish, Martin A. and Shane Nugent, "The Dormant Commerce Clause and the Constitutional Balance of Federalism." *Duke Law Journal*, Volume 1987, No. 4 (Sept. 1987) pp 569-617.

Roach, Kent. *The Supreme Court on Trial: Judicial Activism or Democratic Dialogue?* (Toronto: Irwin Law, 2001.

Rabkin, Jeremy. "The Secret Life of the Private Attorney General." *Law and Contemporary Problems* Vol. 61, No. 1 (Winter, 1998) pp 179-203.

--- *Judicial Compulsions: How Public Law Distorts Public Policy*. (New York: Basic Books, 1989.

Resnick, Phillip. *The European Roots of Canadian Identity* Peterborough, Ontario: Broadview Press, 2005.

Rohrschneider, Robert and Russell Dalton. "A Global Network? Transnational Cooperation Amongst Environmental Groups." *The Journal of Politics*. Volume 64, Number 2. May 2002. pp 510-533.

Rose-Ackermann, Susan. *Controlling Environmental Policy: The Limits of Public Law in Germany and the United States*. New Haven: Yale University Press, 1995.

Rosen, Deborah A. *American Indians and State Law*. Lincoln: University of Nebraska Press, 2007.

Rosenberg, Gerald. *The Hollow Hope: Can Courts Bring About Social Change?* Chicago: University of Chicago Press, 1991.

Rosenbloom, David H. "Retrofitting the Administrative State to the Constitution: Congress and the Judiciary's Twentieth Century Progress." *Public Administration Review.* Vol. 60, No. 1 (Jan. 2000) pp 39-46.

Rossum, Ralph. *Federalism, the Supreme Court, and the Seventeenth Amendment.* Lanham, Md.: Lexington Books, 2001.

Russell, Dan. *A People's Dream: Aboriginal Self-Government in Canada.* Vancouver: UBC Press, 2000.

Russell, Peter H. *Constitutional Odyssey: Can Canadians Become a Sovereign People?* Toronto: University of Toronto Press, 1992.

Sanders, Douglas. "The Indian Lobby." in Keith Banting and Richard Simeon, e.d *Canada Notwithstanding: Federalism, Democracy, and the Constitution Act.* Toronto: Methuen Press, 1983.

Sandler, Ross and David Schoenbrod. *Democracy by Decree.* New Haven: Yale University Press, 2003.

Savoie, Donald. *Governing from the Center: The Concentration of Power in Canadian Politics.* Toronto: University of Toronto Press, 1999.

Scalia, Antonin. *A Matter of Interpretation.* Princeton: Princeton University Press, 1997.

Schneiderman, David. "Harold Laski, Viscount Haldane, and the Law of the Canadian Constitution in the Early Twentieth Century." *The University of Toronto Law Journal*, Vol. 48, No. 4 (Autumn, 1998)

Schoenbrod, David. *Power without Responsibility: How Congress abuses the people through delegation.* New Haven: Yale University Press, 1993.

Schoenbrod, David. "The Delegation Doctrine: Could the Court Give it Substance?" *Michigan Law Review.* Vol. 98, No. 2 (April, 1985) pp 1223-1290.

Schuck, Peter H. and E. Donald Elliott. "To the Chevron Station: An Empirical Study of Federal Administrative Law." *Duke Law Journal.* Vol. 1990, No. 5 (Nov., 1990) pp 984-1077.

Schwartz, Mildred A. *Party Movements in the United States and Canada* Lanham, Md.: Rowan and Littlefield, 2006.

Schwartz, Mildred A. "Canadian Policy Studies in Comparative Perspective," in *Policy Studies in Canada: The State of the Art* ed. Laurent Dobuzinskis, Michael Howlett, and David Laycock. Toronto: University of Toronto Press, 1996.

Segal, Jeffrey A. and Harold J. Spaeth. *The Supreme Court and the Attitudinal Model Revisited.* Cambridge: Cambridge University Press, 2002.

Shapiro, Martin. "Juridicalization of Politics in the United States." *International Political Science Review.* Vol. 15, No. 2 (April, 1994) pp 101-112.

---. *Who Guards the Guardians? Judicial Control of Administration.* Athens, Ga.: University of Georgia Press, 1988.

--- *Courts: A Comparative and Political Analysis.* Chicago: University of Chicago Press, 1986.

--- *Law and Politics in the Supreme Court: New Approaches to Political Jurisprudence.* New York: Free Press of Glencoe, 1964.

Shapiro, Martin and Alec Stone Sweet, *On Law, Politics, and Judicialization*. Oxford: Oxford University Press, 2002

Silverstein, Mark. *Judicious Choices: The New Politics of Supreme Court Appointments*. New York: Norton Press, 1994.

Simeon, Richard. *Federal-Provincial Diplomacy: The Making of Recent Policy in Canada*. Toronto: University of Toronto Press, 1972.

Skogstad, Grace and P. Kopas. "Environmental Policy in a federal system: Ottawa and the provinces." In *Canadian Environmental Policy: Ecosystems, politics, and process*. Ed. R. Boardman. Toronto: Oxford University Press, 1992.

Skrentny, J.D. "Concern for the Environment: A Cross-National Perspective." *International Journal of Public Opinion Research* Volume 5, Number 4, 1993. pp 335-352).

Smith, Joseph L. "Congress Opens the Courthouse Door: Statutory Changes to Judicial Review Under the Clean Air Act." *Political Research Quarterly*. Volume 58, Number 1, 2005. pp 139-149.

Stearns, Maxwell L. "Standing Back from the Forest: Justiciability and Social Choice." *California Law Review*. Vol. 83, No. 6 (Dec., 1995) pp 1309-1413.

Stern,Theodore. *The Klamath Tribe: A People and Their Reservation*. Seattle: University of Washington Press, 1965.

Sunstein, Cass. "Law and Administration After Chevron." *Columbia Law Review*. Vol. 90, No. 8. (Dec. 1990) pp 2071-2120.

Sunstein, Cass. "What's Standing After Lujan? Of Citizen Suits, 'Injuries,'and Article III." *Michigan Law Review*, Vol. 91, No. 2 (Nov. 1992) pp 163-236.

Sunstein, Cass. *After the Rights Revolution: Reconceiving the Regulatory State*. Cambridge: Harvard University Press, 1990.

Sutherland, S.L. "Responsible Government and Ministerial Responsibility: Every Reform its Own Problem." *Canadian Journal of Political Science*. Vol. 24, No. 1, (Mar., 1991) pp 91-120

Swinton, Katherine. "Federalism Under Fire: The Role of the Supreme Court of Canada." *Law and Contemporary Problems*. Vol. 55, No. 1, pp 121-145.

Tate, C. Neal and Torbjorn Vallinder,editors. *The Global Expansion of Judicial Power*. New York: NYU Press, 1995.

Teeple, Gary. *Capitalism and the National Question in Canada*. Toronto: University of Toronto Press, 1972.

Toqueville, Alexis de. *Democracy In America*, Translated by Harvey Mansfield and Delba Winthrop. Chicago and London: University of Chicago Press, 2000.

Tully, James. "A Just Relationship between Aboriginal and Non-Aboriginal Peoples of Canada." in *Aboriginal Rights and Self-Government: the Canadian and Mexican experience in North American Perspective.* Montreal and Ithaca: McGill-Queen's University Press, 2000.

Tushnet, Mark. *Taking the Constitution Away from the Courts*. Princeton: Princeton University Press, 1999.

Valiant, Marcia. "The Legal Foundations of Canadian Environmental Policy." Debora L. VanNijnatten and Robert Boardman, editors. *Canadian Environmental Policy: Context and Cases*. Oxford: Oxford University Press, 2002.

Vipond, Robert. *Liberty and Community: Canadian Federalism and the Failure of the Constitution* Albany: State University of New York Press, 1991.

Waldron, Jeremy. *The Dignity of Legislation* Cambridge: Cambridge University Press, 1999.

Watts, Ronald L. "Canada: Three Decades of Periodic Federal Crises." *International Political Science Review*. Vol. 17. No. 4, (Oct, 1996) pp 353-371.

Watts, Ronald L. "The American Constitution in Comparative Perspective: A Comparison of Federalism in Canada and the United States." *The Journal of American History*. Vol. 74, No. 3 (December, 1987) pp 769-792.

Weinrib, Lorraine. "Canada's Constitutional Revolution: From Legislative to Constitutional State." *Israel Law Review*. Volume 33, Number 1, 1999 pp 13-50.

Weinrib, Lorraine. "The Supreme Court of Canada and Section One of the Charter." The *Supreme Court Law Review*. Volume 10, 1998 pp 469-513.

West, Thomas "Progressivism and the Transformation of American Government." In Marini and Masugi, editors, *The Progressive Revolution in Politics and Political Science: Transforming the American Regime*. Lanham, Md.: Rowman and Littlefield, 2005. pp 13-35

White, G. Edward. "The Inevitability of Critical Legal Studies." *Stanford Law Review*. Volume 36, Number 2, pp 649-672.

Williams, Robert A., Jr. *Like a Loaded Weapon: The Rehnquist Court, Indian Rights, and the Legal History of Racism in America*. Minneapolis: University of Minnesota Press, 2005.

Wilkins, David, and K. Lomawaima. *Uneven Ground: American Indian Sovereignty and Federal Law.* Norman: University of Oklahoma Press, 2001.

Wilson, Jeremy. "Continuity and Change in the Canadian Environmental Movement: Assessing the Effects of Institutionalization." in Debora L. VanNijnatten and Robert Boardman, editors, *Canadian Environmental Policy: Context and Cases.* (Oxford: Oxford University Press, 2002) pp 46-65.

Winfield, Mark. "The Ultimate Horizontal Issue: The Environmental Policy Experiences of Alberta and Ontario, 1971-1993." *The Canadian Journal of Political Science.* Vol. 27, No. 1, (Mar., 1994). pp 129-152.

Wolfe, Christopher. *The Rise of Modern Judicial Review: From Constitutional Interpretation to Judge-Made Law.* Lanham, Md.: Rowan and Littlefield, 1994.

Index